Oxford Applied Mathematics
and Computing Science Series

General Editors
J. N. Buxton, R. F. Churchhouse, and A. B. Tayler

OXFORD APPLIED MATHEMATICS AND
COMPUTING SCIENCE SERIES

JULIAN ULLMANN
University of Sheffield

A Pascal database book

CLARENDON PRESS · OXFORD
1985

Oxford University Press, Walton Street, Oxford OX2 6DP.
Oxford   New York   Toronto
Delhi   Bombay   Calcutta   Madras   Karachi
Kuala Lumpur   Singapore   Hong Kong   Tokyo
Nairobi   Dar es Salaam   Cape Town
Melbourne   Auckland
and associated companies in
Beirut   Berlin   Ibadan   Nicosia

Oxford is a trade mark of Oxford University Press

Published in the United States
by Oxford University Press, New York

British Library Cataloguing in Publication Data
Ullmann, Julian R.
A Pascal database book—(Oxford applied
mathematics and computing science series)
1. Data base management   2. File organization
(Computer science)   3. PASCAL (Computer program
language)
I. Title
001.64'42   QA76.9.D3
ISBN 0–19–859643–X
ISBN 0–19–859642–1 (Pbk.)
Library of Congress Cataloging in Publication Data
Ullmann, Julian R. (Julian Richard), 1936–
A Pascal database book
(Oxford applied mathematics and computing
science series)
Includes index.
1. Data base management.   2. PASCAL (Computer
program language) 1. Title. II. Series.
QA76.9.D3U45   001.64'2   85–4775
ISBN 0–19–859643–X
ISBN 0–19–859642–1 (Pbk.)

Typeset by Latimer Trend & Company Ltd, Plymouth
Printed in Great Britain at the University Press, Oxford
by David Stanford, Printer to the University

Preface

Database technology is of immense importance in practical computing. Indeed, for many students it will prove to be one of the areas of computer science that is most relevant vocationally.

This book has been written primarily for students at universities and polytechnics who use Pascal as their principal programming language. One of the main aims of this book is to teach database technology so that its relation to a Pascal cultural framework can be clearly seen, thus improving the coherence of a student's overall view of computer science and avoiding unhelpful but traditional compartmentalization.

Another main aim of this book is to enable database technology to be taught earlier in the computer science curriculum than has been usual hitherto. We have found that concepts such as fifth normal form and CODASYL data structures are within the grasp of good first-year students. Reasons for teaching database technology early are as follows.

(a) Near the beginning of a computer science course it is particularly important to introduce practical applications of computing, and the database field provides plenty of opportunities for this.

(b) Database technology includes some intellectually appealing concepts, for example in normalization theory. This may help to motivate further study of computer science.

(c) Full details of database management systems such as CODASYL systems are apt to be complicated, and are perhaps not the kind of material that an undergraduate should be expected to learn. By teaching earlier we feel more free to concentrate on principles rather than non-academic although vocationally important details.

(d) Early in a computer science curriculum a database course can serve as a useful vehicle for programming practice, particularly with files, records, pointers, and uses of indirection.

(e) An early database course also serves to introduce important general features of computer science, for example the distinction between higher and lower levels of programming.

(f) If the teaching of database technology is delayed until the final stages of the curriculum this may preclude subsequent teaching of database architectures.

Yet another aim of this book is to introduce rudiments of data processing in the same context as database technology, rather than in a separate educational compartment. For example Chapter 8 introduces check digits in the same context as database integrity constraints. Chapter 5 introduces batch processing as well as B-trees: B-trees are used later to implement database access paths.

An introduction to database technology is surely most convincing if built on at least an elementary grasp of practical uses of files. For this reason Chapter 1 concentrates simply on typical data and its uses. At the same time, Chapter 1 is intended to provide a meaningful initial introduction to files, records, fields, and keys.

A relational view of a database is at a higher level than a view in which access paths are visible. A purely relational view should be taught first to consolidate understanding of uses of files, and to show that a relational view can be self-contained. A relational view is purer and simpler than a lower-level view, and there is much to be said for introducing simple ideas before elaborate ones. After an introduction to the relational level the student is better equipped to appreciate the access paths that are visible at a lower level, and to see how these can support relational technology. The common but strategically mistaken practice of teaching file organization before relational technology is a reflection of the history of development of the field, rather than being the outcome of a deliberate search for the most effective way to teach the subject.

For the elementary purposes of this book we have chosen to introduce just one relational query language and one lower-level language which is actually an extension of Pascal. At each level we prefer to provide a serviceable introduction to one language, rather than a frustratingly superficial introduction to many.

From the cornucopia of relational query languages we have chosen relational algebra because this is helpful for normalization theory in Chapter 3. Furthermore, the names of operators of relational algebra are very useful in Chapters 6 and 7. We introduce relational algebra as a stand-alone query language which is not embedded in a host language.

At a lower level it is educationally desirable for students to see how database access path programming relates to standard Pascal programming. For this purpose Chapters 4 and 5 introduce a minimal extension to Pascal, including data manipulation language procedures such as INSERT, FIND, and REMOVE; thereby we hope to help bridge any culture gap that may have existed between Pascal programming and commercial data manipulation language programming. This extension of Pascal is deliberately at a lower level than other extensions that endow Pascal with relational query language capabilities in order to increase the power of the tools available to the programmer.

Experience suggests that we should systematically build upon that which the student understands, even if this means proceeding from the particular to the general, having first consolidated understanding of the particular by means of specific detailed examples. This is why this book starts with detail and ends in Chapter 8 with a more abstract introduction to database administration. Students would not find Chapter 8 so palatable if the book started with it, although this would be a fairly traditional starting point.

Chapter 9 is really an appendix. It is an informal introductory outline of standard Pascal data structuring facilities, and is designed to be read before Chapter 4 if required.

Many textbooks on Pascal have identifiers in lower case, or in mixed case as in SalesOrderHeader. The usual convention in the data-processing and database literature is to have identifiers in upper case. In this book we should like to follow the convention that has been established with the programming language ADA, but because standard Pascal does not allow underbars in identifiers, as in SALES_ORDER_HEADER, we close up spaces, as in SALESORDERHEADER, in programs and expressions. Otherwise we leave spaces within identifiers, as in SALES ORDER HEADER, for readability. This inconsistency appears to be the most palatable of the available options.

Thanks are due to Siobhan North, Hugh Lafferty, Jim McGregor, and Laurence Atkinson for helpful comments on various parts of the manuscript. The Pascal enhancement introduced in this text has been fully implemented (on a Prime 750 under PRIMOS) by Siobhan North (see A Pascal database management system, *Journal of Pascal, Ada and Modula 2*, Vol. 3, No. 6 (1984), pp 15–22).

Sheffield   J.R.U.
December 1984

Contents

1 An introduction to data processing

1.1. An introduction to data that is processed

Information in industry and commerce can be as vital as finance. Competitiveness may depend on efficiency of management of information, and efficiency may depend on computerization. The aim of this text is to introduce various general methods for computerized management of information. Although we shall often be concerned with commercial examples, the usefulness of the technology extends beyond industry and commerce.

We shall omit computers at first, and just concentrate on typical information. We shall give examples of *what* this information is, *where* it comes from, and *how, when,* and *why* it is used. When we understand what we want to computerize, we are in a better position to understand *how* to computerize.

Our first introductory examples are based on the (simplified) working of a fairly typical (fictitious) company called Typico. Typico is a wholesaler that buys goods from manufacturers, paying relatively low prices because the quantities are large. A wholesaler such as Typico profits by selling the goods at higher prices, but in smaller quantities, to retailers. These retailers are the wholesaler's customers. For example, the name of one of Typico's customers is Smithson Electric.

1.2. Order entry

1.2.1 A purchase order from a customer

We shall start by considering customers' orders and invoicing. Typico's catalogue gives reference numbers for all items that Typico supply. Item reference numbers are useful because, for example, Typico can supply many different types of electric kettle made by different manufacturers. Each type of electric kettle is identified by a different item reference number, as shown in Typico's catalogue. After consulting the catalogue, customers send purchase orders by

mail or telephone asking Typico to supply a list of goods. Figure 1.1
shows an example of a purchase order.

PURCHASE ORDER	OUR PURCHASE ORDER NO: 58311
	OUR SUPPLIER NO: 214

FROM: SMITHSON ELECTRIC
      17, HIGH STREET
      PEEMARSH AVON   Date 3.5.91

BUYER NAME: TELEPHONE 0691-322178
MR.J.BLOODWORTH

TO: DELIVERY INSTRUCTIONS:
TYPICO PLC   Ship to above address
INDUSTRIAL ESTATE
GATESHEAD
TYNE & WEAR

QUANTITY	ITEM REF NUMBER	DESCRIPTION	UNIT PRICE
2	6PK9F1	Electric Kettle	10.17
100	F8431P	Pack of three 5A fuses	0.30
1	J496B5	Electric soldering iron	2.90
150	775Y94	13A plug	0.46
4	8KJ652	Toaster	8.62

Fig. 1.1. Example of a customer's purchase order.

1.2.2. *File definitions*

The list of goods in Smithson Electric's purchase order is a simple
example of a file. For present purposes a *file* is an ordered set of
records. Each line in Smithson Electric's list of goods is an example
of a record. A *record* is an ordered set of field values. Within each
record the entries in successive columns of the purchase order are the
field values that make up the record. For example the third record in
the file consists of the four field values 1, 'J496B5', 'Electric soldering
iron', and 2.90. It is important that a string of characters such as
'Electric soldering iron' can possibly be a value, just as the number
2.90 can possibly be a value.

A column heading such as UNIT PRICE is a *field name*. In the purchase order in Fig 1.1 the successive values of the UNIT PRICE field are

10.17
0.30
2.90
0.46
8.62

The possible values of any given field are restricted to a specific domain, which is called the *type* of the field. For example the QUANTITY field has values that must be integers, and therefore this field is of integer type. The UNIT PRICE field is of real-number type, because its values are real numbers. The DESCRIPTION field is of string-of-characters type. We usually say, more briefly, that a field such as DESCRIPTION is of type *string*.

For the sake of introductory simplicity the present text always assumes that all of the records in any given file have the same field names and field types.

1.2.3. Files involved in order entry

1.2.3.1. Customers file.

Typico keep the names, addresses, and other particulars of their customers in a file that is called the CUSTOMERS file. Upon receiving a purchase order from Smithson Electric, one of Typico's first actions is to look up Smithson Electric in the CUSTOMERS file to check that the mailing address is correct and that the credit limit has not been exceeded. For the CUSTOMERS file the field names are as follows. Text that is enclosed between braces is always explanatory comment that is intended to facilitate the reader's understanding and is not part of a record or program.

CUSTOMERS file field names

CUSTOMER NUMBER	{a unique serial number that Typico assigns to each customer}
NAME	{of customer company}
BILLING ADDRESS	{where Typico should send invoices etc.}

CREDIT LIMIT
SALES AREA   {TYPICO divide the whole country
                                                  into seven areas; the SALES AREA
                                                  field says which area each customer
                                                  is in}
SALES PERSON EMPLOYEE NO. {identifies the TYPICO employee
                                                  who is responsible for sales to this
                                                  customer}

For each customer this file contains one record. For Smithson
Electric the actual record could be as follows.

6391   {CUSTOMER NUMBER}
SMITHSON ELECTRIC   {NAME}
17 HIGH STREET, PEEMARSH,
AVON   {BILLING ADDRESS}
5000   {CREDIT LIMIT}
SW   {SALES AREA}
78631   {SALES PERSON EMPLOYEE
                                  NO}

Another example of a record in the CUSTOMERS file is as
follows.

6433   {CUSTOMER NUMBER}
BLUNDELLS   {NAME}
302 QUEENS ROAD,
BRIGHTON   {BILLING ADDRESS}
10000   {CREDIT LIMIT}
SE   {SALES AREA}
78631   {SALES PERSON EMPLOYEE
                                  NO}

A *candidate key* of a given file is a minimal set of fields such that a
value of a candidate key identifies exactly one record in the file. This
set (of one or more fields) is minimal in the sense that, if any field is
deleted from it, it is not a candidate key. For the CUSTOMERS file
CUSTOMER NUMBER is a candidate key, because Typico arrange that each customer has a unique CUSTOMER NUMBER. In
our example the CUSTOMER NUMBER 6391 distinguishes
Smithson Electric's CUSTOMERS record from all others.
    It is possible that more than one customer has the same name. For
example, besides Smithson Electric in Peemarsh there could be

another customer named Smithson Electric in Brighton. This means that customer NAME is not a candidate key, because it does not identify a unique customer. However, we can reasonably assume that Typico will not have more than one customer with the same name at the same address, so the *pair* of fields NAME and BILLING ADDRESS together constitute a candidate key. Values of these two fields together distinguish a unique customer record, and Typico can use this to look up in the file a customer's CUSTOMER NUMBER, should this be required.

We have seen that the CUSTOMERS file has two candidate keys. One of these is CUSTOMER NUMBER and the other is the pair of fields NAME and BILLING ADDRESS. This example illustrates the general fact that a file may have more than one candidate key. It is common practice to select one of the candidate keys for normal routine use, and to refer to this selected candidate key as the *primary key* of the file. For example, Typico use CUSTOMER NUMBER as the primary key of the CUSTOMERS file.

1.2.3.2. Inventory file

Typico maintain an INVENTORY file in which there is one record for each item that Typico may supply to customers (or consume in other ways).

INVENTORY file field names

ITEM REF NO	{A unique reference number serves as primary key to identify an item}
BIN NUMBER	{This indicates where the item is physically stored in (which) one of Typico's warehouses}
DESCRIPTION	{a brief verbal description of item}
UNITS	{in which quantity is measured, e.g. items, or kilograms, or metres}
QUANTITY IN WAREHOUSE	{physically now}
QUANTITY ALLOCATED	{to agreed shipments that have not yet been physically carried out}
REORDER LEVEL	{when quantity in warehouse minus quantity allocated plus quantity currently on order falls below reorder level, the item should be reordered from suppliers}

QUANTITY TO ORDER   {this says how many units to order
                                 when the item is reordered from a
                                 supplier}
QUANTITY ON ORDER   {order accepted by supplier but not
                                 yet shipped to Typico}
STANDARD SELLING PRICE PER UNIT   {To Typico's customers}

1.2.3.3.   *Sales order header and detail files*

Upon receiving a purchase order from a customer such as Smithson
Electric, Typico check the details of the order as we shall explain
later. If Typico decide to accept the order and therefore supply the
specified goods they create a *sales order* for their own internal use. A
sales order states what Typico is going to supply to whom as the
result of accepting a purchase order.

   A sales order could be stored by Typico as a single record in a file
of sales orders. In this case the number of field values per record
would generally not be the same for all sales orders, because
different sales orders may specify different numbers of different
items. It may be possible to cope with this variation, but usually at
the cost of inefficiency for reasons that will be explained later. To
avoid this inefficiency it is usual practice to store the sales order
information in two files: SALES ORDER HEADER and SALES
ORDER DETAIL. In the HEADER file Typico store detail-
independent information such as which customer placed the order
and the date of the order. The DETAIL file gives details of items
ordered. Field names for these files are as follows.

SALES ORDER HEADER file field names

SALES ORDER NUMBER   {primary key value assigned by
                               Typico for identification of a sales
                               order header}
CUSTOMER NUMBER   {same as in CUSTOMERS file}
CUSTOMER's PURCHASE ORDER NUMBER
BUYER NAME   {name of member of staff of
                               customer company who was
                               responsible for their purchase order}
BUYER TELEPHONE NUMBER
DELIVERY ADDRESS   {where customer wishes goods to be
                               delivered}

DATE OF ORDER	{date of creation of sales order by Typico}
ACKNOWLEDGEMENT FLAG	{has value 'yes' if Typico have sent an acknowledgement of the order to the customer, and 'no' otherwise}

SALES ORDER DETAIL file field names

SALES ORDER NUMBER	{same as in SALES ORDER HEADER file}
LINE NUMBER	{there is one record in this file for each item in a sales order. Each such record is called a *line* of the order and is given a unique line number within this particular order. SALES ORDER NUMBER and LINE NUMBER *together* constitute the primary key of the SALES ORDER DETAIL file}
ITEM REF NO	{same as in Typico's INVENTORY file}
DESCRIPTION	{a brief verbal description may be useful for checking for mistakes}

QUANTITY ORDERED
QUANTITY NOT YET DELIVERED

{in case more than one shipment is necessary}

PRICE CHARGED PER UNIT

1.2.4. Order entry routine

The order entry routine is a process by which Typico check a purchase order from a customer and, if the order is acceptable, create a corresponding sales order. There are three main steps in the process.

Customer identification. The customer's CUSTOMERS record is looked up in the CUSTOMERS file, using CUSTOMER NUMBER or NAME and BILLING ADDRESS as key. If this is a new customer then a new CUSTOMERS record is created, which includes a credit limit determined by Typico's management. By accessing the CUSTOMERS file at this time Typico (a) check that the billing address in the file and on the purchase order agree, (b) obtain the CUSTOMER NUMBER that will be entered in the SALES ORDER HEADER (the remaining information for the SALES ORDER HEADER record is obtained from the customer's purchase order), and (c) obtain the customer's credit limit from the CUSTOMERS file.

Product identification. Each item in the customer's purchase order is looked up in the Typico INVENTORY file. If there is any discrepancy between the customer's description and the inventory description of the item, or if there is any difference between the prices specified by the customer and the inventory, then Typico query the customer (possibly by telephone). Otherwise information is assembled for a SALES ORDER DETAIL record and the cost of this item is added into a grand total for this particular purchase order.

Credit check. If the total price of this purchase order plus this customer's currently outstanding debts to Typico exceed this customer's credit limit then Typico send the purchase order back to the customer, explaining that it should be resubmitted after previous invoices have been paid. Otherwise, if the credit limit has not been exceeded, Typico enter the SALES ORDER HEADER record in the SALES ORDER HEADER file and also enter SALES ORDER DETAIL lines into the SALES ORDER DETAIL file, thus *creating* the sales order.

At Typico the sales order entry routine is executed by a clerk using a computer terminal. We shall not now say just how much of the job the computer does and how much the clerk does.

1.3. Shipping and invoicing

1.3.1. Picking

Typico always deliver goods using their own vans, not by mail nor by other carriers. Each day vans from Typico deliver goods to certain areas, but not all areas of the country. Typico vans never deliver to the same area on consecutive days. The arrangements are intended to help Typico deliver goods to more than one customer in one van trip.

Each night, for each area to which vans will deliver the next day, Typico review all unsatisfied sales orders for customers in the area. For each customer, items in the sales order detail lines are looked up in the inventory and a report is sent to a junior manager, showing him the quantity and price of goods ordered that Typico could supply from (non-allocated) stock. If sufficient goods cannot be supplied from stock, Typico mail a purchase order acknowledgement to the customer, if an acknowledgement has not already been sent, but do not prepare a shipment (i.e. delivery). When Typico send an acknowledgement they give the value 'yes' to the ACKNOWLEDGEMENT FLAG in the SALES ORDER HEADER, and this is used to prevent any given sales order from being acknowledged more than once.

If the junior manager decides to proceed with a delivery to a given customer, then Typico prepare three separate documents relating to the delivery. The three documents are the picking list, the delivery note, and the invoice. While preparing these documents, Typico consult the INVENTORY file, and for each item that will be shipped they increase the QUANTITY ALLOCATED by the number of units that will be included in this shipment. A simple example of a picking list is shown in Fig. 1.2.

TYPICO PICKING LIST

DELIVERY TO: Smithson Electric, 17 High Street, Peemarsh, Avon
DELIVERY DATE: 7:5:91

BIN NO	ITEM REF NO	DESCRIPTION	QUANTITY
2	F8431P	pack of three 5 A fuses	50
2	775Y94	13 A plug	150
5	8K1143	100 W plain bulb	100
8	6NF31K	Electric fan	5
9	6PK9F1	Electric kettle	2

Fig. 1.2. Example of a picking list.

A picking list tells the warehouse staff which items to take (*pick*) from the warehouse to make up the shipment. On the picking list the items are listed in the *sequence* in which they will be physically found by someone travelling round the warehouse. If the picking list includes many items this sequencing significantly reduces the time spent by staff physically travelling round the warehouse. After picking up all the items on the picking list, the warehouse staff appropriately reduce the QUANTITY IN WAREHOUSE and QUANTITY ALLOCATED in the INVENTORY record for each item that has been picked. If, owing to a mistake somewhere, the quantity of an item on the picking list is not physically found in the warehouse, then the delivery note and invoice are modified accordingly, and this mistake is included in a report to Typico's management.

Picking lists for more than one customer can be created before the warehouse staff actually pick the goods from the warehouse for delivery to any of these customers. The QUANTITY ALLOCATED field in the INVENTORY file is intended to prevent the same goods being allocated to more than one customer. For example, if there were only four electric kettles in the warehouse and three of these had been allocated to Blundells of Bristol, then it would be a mistake to allocate two to Smithson Electric at this time.

We might consider whether Typico should simplify their procedures by creating a picking list, delivery note and invoice directly from a customer's purchase order at the time of creating a sales order. One reason why Typico do *not* work this way is that their vans only deliver to any given customer on one or two days in each week, and it is usually better to allocate goods to customers to whom delivery is soonest rather than to customers in the sequence in which purchase orders are received. Between the time of receiving a customer's purchase order and the time of making a delivery to that customer, some of the required items may be delivered *to* Typico by suppliers.

1.3.2. *Invoicing*

Typico create an invoice at the same time as they create the picking list for a delivery to a customer. An example of an invoice, which is a demand for payment, is shown in Fig. 1.3. While creating the invoice, Typico also create a delivery note, which looks like the invoice but has the heading DELIVERY NOTE or PACKING SLIP instead of INVOICE and bears the customer's address for delivery, which may not be the billing address.

TYPICO PLC

INDUSTRIAL ESTATE, GATESHEAD, TYNE & WEAR

INVOICE

CUSTOMER   INVOICE NO:61192

SMITHSON ELECTRIC
17 HIGH STREET   DATE: 10:5:91
PEEMARSH   VAT Reg: 86872194
AVON

ITEM REF NO	DESCRIPTION	QUANTITY	YOUR PURCHASE ORDER NO	PRICE
6NF31K	Electric fan	5	76132	26.25
8K1143	100-watt plain bulb	100	76132	33.50
6PK9F1	Electric kettle	2	58311	20.34
F8431P	Pack of 3A fuses	50	58311	12.00
775Y94	13A plug	150	58311	69.30
			GOODS TOTAL	161.39
			DELIVERY CHARGE	20.00
			VAT 10%	18.14
			TOTAL DUE	199.53

Fig. 1.3. Example of an invoice.

When a van driver takes a shipment of goods from Typico he signs a copy of the delivery note. Upon receiving the goods the customer also signs a copy of the delivery note, and the driver takes this copy back to Typico, who then mail the invoice to the customer. Typico do not mail the invoice to the customer *until* they have received the delivery note signed by the customer in case the customer's premises have burnt down or the customer has refused to accept delivery for some other reason, or Typico's van disintegrated before reaching the customer.

At the time they create the invoice and delivery note, Typico enter the invoice information in two files: the INVOICE HEADER file and INVOICE DETAIL file. The reason for using two files instead of one is the same as it was in the case of sales orders, i.e. to avoid using a single file whose records are apt to vary greatly in length. The field names are as follows.

INVOICE HEADER file field names

INVOICE NUMBER	{primary key}
CUSTOMER NUMBER	{same as in CUSTOMERS file}
DELIVERY CHARGE	
VAT CHARGE	
TOTAL AMOUNT	{total demanded by invoice}
SHIPMENT DATE	
INVOICE DATE	{normally the day after shipment}
INVOICE DESPATCHED FLAG	{has value 'yes' if invoice has been mailed to customer, and 'no' otherwise}

INVOICE DETAIL file field names

INVOICE NUMBER	{for a given invoice this is same as in INVOICE HEADER}
INVOICE LINE NUMBER	{for a given invoice number the invoice detail records are assigned successive line numbers 1, 2, 3, ..., so that the LINE NUMBER and INVOICE NUMBER *together* constitute the primary key for this file}
SALES ORDER NUMBER	{may not be the same for all items on any given Typico invoice}
ITEM REF NO	{there is one INVOICE DETAIL record for each item, or set of identical items, on the invoice}
DESCRIPTION	
QUANTITY	
PRICE CHARGED PER UNIT	

When the van returns from delivery the invoice is mailed to the customer if the delivery has been accepted, as we have said previously. In this case the INVOICE DATE is entered into the INVOICE HEADER and the INVOICE DESPATCHED FLAG is set to 'yes'. Otherwise the INVOICE HEADER and DETAIL records for this delivery are deleted from the files and the goods are returned to the warehouse, the INVENTORY file being updated accordingly.

The INVOICE HEADER and DETAIL files provide a record of shipments, and therefore a separate file for shipments is not necessary for Typico.

1.3.3. *Sales order history file*

When a sales order has been entirely fulfilled by the customer's acceptance of a shipment, the SALES ORDER HEADER and DETAIL records are copied into a SALES ORDER HISTORY file and are then deleted from the current SALES ORDER HEADER and SALES ORDER DETAIL files. The history file and the customers' actual purchase orders, which are kept for several years, serve as data for the resolution of disputes and answering queries.

If a sales order has been only partially fulfilled by a shipment, a copy of the SALES ORDER HEADER together with SALES ORDER DETAIL lines that say what was actually supplied are entered into the SALES ORDER HISTORY file. The SALES ORDER DETAIL records for items that have not been fully delivered are amended to show the quantities that Typico must deliver in the future. Thus the SALES ORDER HEADER and DETAIL lines tell Typico what has been ordered and not yet delivered.

1.4 Purchase orders from Typico to suppliers

1.4.1. *Suppliers*

We now turn our attention to suppliers of goods to Typico. Typico maintain a SUPPLIERS file that has one record for each supplier. The field names are as follows.

SUPPLIERS file field names
_____

SUPPLIER NUMBER   {primary key}
SUPPLIER NAME
ADDRESS FOR PAYMENTS TO SUPPLIER
SUPPLIERS CUSTOMER NUMBER   {assigned to Typico by the
                                 supplier}

SALES PERSON NAME   {supplier employee responsible for
                                  sales to Typico}
TELEPHONE NUMBER   {of sales person}

Any given supplier may supply more than one item, and any given
item may be available from more than one supplier. Typico maintain
a SOURCES file that shows which suppliers supply which item. The
field names are as follows.

SOURCES file field names

ITEM REF NO   {Typico's}
SUPPLIER NUMBER
SUPPLIERS PRODUCT NO   {corresponds to Typico's item ref.
                                  no.}
SUPPLIERS PRICE PER UNIT
NUMBER OF UNITS SUPPLIED DURING LAST SIX
                                  MONTHS   {by this supplier}
NUMBER OF UNITS FOUND FAULTY DURING LAST SIX
                                  MONTHS

1.4.2. Purchase order creation

To find out which items to order from suppliers, Typico scan
through their INVENTORY file twice per week. An item should be
ordered if its QUANTITY IN WAREHOUSE minus QUANTITY
ALLOCATED plus QUANTITY ON ORDER is less than the
REORDER LEVEL. Each item that should be ordered is looked up
in the SOURCES file, and a Typico employee (who is called a *buyer*)
decides which supplier this item should be ordered from. This
decision depends on the unit price, the reputation of the supplier,
and whether Typico can now place a large enough order to obtain a
good discount. For each supplier from whom the buyer decides to
order goods, Typico create a purchase order. A Typico purchase
order looks like Smithson Electric's purchase order, but quantities
of goods are generally far larger.

   Typico maintain PURCHASE ORDER HEADER and DETAIL
files that are analogous to SALES ORDER HEADER and
DETAIL files. When a Typico purchase order is created, a
PURCHASE ORDER HEADER record is entered into the

PURCHASE ORDER HEADER file, and detail records are entered into the PURCHASE ORDER DETAIL file. The field names are as follows.

PURCHASE ORDER HEADER file field names

PURCHASE ORDER NUMBER	{primary key}
SUPPLIER NUMBER	{of supplier with whom Typico is placing this order}
SUPPLIER SALESPERSON NAME	
	{supplier employee responsible for this purchase by Typico}
BUYER EMPLOYEE NO	{identifies Typico manager responsible for this purchase}
PURCHASE ORDER DATE	

PURCHASE ORDER DETAIL file field names

PURCHASE ORDER NUMBER	
PURCHASE ORDER LINE NUMBER	
ITEM REF NO	{Typico's}
SUPPLIERS ITEM REF NO	{obtained by Typico from supplier's catalogue}
QUANTITY	
STANDARD PRICE PER UNIT	
DISCOUNT PER CENT ON ORDERED QUANTITY	

When Typico have received and paid for all goods listed on a purchase order, HEADER and DETAIL records are transferred to a PURCHASE ORDER HISTORY file that is analogous to the SALES ORDER HISTORY file.

1.4.3. Receipt of goods

When Typico receive a shipment of goods from a supplier, the goods are checked to see whether they have arrived in acceptable condition. For each batch of identical items accepted by Typico, a record is entered in the GOODS RECEIPTS file, for which the field names are as follows.

GOODS RECEIPTS file field names

PURCHASE ORDER NUMBER
PURCHASE ORDER LINE NUMBER
SUPPLIER'S INVOICE NUMBER

{this together with the two previous
fields constitutes the primary key;
there may be receipts on different
dates that have the same purchase
order number and line number}

DATE OF RECEIPT
QUANTITY ACCEPTED

If the supplier supplies in one shipment a set of identical goods
ordered in different purchase orders, then a separate record is
entered into the GOODS RECEIPTS file corresponding to each of
these purchase orders. When goods are accepted by Typico the
appropriate QUANTITY IN WAREHOUSE field values in the
INVENTORY file are updated accordingly.

1.5. Aspects of accounting

1.5.1. *An account is a file*

For present purposes an account is a file that has field names
something like the following.

DATE   {of transaction}
AGENT   {debtor or creditor name or
                                reference number}
TRANSACTION REFERENCE NO
                                {e.g. INVOICE NO}
AMOUNT DEBIT   {account *increased* by this amount}
AMOUNT CREDIT   {account *decreased* by this amount}

One of the last two field values (i.e. DEBIT or CREDIT) is normally
blank. It is a well-established, but possibly surprising, convention
that an AMOUNT DEBIT is an amount of *income* into an account,
and an AMOUNT CREDIT is an amount of *outflow*.

1.5.2. *Accounts receivable*

1.5.2.1. *Receipt of payments to Typico*

Customers pay for goods by sending cheques to Typico. Typico pay cheques into their bank in batches (e.g. all cheques received between noon on one day and noon the next day are paid in one batch). Successive batches are given successive batch numbers, 1, 2, 3, ...

Corresponding to each cheque received, a Typico clerk enters a record into a CASH RECEIPTS JOURNAL file that has the following field names.

CASH RECEIPTS JOURNAL file field names

CUSTOMER NUMBER
CHEQUE NUMBER   {as printed on the cheque}
BATCH NUMBER
DATE
TIME   {of receipt}
INVOICE NUMBER   {of invoice that demanded this
                                payment}
PAYMENT AMOUNT
EMPLOYEE NUMBER OF PERSON WHO ENTERED THIS
                        RECORD   {into the file; if
                                something goes wrong, Typico will
                                know who to ask about it}

When a batch is complete, ready to be taken to the bank, payment amounts in the CASH RECEIPTS JOURNAL records for the batch are totalled. The total amount is (not surprisingly) called the *batch total*. The bank teller who receives the batch of cheques totals them independently, and if the resulting total does not agree with Typico's total then the bank and Typico look for a mistake. This is a classical example of the use of a batch total as a safeguard against clerical errors, e.g. typing errors in CASH RECEIPTS JOURNAL records.

1.5.2.2. *Accounts receivable file*

For each customer, Typico maintain an account of what the customer has paid and what the customer owes Typico. These

accounts are all held in the same file, which is called the
ACCOUNTS RECEIVABLE FILE. Actually ACCOUNTS
RECEIVABLE is American terminology: corresponding British
terminology is DEBTORS. Typico's ACCOUNTS RECEIVABLE
file has the following field names.

ACCOUNTS RECEIVABLE file field names

CUSTOMER NUMBER	
DATE	
AMOUNT DEBIT	{income that *increases* the account}
CHEQUE NUMBER	{of cheque making payment *into* this account; this field and AMOUNT DEBIT field are blank in a record that records a *decrease* in the account}
AMOUNT CREDIT	{outflow that *decreases* the account}
INVOICE NUMBER	{this field and the AMOUNT CREDIT field are blank in a record that records an *increase* in the account}
BALANCE OF ACCOUNT	{the value of this field includes a sign: + if the customer owes a balance to Typico; − if Typico owes a balance to the customer}

Corresponding to each CASH RECEIPTS JOURNAL record, an
ACCOUNTS RECEIVABLE record is created and entered into the
ACCOUNTS RECEIVABLE file. This copying of transaction data
into the ACCOUNTS RECEIVABLE file is called *posting* the
transaction entry to the ACCOUNTS RECEIVABLE file. It may be
convenient to delay this posting until some time after the creation of
the CASH RECEIPTS JOURNAL record.

Corresponding to each invoice mailed to a customer, a record is
created in the ACCOUNTS RECEIVABLE file to show the sum
now owed to Typico by the customer in respect of this invoice. The
supply of goods, as evidenced by invoicing, is regarded as an outflow
that decreases the account.

Each month the ACCOUNTS RECEIVABLE file is scanned to
provide information to make up monthly statements for customers.
A statement summarizes the customers' payments and debts to
Typico during the month. A simple example of a statement is shown
in Fig. 1.4.

TYPICO PLC

Industrial Estate
Gateshead, Tyne & Wear

CUSTOMER   MONTHLY STATEMENT

SMITHSON ELECTRIC
17 HIGH STREET
PEEMARSH
AVON   for month ended 30th June 1991

DATE	DESCRIPTION	AMOUNT
	BALANCE BROUGHT FORWARD	210.31
2.6.91	INVOICE NO. 61924	395.60
11.6.91	INVOICE NO. 64382	184.72
15.6.91	CHEQUE	500.00 −
20.6.91	INVOICE NO. 65112	221.02
28.6.91	INVOICE NO. 68925	166.53
	BALANCE DUE	1,678.18

Fig. 1.4. Example of a customer's monthly statement.

In the AMOUNT column, a minus sign denotes a payment by the customer. Besides producing statements, the ACCOUNTS RECEIVABLE file is also scanned to provide a report showing which customers are slow payers, which are quick payers who possibly therefore deserve larger discounts, and which have debts so long outstanding that they deserve special chasing. This is an example of *exception reporting*.

1.6. Accounts payable

1.6.1. *Invoice receipt*

When Typico receive an invoice from one of their suppliers they process it as follows.

(a) Find the corresponding record (or records) in the PUR-CHASE ORDER HEADER file.
(b) Use the SUPPLIER NUMBER found in the PURCHASE ORDER HEADER record to find the supplier name and address in

the SUPPLIERS file, and check that this name and address is the same as on the invoice.

(c) Check the invoice line by line with the PURCHASE ORDER DETAIL and the GOODS RECEIPTS file to make sure that the invoiced quantities of goods have actually been ordered, received and accepted by Typico.

(d) Work out on what date the invoice should be paid to avoid losing worthwhile discount.

(e) If Typico accept that the invoice should be paid, create and store a record in the PENDING INVOICE FILE for which the field names are as follows.

PENDING INVOICE file field names

SUPPLIER NUMBER	
INVOICE NUMBER	{given by the supplier}
PURCHASE ORDER NUMBER	{Typico's}
INVOICE DATE	{date of issue of invoice}
DUE DATE	{when Typico should pay}
AMOUNT	{payable by Typico}

1.6.2. Payments to suppliers

The records in the PENDING INVOICE file are kept in order of DUE DATE, so that all invoices which should be paid on a particular day will have consecutive records. This set of consecutive records will be followed, in the PENDING INVOICE file, by a set of consecutive records for invoices that should be paid tomorrow, and so on.

Each day, a Typico accountant uses the PENDING INVOICE file to find which invoices should now be paid, and decides which to pay and which to defer, bearing in mind the amount of cash that Typico currently has available for payment to suppliers. For each invoice that is to be paid by Typico, a cheque is sent to the supplier and this payment is recorded in a file called the CASH PAYMENTS JOURNAL.

1.7. The general ledger

1.7.1. Chart of accounts

The general ledger is a collection of accounts that show the financial position of the company (for purposes such as calculation of profitability). The general ledger may include separate accounts for each of the following.

Capital funds	{money put into company by owners}
Capital assets	{e.g. vans, furniture, buildings}
Bank account	{normally a company has more than one}
Accounts payable	{general ledger contains only summary totals}
Accounts receivable	{general ledger contains only summary totals}
Rents and rates	
Gas, electricity and water	
Salaries and wages	
Sales	{what Typico has charged customers}
Inventory	{cost of stock}
Cost of goods sold	{what Typico paid for them}

This is not a complete list. The accounts in the general ledger and elsewhere are specified in a document that is called the *chart of accounts*. The chart of accounts defines the company's accounting procedures and the degree of detail of each account.

A *transaction* is an event such as receipt of payment from a customer, payment by Typico of an electricity bill, purchase by Typico of a van, receipt by Typico of goods on credit from a supplier, etc. The general ledger accounts are set up so that every transaction is included in a total that is shown in at least two different accounts. In the following simplified introductory example, every transaction is explicitly recorded in at least two accounts, instead of merely being included in totals that are included in these accounts.

If a transaction is recorded in exactly two accounts, then it is recorded in one of these accounts as a *debit* entry that *increases* the balance of the account, and in the other account as a *credit* entry that *decreases* the value of the account. It is vital that the debit entry and the credit entry sum to zero: one is positive and the other is negative by the same amount. If a transaction is recorded in more than two accounts, the sum of the entries in all these accounts must be zero. This method of book-keeping, which ensures that the sum of all entries for one transaction is zero, is called *double-entry book-keeping*. One of its advantages is that clerical errors can be detected by checking that the sum of the balances of all accounts is zero.

Figure 1.5 shows some simplified examples of transactions, show-

Transaction	Amount	Account name	+ or −
Owners provide capital	10000	Capital funds	−
	10000	Bank account	+
Typico buy van	3000	Capital assets	+
	3000	Bank account	−
Typico pay rates	1200	Rents and rates	+
	1200	Bank account	−
Receive goods on credit	5000	Inventory	+
	5000	Accounts payable	−
Pay wages	1500	Salaries and wages	+
	1500	Bank account	−
Receive goods on credit	2000	Inventory	+
	2000	Accounts payable	−
Sell for 1100 on credit goods that cost 800	800	Inventory	−
{note there are entries in four accounts for this one transaction}	800	Cost of goods sold	+
	1100	Sales	−
	1100	Accounts receivable	+
Pay a supplier	3000	Bank account	−
	3000	Accounts payable	+
Receive payment from customer	1000	Accounts receivable	−
	1000	Bank account	+

Fig. 1.5. A list of transactions.

ing the two (or in one case four) associated entries in accounts. In this figure + means *debit* which *increases* an account, and − means *credit* which *decreases* an account. Making an entry in an account, as the result of a transaction, is called *posting* to the account. In the above example there were, for instance, three postings to the inventory account, and consequently the inventory account could be as shown in Fig. 1.6. It is easy to work out what the other accounts will look like, assuming that they start from zero.

General ledger accounts for headings such as Accounts Payable, Accounts Receivable and Inventory do not show the fine details of every transaction. Instead, detail is shown in *subsidiary ledgers*. The ACCOUNTS RECEIVABLE file that we have introduced previously is an example of a subsidiary ledger. The Accounts Receivable general ledger account at Typico is a summary of the

Inventory account

DATE	DETAIL	DEBIT	CREDIT
6:9:90	WILLIAMS CABLES	5000	
10:9:90	WIZARD FITTINGS	2000	
12:9:90	SMITHSON ELECTRIC		800

Fig. 1.6.   Example of an inventory account.

ACCOUNTS RECEIVABLE file and it merely shows the value of goods supplied to each customer on credit each month, and the total amount that each customer has actually paid to Typico each month. This illustrates the idea that a general ledger account is usually a bird's-eye-view summary rather than a completely detailed account: the detail is delegated to subsidiary ledgers. At Typico the ACCOUNTS RECEIVABLE file is a subsidiary ledger that lists individual invoices and payments (not shown individually in the general ledger) but does not show individual lines of invoice detail. This level of fine detail is delegated to the INVOICE DETAIL file.

We shall not describe mechanisms for posting to general ledger accounts. The list of transactions and their postings, which was given above by way of example, was very much simplified for introductory purposes.

1.7.2.   *Audit trails*

In order to prevent loss or theft of goods or money and to check the accuracy and completeness of accounts, Typico and their auditors must be able to check the origin of every entry in every account. In other words, auditors must be able to check how each entry was arrived at. For this purpose the details of processing and posting of transactions are recorded in JOURNAL files, such as Typico's GOODS RECEIPTS, CASH RECEIPTS JOURNAL and CASH PAYMENTS JOURNAL that we have mentioned previously. A chain of file entries leading from an individual invoice or cheque to an entry in a general ledger account is an example of an *audit trail*. An audit trail is the history of the processing of a transaction. An accounting and filing system should be set up so that an audit trail is available for every transaction. Typico keep SALES ORDER

HISTORY and PURCHASE ORDER HISTORY files for audit purposes, as well as for answering queries.

1.8. Employees file and payroll

1.8.1. *Employees file*

Typico maintain a file that has one record for each employee. The field names are as follows.

EMPLOYEES file field names

EMPLOYEE NUMBER	{primary key}
SURNAME	
FORENAMES	
TITLE	{Mr, Mrs, etc.}
HOME ADDRESS	
OFFICE ADDRESS	{which room in which building of Typico's premises}
OFFICE TELEPHONE	
APPOINTMENT NUMBER	{see Section 1.8.4}
DATE OF ENTRY TO THIS APPOINTMENT	
PART TIME PER CENT	{100 if full-time}
DATE OF BIRTH	
WHETHER TEMPORARY	{yes or no}
DATE OF EXPIRY OF TEMPORARY APPOINTMENT	{blank if not temporary}
WHETHER ON PROBATION	{yes or no}
DATE OF END OF PERIOD OF PROBATION	{a blank if not on probation}
DATE OF LAST REVIEW OF PERFORMANCE	
SKILL DESCRIPTION	{e.g. clerk, accountant, driver}
HIGHEST QUALIFICATION	{e.g. B.Sc. Computer Science}
MARITAL STATUS	{single, married, divorced or widowed}
SEX	{M or F}
GROSS PAY THIS MONTH	{before any deductions}
EMPLOYEES MONTHLY SUPERANNUATION CONTRIBUTION	{towards pension}
TAXABLE PAY THIS YEAR TO DATE	{total gross pay less total superannuation contribution}

TAX CODE   {determines amount of income tax withheld from pay and subsequently paid direct to Inland Revenue by employer}

INCOME TAX FOR THIS MONTH   {amount deducted from pay by employer}

INCOME TAX THIS YEAR TO DATE   {total over all months so far this year}

NATIONAL INSURANCE   {contribution paid monthly by employee}

NATIONAL INSURANCE THIS YEAR TO DATE

REASON FOR OTHER DEDUCTION   {e.g. union subscription or court order}

AMOUNT OF OTHER DEDUCTION

ARREARS OF PAY   {e.g. backdated pay rise}

NET PAY THIS MONTH

EMPLOYEE BANK NAME

EMPLOYEE ACCOUNT NUMBER

Typico can use this file to obtain reports that list employees who satisfy various criteria: the given criteria constitute a *profile*. For example, Typico can in this way obtain a list of names of employees who are 60 years old or older. A more elaborate example is that Typico can obtain a list of their employees who match the following profile:

(1) skill description is 'electrical engineer';
(2) home address is in Newcastle;
(3) gross pay per annum exceeds £10 000.

Another example is that Typico can use the EMPLOYEES file to obtain a report that lists the employees on probation whose probationary period ends within three months, and whose performance should therefore be subject to urgent review so that Typico can decide whether to offer them permanent jobs.

1.8.2. *Payroll processing*

1.8.2.1. *EMPLOYEES file update*

A company usually has some employees who are paid cash each week, and others who are paid monthly by direct transfer of funds from a company bank account to the employee's bank account. We shall consider only the second of these modes of operation.

Typico use their EMPLOYEES file each month to work out how much should be paid to each employee. As a preliminary step, before the payment calculations, the EMPLOYEES file is updated routinely each month. For example any changes in any employee's basic pay, tax code, trade union subscriptions, or National Insurance contributions should be incorporated in the EMPLOYEES file. Similarly, details of dates of starting a job or leaving a job must be entered into the file so that pay can be adjusted accordingly: an employee may start or leave a job at a date that is not at the end or beginning of a month. Arrears of pay arising from backdated pay increases must also be incorporated into the EMPLOYEES file.

When the EMPLOYEES file is updated a report of all changes that have been made is produced so that changes can be checked by staff. This record of changes forms part of an audit trail. Payment data in the EMPLOYEES file constitutes a subsidiary ledger.

1.8.2.2. *Payment calculation*

The net pay, i.e. the amount that an employee actually receives, is made up as follows:

net pay = basic pay + arrears of pay − superannuation
            contribution − income tax − other deductions (such as
            union subscriptions)

As well as calculating net pay for each employee each month prior to payment, Typico also compute the total pay and income tax for the (financial) year up to and including that month. This helps Typico to report at the end of the year to the tax authorities the payments to, and tax withheld from, employees.

When the net pay calculation has been completed, it should preferably be checked manually by an accountant to guard against errors.

1.8.2.3. *Actual payment of employees*

After calculation and checking of net pay, employees are paid on the last day of the month by direct transfer of funds from a Typico bank account to the employees' private bank accounts. This transfer of funds is not done by cheque but by electronic funds transfer, which we shall not now explain. At the same time a printed pay slip, which itemizes gross pay, net pay, and the amounts of various deductions such as tax, is sent to each employee.

During the payment process, Typico record in accounts that we have not previously mentioned the total amounts paid to various categories of employees such as sales-persons, warehouse persons, van drivers, accounts staff, and managers. This helps Typico to see where it spends its money.

1.8.2.4. Tax reporting

Income tax withheld from employees must be forwarded to the tax authorities together with tax and payment details for all employees. After the end of the tax year, Typico has a legal obligation to give each employee a formal statement of total gross pay and total income tax deducted during that year. Typico must also forward reports and superannuation contributions to the financial institutions who look after pension provision. Furthermore, Typico must send reports and payments to trade unions and other organizations on whose behalf there have been deductions from employees' pay.

1.8.3. Employee history file

When an employee leaves, or is promoted, or changes job within Typico, data from his EMPLOYEES file record is copied into a newly created record in the EMPLOYEE HISTORY file. If the employee has left, his record is deleted from the EMPLOYEES file; otherwise it is updated to show his present appointment.

1.8.4. ESTABLISHMENT file

For simplicity we have not previously mentioned that Typico has a number of departments, such as sales, purchasing, warehouse, finance, and transport. Each department has a certain number of posts for employees, e.g. the sales department has a certain number of senior salesmen, a certain number of junior salesmen, a certain number of senior secretaries, and so on. These numbers constitute the *establishment* of the department. Typico have an ESTABLISHMENT file that records the establishment that has been agreed by management for each department. At any given time, some of the posts specified in the ESTABLISHMENT file may be vacant and others may be filled by more than the agreed number of employees.

The primary key to the ESTABLISHMENT file is APPOINT-MENT NUMBER. For any given APPOINTMENT NUMBER value there may be more than one employee, and all such employees have this APPOINTMENT NUMBER value in their EMPLOYEES record. A record in the ESTABLISHMENT file shows, among other things, the department and title of each post. An example of a title of a post is CLERICAL ASSISTANT.

1.9. Exercises

1. Make up one fictitious record that could belong to Typico's INVEN-TORY file.

2. Make up one Typico SALES ORDER HEADER record and a collection of SALES ORDER DETAIL records that could possibly correspond to Smithson Electric's purchase order in Section 1.2.1.

3. Ideally a SALES ORDER DETAIL record could be uniquely identified by values of the two fields SALES ORDER NUMBER and ITEM REFERENCE NUMBER. It is common practice to give DETAIL records LINE NUMBERs. Why do you think this is done? (Bear in mind that sometimes hundreds of DETAIL records may correspond to a single HEADER record.)

4. Assuming that file contents will never change, list all candidate keys for each of the following two files:

(a)

FIELD 1	FIELD 2	FIELD 3	FIELD 4
a	1	x	p
b	3	z	p
c	3	y	p
d	2	w	q

(b)

FIELD 1	FIELD 2	FIELD 3	FIELD 4
a	1	x	p
b	3	y	p
c	3	z	p
d	2	x	q

5. For each of the following Typico files, list all candidate keys:

   (a) SALES ORDER HEADER;
   (b) SALES ORDER DETAIL;
   (c) SUPPLIERS;
   (d) SOURCES;
   (e) GOODS RECEIPTS;
   (f) PENDING INVOICE;
   (g) EMPLOYEES.

6. Suggest field names for the records in

   (a) Typico's CASH PAYMENTS JOURNAL (Section 1.6.2).
   (b) Typico's ESTABLISHMENT file (Section 1.8.4).

2 Relational algebra

2.1. Introduction

If a collection of files are stored in computer memory, we cannot read them and update them directly as we could if they were stored in the old-fashioned way on paper. Instead we have to tell the computer system to read them and update them on our behalf. Often we shall wish to program things that are awkward or impossible in standard Pascal, and instead it may be expedient to use a *data manipulation language* which is a specially enhanced version of an ordinary programming language. Alternatively we may wish to use a higher level *query language* which is a special-purpose file-accessing language. The distinction between query languages and data manipulation languages is not very clear, and some people prefer not to make this distinction at all.

Relational algebra is a primitive example of a query language. There are more sophisticated query languages that are more comfortable to use, are closer to ordinary English, and have greater technical capabilities. We concentrate initially on relational algebra because this provides a basic well-known starting point for dealing with a collection of files, and gives names to fundamental operations that have to be performed anyway, whatever language is used.

2.2. Music files

As illustrative examples for use in an introduction to relational algebra, Typico files would be unnecessarily complicated. We shall instead use the following collection of artificially simple files which we shall refer to as *music files*.

The music files contain information about musicians, musical compositions, and specific performances. An *ensemble* is a group of musicians functioning as an entity: for example, a band, an orchestra, or a quartet. A musician can be a performer on one or more instruments, and/or a composer, and/or a director (i.e. conductor) of performances, and/or a manager of ensembles.

All dates in the files are in the form of an eight-digit number in which the four leftmost digits are the year number, the next two digits are the month number, and two rightmost digits are the day number. For example 19910507 means May 7 1991. An advantage of this representation of dates is that they can be used directly as operands of greater than and less than comparisons, e.g. if $d = 19891102$ then it is true that $19910507 > d$.

The file names and field names for the music files are as follows.

MUSICIANS	{is file name; this file gives personal details of musicians; field names are as follows}
MNO	{musician number, which is the primary key of this file and is used for cross referencing}
MNAME	{musician name: for simplicity just one name per musician}
BDATE	{date of birth}
BCOUNTRY	{country of birth}

COMPOSITIONS	{is file name; this file gives details of individual compositions; field names are as follows}
CNO	{composition number, which is the primary key of this file and is used for cross referencing}
TITLE	{of composition}
MNO	{of musician number of composer}
CDATE	{date of composition}

ENSEMBLES	{is file name; this file gives details of ensembles; field names are as follows}
ENO	{ensemble number, which is the primary key of this file and is used for cross referencing}
ENAME	{ensemble name}
ECOUNTRY	{home country of ensemble}
MNO	{musician number of manager of ensemble}

PERFORMANCES	{is file name; this file gives details of performances of compositions; field names are as follows}
CNO	{composition number of composition that was performed}
PDATE	{date of performance}
TOWN	{location of performance}
COUNTRY	{of town}

| MNO | {musician number of director of performance} |
| ENO | {ensemble number of ensemble that performed} |

PERFORMERS	{is file name; this file tells us which musician plays which instrument and how well; some musicians play more than one instrument and others play none; field names are as follows}
PNO	{performer number, which is the primary key of this file and is used for cross referencing}
MNO	{musician number}
INSTRUMENT	{played by musician}
GRADE	{how well musician plays}

ENSEMBLE MEMBERS	{is file name; this file says which performer plays in which ensemble; field names are as follows}
ENO	{ensemble number}
PNO	{performer number}

To make it easy to see what is going on we now give a very simple example of complete contents of the music files, with only a few records in each file. The practical usefulness of relational algebra would be more obvious in an example where there were tens of thousands of records, but the quantity of data would increase the difficulty of seeing what was happening. Expressions in relational algebra should be equally valid whether the files actually contain tens of thousands of records or only a few as in the following example.

MUSICIANS   {file name}

MNO	MNAME	BDATE	BCOUNTRY
M1	AYBEESKY	19410609	WYLAND
M2	BEESEESKY	18181211	ZEDLAND
M3	SEEDEESKY	18980404	EXLAND
M4	AYBEESKY	19360621	WYLAND
M5	AYEFSKY	19510919	ZEDLAND
M6	BEEDEESKY	19021025	TEELAND
M7	AYSEESKY	19471104	WYLAND
M8	SEEDEESKY	18980404	TEELAND
M9	DEEBEESKY	19540130	WYLAND

COMPOSITIONS {file name}

CNO	TITLE	MNO	CDATE
C1	ELPIECE	M5	19830605
C2	EMTUNE	M9	19851108
C3	KAYSONG	M3	19340120
C4	AITCHTUNE	M5	19840929
C5	ELPIECE	M3	19290530
C6	KAYSONG	M5	19821204

ENSEMBLES {file name}

ENO	ENAME	ECOUNTRY	MNO
E1	THE AYS	EXLAND	M7
E2	THE BEES	EXLAND	M5
E3	THE CEES	TEELAND	M7
E4	THE AYS	ZEDLAND	M4
E5	THE DEES	EXLAND	M5
E6	THE EFS	EXLAND	M5
E7	THE BEES	ZEDLAND	M4

PERFORMANCES {file name}

CNO	PDATE	TOWN	COUNTRY	MNO	ENO
C5	19860530	TEETON	TEELAND	M9	E3
C1	19860615	ARBY	EXLAND	M1	E6
C5	19860622	ESTON	EXLAND	M9	E5
C3	19860622	ESFIELD	EXLAND	M1	E1
C5	19860703	ESTON	TEELAND	M9	E5
C6	19860705	ARBY	ZEDLAND	M7	E4
C1	19860711	TEEBY	EXLAND	M1	E1
C4	19860719	ARTON	WYLAND	M4	E2

PERFORMERS {file name}

PNO	MNO	INSTRUMENT	GRADE
P1	M1	SAXOPHONE	GOOD
P2	M1	FLUTE	AVERAGE

cont.

P3	M1	PIANO	AWFUL
P4	M4	TRUMPET	GOOD
P5	M5	VIOLIN	GOOD
P6	M5	VIOLA	WEAK
P7	M9	CLARINET	GOOD
P8	M9	SAXOPHONE	AWFUL
P9	M7	PIANO	AVERAGE

ENSEMBLE MEMBERS   {file name}

ENO	PNO
E1	P5
E1	P8
E1	P9
E2	P5
E2	P3
E3	P9
E4	P4
E4	P1
E4	P7
E5	P5
E5	P9
E6	P1
E6	P7
E7	P3
E7	P5

2.3. Operators and operands

The names and types of fields of a record constitute the record's *type*. An unordered set of (non-variant) records that all have the same type is a *relation*. The concept of a *file* is more general than a relation: a file may contain records of more than one type, although we shall ignore this possibility in this text. Furthermore, the sequence of records in a file is generally defined and meaningful.

Before introducing the operands of relational algebra, it may be helpful to note that in the Pascal statement

F: = (A + B)*C − D

A, B, C, and D are *operands*, and + , *, and − are *operators*. The *result* is assigned to F.

In relational algebra the operands and results of expressions are relations. For the purposes of this text we shall also regard operands and results of expressions in relational algebra as *files*. The ordering of records in operand files is disregarded by the operators of relational algebra, and the ordering of records in files that are results of expressions in relational algebra should be regarded as random.

In the context of relational theory and relational algebra, records are sometimes known as *tuples*, and types of fields are sometimes known as *domains*, but this terminology will not be used in the present text.

We now introduce the operators of relational algebra.

2.4. Projection

The projection operator has a single operand that we shall denote by FNAME. FNAME can be either a data file or the result of a relational algebra expression. We shall denote the projection operation by

proj list of field names (FNAME).

In the list of field names that follows **proj**, all the names must be of fields of FNAME. The result of the projection operation is obtained by

(a) deleting from FNAME all fields that are *not* included in the list of field names, and
(b) deleting from the result of (a) all repetitions so that in the result of (b) no two records are identical.

For example the result of **proj** INSTRUMENT (PERFORMERS) is

SAXOPHONE
FLUTE
PIANO
TRUMPET
VIOLIN
VIOLA
CLARINET

in which no instrument occurs more than once. As a further example, the result of **proj** MNAME,BCOUNTRY (MUSICIANS) is

AYBEESKY	WYLAND
BEESEESKY	ZEDLAND
SEEDEESKY	EXLAND
AYEFSKY	ZEDLAND
BEEDEESKY	TEELAND
AYSEESKY	WYLAND
SEEDEESKY	TEELAND
DEEBEESKY	WYLAND

2.5. Selection

Like projection, the selection operator has a single operand which can be either a data file or the result of relational algebra expression. We shall denote the selection operation by

sel condition (FNAME).

The result of this operation is obtained by deleting from FNAME all records that do not satisfy the condition. For example the result of **sel** BCOUNTRY = 'WYLAND' (MUSICIANS) is

M1	AYBEESKY	19410609	WYLAND
M4	AYBEESKY	19360621	WYLAND
M7	AYSEESKY	19471104	WYLAND
M9	DEEBEESKY	19540130	WYLAND

In

sel BCOUNTRY = 'WYLAND' (MUSICIANS) is

WYLAND is enclosed by quotes because it is a character string that is a literal value of the field BCOUNTRY. BCOUNTRY is not in quotes because it is a field name. In general, characters and character strings that are literal values must always be enclosed in quotes to distinguish them from names of fields, variables, etc., which must not be enclosed within quotes. A numeric value must not be enclosed between quotes unless it is being regarded as a string of characters. For example we can obtain the MUSICIANS records for all musicians born in 1946 or later by writing

sel BDATE > 19451231 (MUSICIANS)

in which 19451231 is not in quotes because here it is an integer and not a character string.

In a selection operation the condition can include the comparison operators $<$, $=$, $>$, $<=$, $<>$, and $>=$, and the logical operators **and**, **or**, and **not**. The condition must not, however, include arithmetical operators such as $+$, $-$, $*$, and $/$. Within a condition an operand cannot itself be the result of a relational algebra expression. We shall write conditions in accordance with the rules of standard Pascal.

For example, to obtain the MUSICIANS records of all musicians born in WYLAND later than December 31 1945 we can write

sel (BCOUNTRY = 'WYLAND') **and**
(BDATE > 19451231)(MUSICIANS)

which yields

M7	AYSEESKY	19471104	WYLAND
M9	DEEBEESKY	19540130	WYLAND

2.6. Very simple queries

By applying a projection operation to the result of a selection operation we can extract information from a file to answer a very simple practical query as shown in the following example.

Query: find the names of all musicians born in 1946 or later.

This can be answered by
proj MNAME (**sel** BDATE > 19451231 (MUSICIANS)).

Another example is as follows.

Query: find the musician number of every musician who plays the piano and is not graded AWFUL.

This can be answered by

proj MNO (**sel** (INSTRUMENT = 'PIANO') **and** (GRADE
< > 'AWFUL')(PERFORMERS)).

The answer is M7 which is a single value. In fact it is legitimate for an answer to be null, i.e. to contain nothing. Yet another simple example is the following.

Query: find the town and country of every performance that took place on June 22 1986.

This can be answered by

proj TOWN, COUNTRY (**sel** PDATE = 19860622
(PERFORMANCES)).

2.7. Join

2.7.1. *Natural join on a single field*

In relational algebra there is a family of join operators. We shall be concerned only with a special kind of join called a *natural* join, and we shall use *join* to mean *natural join* unless we specify the contrary.

We need to know that, like a Pascal variable, a field of a record has a *type* such as INTEGER, REAL, or character STRING. A join has two operands, which we shall denote by FNAME1 and FNAME2. These can be either data files or the results of relational algebra expressions: this is always to be understood henceforward. For initial simplicity we shall assume that FNAME1 and FNAME2 have in common exactly one field that has the same name and type in FNAME1 and FNAME2. For example, MUSICIANS and COMPOSITIONS files have in common exactly one field which is MNO. DATE is not common because it has the name BDATE in MUSICIANS and CDATE in COMPOSITIONS.

As an even simpler example, suppose that FNAME1 has fields G1 and F1 and contains

G1	F1
d	3
h	7
y	4

and FNAME2 has fields F1 and G2 and contains

F1	G2
3	A
3	B
7	A
4	C
4	B

The result of the operation FNAME1 **join** FNAME2 is obtained by concatenating every record in FNAME2 with every record in FNAME1 that has the same value in the common field, and showing the common field only once in the result. *Concatenate* means *string together*.

In our example we string together the records

F1	G2
3	A
3	B

of FNAME2 with the record

G1	F1
d	3

of FNAME1, because these have the same value (actually 3) in the common field F1. As a result of this concatenation FNAME1 **join** FNAME2 contains

G1	F1	G2
d	3	A
d	3	B

and also further records as we shall see. The only record of FNAME2 that can be concatenated with

G1	F1
h	7

in FNAME1 is

F1	G2
7	A

because this is the only one that has the same value (actually 7) of the common field F1. Furthermore, the result of the join will also contain the concatenation of the two records

F1	G2
4	C
4	B

of FNAME2 with the record

G1	F1
y	4

of FNAME1 because these have the same value (actually 4) of the common field F1. Finally, the complete result of FNAME1 **join** FNAME2 is

G1	F1	G2
d	3	A
d	3	B
h	7	A
y	4	C
y	4	B

2.7.2. *The use of join in answering queries*

The expression **proj** MNO (COMPOSITIONS) gives us the MNO of every composer, i.e. of every musician who has composed at least one composition. In order to find the MNAME of every composer we need to associate the MNAME with the MNO for each COMPOSITION record. This association can be achieved by joining COMPOSITIONS with MUSICIANS, and thus concatenating each COMPOSITIONS record with the composer's MUSICIANS record.

proj MNAME (COMPOSITIONS **join** MUSICIANS)

gives us the names of all composers. Further, the query

Query: give the name and date of birth of every composer of a piece entitled KAYSONG

can be answered by

proj MNAME, BDATE (**sel** TITLE = 'KAYSONG' (COMPOSITIONS)
join MUSICIANS).

The selection operation picks out from the COMPOSITIONS file the compositions entitled KAYSONG. The join operation strings MUSICIANS information together with selected COMPO-SITIONS information. The requirement for agreement in the common field MNO means that the MUSICIANS information that is concatenated with a particular COMPOSITIONS record belongs to that particular composition's composer. For our example data, the final result of the relational algebra expression is

```
SEEDEESKY    18980404
AYEFSKY      19510919
```

which is the correct answer to the query.

There are queries that can be answered by using two or more join operations. For example

Query: list all the instruments played in the ensemble named THE AYS OF ZEDLAND.

A relational algebra expression for this is:

proj INSTRUMENT (**proj** ENO (**sel** (ENAME = 'THE AYS') **and** (ECOUNTRY = 'ZEDLAND') (ENSEMBLES)) **join** ENSEMBLE MEMBERS **join** PERFORMERS)

The first (i.e. leftmost) join brings in the PNOs of all the performers in the ensemble. The second join brings in the names of instruments of the performers.

A relational algebra expression may involve selection operations on more than one file. For instance

Query: give the date of every performance in EXLAND of any composition entitled EMTUNE.

A relational algebra expression for this is:

proj PDATE (**sel** COUNTRY = 'EXLAND' (PERFORMANCES) **join**
proj CNO (**sel** TITLE = 'EMTUNE' (COMPOSITIONS)))

The following example goes a step further, requiring a second join

Query: give the name of the composer of any composition entitled EMTUNE that has been performed at any time on EXLAND.

A relational algebra expression for this is

proj MNAME (**proj** CNO (**sel** COUNTRY = 'EXLAND' (PERFORMANCES)) **join sel** TITLE = 'EMTUNE' (COMPOSITIONS) **join** MUSICIANS).

This may look complicated: many people find relational algebra easier to write than to read.

2.7.3.   Natural join on more than one field

The join of two files that have no common field is null. The join of two files FNAME1 and FNAME2 that have more than one common field is obtained by concatenating each record of FNAME1 with every record of FNAME2 that has the same values of the common fields.

For example, if FNAME1 contains

G1	F1	F2
d	3	H
h	7	N
y	4	H

and FNAME2 contains

F1	F2	G2
3	H	A
3	H	B
7	N	A
4	H	C
4	H	B

then the result of FNAME1 **join** FNAME2 is

G1	F1	F2	G2
d	3	H	A
d	3	H	B
h	7	N	A
y	4	H	C
y	4	H	B

The common fields are shown only once in the result of the join. In the following example one of the joins is on two fields.

Query: give the name and country of every ensemble of which the manager is also one of the performers.

This can be answered by

proj ENAME, ECOUNTRY (ENSEMBLES **join** PERFORMERS **join** ENSEMBLE MEMBERS).

An interpretation of this is that, for each ensemble, if the manager is a performer then the first join concatenates his PNOs with the ensemble's ENO. An ensemble whose manager is not a performer is absent from the result of the first join. The second join is on the two fields ENO and PNO and eliminates from the result of the first join any record that contains an ENO, PNO pair which is not in ENSEMBLE MEMBERS. Thus the second join eliminates ensembles whose manager does not also play in the ensemble.

2.8. Exercises

1. Write expressions in relational algebra to answer the following queries:

   (a) In which towns in EXLAND have there been performances?
   (b) Give the date of composition of every piece entitled KAYSONG.
   (c) Give the names of all saxophone players.
   (d) Give the titles of all compositions by AYEFSKY.
   (e) Give the dates of all performances of pieces composed by composers who were born in ZEDLAND.
   (f) Give the name of the manager of each ensemble that includes a SAXOPHONE.

2. Using Typico files, write relational algebra expressions to answer the following queries:

   (a) Give the DESCRIPTION of the item that has ITEM REF NO = '95PA42'.
   (b) Give the CUSTOMER NUMBER and CREDIT LIMIT of SMITH-SON ELECTRIC whose billing address is 17 HIGH STREET, PEEMARSH.
   (c) Give the CUSTOMER NUMBER of every customer for whom there

is any sales order that includes the item that has ITEM REF
NO = '95PA42'.

(d) Give the name and billing address of every customer for whom there
is at least one sales order that includes at least 10 units of the item that
has ITEM REF NO = '95PA42'.

3. Using music files, write relational algebra expressions to answer the
following queries.

(a) Give the name of every ensemble of EXLAND that includes a
saxophone.

(b) Give the names of all towns in EXLAND where any piece composed
later than 19491231 has been performed.

(c) Give the date, town, and country of every performance directed by
the composer of the composition performed.

2.9. Union

As well as select, project, and join operators, relational algebra has
union, intersection, difference, division, and product operators.
Union, intersection, and difference operations are only applicable to
files that have the same field names and field types. In other words,
the operand files must have the same record type.

The result of

FNAME1 **union** FNAME2

comprises all the records that are in at least one (possibly both) of
FNAME1 and FNAME2. For example, if FNAME1 contains

F1	G1
a	4
b	5
c	6

and FNAME2 contains

F1	G1
d	2
b	5
e	4
c	6

then FNAME1 **union** FNAME2 contains

F1	G1
a	4
b	5
c	6
d	2
e	4

There are queries that can be answered by including '**or**' in a selection condition, instead of using a union. For example

Query: give the names of all musicians born in WYLAND or ZEDLAND, which can be answered by

proj MNAME (**sel** BCOUNTRY = 'WYLAND') **or** (BCOUNTRY = 'ZEDLAND')(MUSICIANS)).

We need a union operation when the operands are not selected from the same file by a selection operation. For example

Query: give the names of all musicians who were born in WYLAND or who have composed a piece entitled KAYSONG, which can be answered by

proj MNAME (**sel** BCOUNTRY = 'WYLAND' (MUSICIANS)) **union** **proj** MNAME (MUSICIANS **join sel** TITLE = 'KAYSONG' (COMPOSITIONS)).

The first operand of the union is the set of MNAMEs for musicians born in WYLAND. The second operand is the set of MNAMEs for composers of any piece entitled KAYSONG.

2.10. Intersection

The result of FNAME1 **intersection** FNAME2 is the set of records that belong to both FNAME1 and FNAME2. For example if FNAME1 contains

F1	G1
a	4
b	5
c	6

and FNAME2 contains

F1	G1
d	2
b	5
e	4
c	6

then FNAME1 **intersection** FNAME2 contains

F1	G1
b	5
c	6

An example of a query that can be answered by using intersection is

Query: give the name of every musician who has composed a piece entitled KAYSONG and a piece entitled ELPIECE. This can be answered by

proj MNAME (MUSICIANS **join** (**proj** MNO (**sel** TITLE = 'KAYSONG' (COMPOSITIONS)) **intersection proj** MNO (**sel** TITLE = 'ELPIECE' (COMPOSITIONS))))).

We do not need intersection to answer

Query: give the name of every musician born in WYLAND before January 1 1946.

Instead of using intersection for this we can use '**and**' in a selection condition (which would not have been possible in the previous example):

proj MNAME (**sel** (BCOUNTRY = 'WYLAND') **and** (BDATE < 19460101)(MUSICIANS)).

2.11. Difference

The result of FNAME1 **difference** FNAME2 is the set of records that are in FNAME1 *and not* in FNAME2. For example if FNAME1 contains

F1	G1
a	4
b	5
c	6
f	5

and FNAME2 contains

F1	G1
d	2
b	5
e	4
c	6

then FNAME1 **difference** FNAME2 contains

F1	G1
a	4
f	5

An example of a query that can be answered by using a difference operation is

Query: give the names of all musicians who are not composers. This can be answered by

proj MNAME ((**proj** MNO (MUSICIANS) **difference proj** MNO (COMPOSITIONS)) **join** MUSICIANS).

Within this the subexpression

proj MNO (MUSICIANS) **difference proj** MNO (COMPOSITIONS)

gives all the MNOs that appear in the MUSICIANS file and not in the COMPOSITIONS file.

2.12. Division

For the division operation FNAME1 **division** FNAME2 every field

of FNAME2 must have the same name and type as a field of
FNAME1. The result of division is a file whose fields are those of
FNAME1 that are not in FNAME2. A record is included in the
result of division if and only if this record occurs in FNAME1
concatenated with *every* record in FNAME2. For example if
FNAME1 consists of

G2	G1	F1
A	d	3
C	h	7
B	h	7
B	y	4
A	y	4
A	h	7
B	d	3
C	y	4

and FNAME2 consists of

G1	F1
d	3
h	7
y	4

then FNAME1 **division** FNAME2 consists of

G2
A
B

in which there is only one field, which is the only one that belongs to
FNAME1 and *not* to FNAME2. The value A of G2 is included in
the result of division because A appears concatenated with *every*
record of FNAME2 in FNAME1; that is to say, FNAME1 includes
all of

G2	G1	F1
A	d	3
A	h	7
A	y	4

The value C of G2 is not included in the result of this division because

C   d   3

does not occur in FNAME1. An example of a query that can be answered using a division operation is

Query: give the ENOs of all ensembles that include all the performers who play in ensemble E6. This can be answered by

ENSEMBLE MEMBERS **division proj** PNO (**sel**
ENO = 'E6'(ENSEMBLE MEMBERS)).

In this the second operand of the division operation is a list of all PNOs of performers in E6.

2.13. Product

The result of FNAME1 **product** FNAME2 is obtained by concatenating every record of FNAME2 with every record of FNAME1. For example if FNAME1 consists of

F1	F2
b	4
d	7

and FNAME2 consists of

F3	F4
A	4
C	R

then FNAME1 **product** FNAME2 consists of

FNAME1.F1	FNAME1.F2	FNAME2.F3	FNAME2.F4
b	4	A	4
b	4	C	R
d	7	A	4
d	7	C	R

In the result the fields have their original field names qualified by their original file name. *Qualified by* means that the file name is written before the field name, and the two names are separated by a full stop. A resulting composite field name such as FNAME1.F1 can be used exactly like a simple field name.

A field name is used to identify a unique field within a record, and therefore no two fields of a record may have the same name. Qualification of field names of a product ensures that in a case such as MUSICIANS **product** COMPOSITIONS the field names are unique. In this example, if the qualifying file names were deleted the field name MNO would illegally occur twice in the product.

One practical reason for employing products in answering queries is to compare values of fields of different files. For example

Query: give the titles of all pieces composed since the birth of AYEFSKY, which can be answered by

proj COMPOSITIONS. TITLE (**sel**
COMPOSITIONS.CDATE > MUSICIANS.BDATE (COMPOSITIONS
product sel MNAME = 'AYEFSKY' (MUSICIANS))).

Another reason for using a product is to pick out pairs of field values from the same file. We would wish to do this to answer

Query: give the names of all pairs of musicians who were born in the same country.

If we take the product of the MUSICIANS file with itself, each qualified field name will occur twice in the product, which is illegal; qualified field names must be unique. A way out of this difficulty is to introduce an alternative name, technically called an *alias* for MUSICIANS. We introduce this new name by writing an **aliases** statement before the relational algebra expression that answers our query:

NEWSICIANS **aliases** MUSICIANS;
proj MUSICIANS.MNAME, NEWSICIANS.MNAME (**sel**
MUSICIANS.BCOUNTRY = NEWSICIANS.BCOUNTRY
(MUSICIANS **product** NEWSICIANS)).

If we wish to ensure that all such pairs of musicians have different names we can use the more elaborate expression

NEWSICIANS **aliases** MUSICIANS;
proj MUSICIANS.MNAME, NEWSICIANS.MNAME (**sel**
(MUSICIANS.BCOUNTRY = NEWSICIANS.BCOUNTRY) **and**
(MUSICIANS.MNO < > NEWSICIANS.MNO) (MUSICIANS **product**
NEWSICIANS)).

2.14. Exercises

1. Using the music files write relational algebra expressions to answer the following queries.

  (a) Give the ENO of every ensemble that includes a saxophone or a clarinet (or both).
  (b) Give the ENO of every ensemble that includes a saxophone and a clarinet.
  (c) Give the ENO of every ensemble that includes a saxophone but not a clarinet.
  (d) Give the name of every musician born later than 19451231 and not born in WYLAND.
  (e) Give the name of every musician born in WYLAND who does not play the saxophone.
  (f) Give the name of every musician who was not born in WYLAND and who does not play the saxophone.
  (g) Give the name of every musician who was born in WYLAND and plays the saxophone.
  (h) List every country in which all of AYEFSKY's compositions have been performed.
  (i) List every country in which none of AYEFSKY's compositions have been performed.
  (j) Give the names of all ensembles who have performed in all countries where any ensemble has performed.
  (k) Give the name of every ensemble that includes either a saxophone or a clarinet but not both.

2. Using Typico files write relational algebra expressions to answer the following queries.

  (a) Give the item reference number of every item that
    (i) is included in any sales order for the customer whose customer number is 6391, and

    (ii) is such that the QUANTITY IN WAREHOUSE of this item is
       less than 5.
  (b) Give the item reference number of every item that is included in at
     least one sales order for customer number 6391 and is also included in
     at least one sales order for customer number 6752.
  (c) Give the item reference number for every item that is included in at
     least one sales order but is not included in any purchase order.
  (d) Give the sales order numbers of all sales orders that include all the
     items ordered in sales order number 1058.

2.15. Query optimization

Hitherto we have said nothing about minimizing the amount of
computation that is required for answering a given query, and we
have not worried about efficiency when writing relational algebra
expressions. *Query optimization* means choosing the *sequence* of
query-answering operations so as to maximize efficiency. For example, if V is a possible value for a field F of file FNAME1 then

(sel F = V (FNAME1)) join FNAME2

selects records from FNAME1 before the join is executed. The
expression

sel F = V (FNAME1 join FNAME2)

yields the same result, but is probably less efficient if the result of the
join contains more than the number of records in FNAME1. We can
expect a selection operation to be slower, and in this sense less
efficient, if it is a selection from a larger number of records.

    If a query is expressed in a query language such as relational
algebra, the optimization of the sequence of operations can be done
automatically by a computer. If a query is answered using the
enhanced version of Pascal that will be introduced in Chapters 4 and
5, automatic maximization of efficiency is very much more difficult,
and this is an important reason for using a special-purpose query
language.

2.16. Numerical capabilities of query languages

Various query languages are more advanced than relational algebra in that they include the following capabilities.

Arithmetic. For example
Query: find the total, over all unpaid invoices, of Smithson Electric's debt to Typico.

Relational algebra cannot answer this. There are other query languages that can find the total, the average, or a count, or some other straightforward numerical result.

Sorted order. Various query languages allow the user to specify the sequence (sorted order) in which records will appear as the result of a query.
Quotas. In the example
Query: give the invoice numbers of the four most recent unpaid invoices to Smithson Electric.

The number four is an example of a *quota*. It specifies an upper limit on the *number* of records that will be included in the reply to a query. Relational algebra does not allow us to specify quotes, but various other query languages do have this facility.

2.17. Query language capabilities other than retrieval

Hitherto we have only indicated capabilities of query languages for retrieving information. A query language should preferably also allow the insertion, deletion, and updating of records. *Updating* means changing various individual fields, without insertion or deletion of entire records.

In this text we shall not introduce stand-alone query languages which have numeric capabilities and capabilities other than retrieval. Instead we shall introduce in Chapters 4 and 5 a powerful extension to Pascal that illustrates how the business of answering queries relates to ordinary Pascal programming.

3 Relational normalization

3.1. Allocation of fields to files

Typico files and music files have hitherto been given as data. We now take a step back to consider how to decide which fields should belong to which files. First we must see what is meant by non-loss decomposition.

3.2. Non-loss decomposition

Consider, for example, a simplified file named ZOOANIMALS that has three fields: ZOO, ANIMAL, and COUNTRYOFORIGIN. Suppose that this file contains just four records:

ZOO	ANIMAL	COUNTRYOFORIGIN
AYTON	KANGAROO	AUSTRALIA
AYTON	CAMEL	ARABIA
BEETON	EMU	AUSTRALIA
BEETON	CAMEL	ARABIA

It is easy to check that

(proj ZOO,ANIMAL (ZOOANIMALS)) **join (proj** ANIMAL, COUNTRYOFORIGIN (ZOOANIMALS))

is identical with the original file ZOOANIMALS. In general a non-loss decomposition of a file is a set of projections of that file whose join is identical with that file. Thus, for example, the two projections **proj** ZOO,ANIMAL (ZOOANIMALS) and **proj** ANIMAL, COUNTRYOFORIGIN (ZOOANIMALS) constitute a non-loss decomposition of the file ZOOANIMALS.

The join of the two projections **proj** ZOO, COUNTRYOFORIGIN (ZOOANIMALS) and **proj** ANIMAL, COUNTRYOFORIGIN (ZOOANIMALS) is

ZOO	ANIMAL	COUNTRYOFORIGIN
AYTON	KANGAROO	AUSTRALIA
AYTON	EMU	AUSTRALIA
AYTON	CAMEL	ARABIA
BEETON	KANGAROO	AUSTRALIA
BEETON	EMU	AUSTRALIA
BEETON	CAMEL	ARABIA

which contains records

AYTON	EMU	AUSTRALIA
BEETON	KANGAROO	AUSTRALIA

that are not in the original file ZOOANIMALS. Therefore this join is not identical with ZOOANIMALS and the two projections **proj** ZOO, COUNTRYOFORIGIN (ZOOANIMALS) and **proj** ANIMAL,COUNTRYOFORIGIN (ZOOANIMALS) do *not* constitute a non-loss decomposition of ZOOANIMALS.

We now introduce relational normalization theory, which does two things:

(a) provides ways of determining whether or not a given set of projections of a file FNAME is a non-loss decomposition of FNAME, and

(b) provides rules for choosing between the alternatives
    (i) simply store a file name FNAME in its present form, or
    (ii) obtain a collection of projections that constitute a non-loss decomposition of FNAME and store these and do not store FNAME (in this case FNAME can be reconstructed from the projections when required).

We shall deal with (b) first, i.e. whether or not to store a file or a non-loss decomposition, and return to (a) later.

3.3. Duplication

3.3.1. Examples of duplication

Sometimes we can avoid undesirable and unnecessary duplication of stored data if we replace a file by a non-loss decomposition.

Consider for example a simplified file named WHOSUPPLIES that
has three fields:

ITEMREFNO   {identifies an item}
NAME   {supplier of this item}
PHONENO   {supplier's telephone number}

For simplicity we shall assume that no two suppliers have the same
name, and that no item has more than one supplier. Suppose that the
file contains the following.

ITEMREFNO	NAME	PHONENO
AA39	JACKSON	3692
AC22	JACKSON	3692
AH84	WILSON	5948
AP83	ROBSON	2514
AZ27	WILSON	5948
DD68	WILSON	5948
FS44	ROBSON	2514
HS41	ROBSON	2514
MM72	WILSON	5948

For reasons that will become clear later the two projections **proj**
ITEMREFNO,NAME (WHOSUPPLIES) and **proj** NAME,PHO-
NENO (WHOSUPPLIES) constitute a non-loss decomposition of
WHOSUPPLIES. This means that their join is identical with
WHOSUPPLIES. The projection **proj** NAME, PHONENO (WHO-
SUPPLIES) contains the following.

NAME	PHONENO
JACKSON	3692
WILSON	5948
ROBSON	2514

Each of these telephone numbers appears only once in this projection, but, for example, WILSON's telephone number occurs four
times in WHOSUPPLIES. This repetition of telephone numbers if
an example of *duplication*. This can be avoided if, instead of storing
WHOSUPPLIES, we store a non-loss decomposition in which each
telephone number appears just once. Similarly, duplication of

CAMEL ARABIA

is avoided if we store an appropriate non-loss decomposition of ZOOANIMALS instead of storing the original file ZOOANI-MALS.

We prefer to avoid duplication because duplication wastes space, and if duplication means n repetitions (e.g. three repetitions of ROBSON's phone number) then all of the n duplicates must be updated when any one of them is updated. For example, if ROB-SON's phone number changes we must change his number in all three of the WHOSUPPLIES records that contain his number. This is undesirable because doing the same thing n times is a waste of time. If we updated fewer than n of the duplicates we would introduce inconsistency, but by avoiding duplication we avoid the risk of inconsistency. There is no risk of inconsistency in **proj** NAME,PHONENO (WHOSUPPLIES) because each phone number is stored exactly once in this projection.

3.3.2. *Candidate keys*

In some cases duplication can be ruled out by replacing a file by a non-loss decomposition. In other cases, replacement of a file by a non-loss decomposition will not be helpful. We now consider how to distinguish between these cases, and thereby decide whether or not replacement by a non-loss decomposition will be helpful.

We shall need to use the concept of a candidate key, which was introduced in Section 1.2.3.1. A candidate key of a file is a minimal set of (one or more) fields whose values uniquely pick out one of the file's records. A candidate key is defined to be minimal in the sense that if any field is deleted from it then it is no longer a candidate key. A file may have more than one candidate key.

For example CUSTOMERNO is a candidate key for the file CUSTADDRESS.

CUSTOMERNO	CUSTNAME	ADDRESS
0391	WILKINSON	19 COBBLE ST
0403	SAMSON	31 HIGH STREET
0569	WILKINSON	31 HIGH STREET
0615	SAMSON	19 COBBLE STREET

The pair of fields CUSTNAME, ADDRESS constitute another candidate key. The projections **proj** CUSTOMERNO, CUST-NAME (CUSTADDRESS) and **proj** CUSTOMERNO, ADDRESS (CUSTADDRESS) constitute a non-loss decomposition that does *not* help to reduce duplication. In this unhelpful decomposition the projections share the candidate key CUSTOMERNO. The sharing of a candidate key is of critical importance. For example, in the non-loss decomposition of WHOSUPPLIES which is helpful for avoiding duplication, the projections do *not* share a candidate key.

We now prove that if the projections that constitute a non-loss decomposition share a candidate key then this decomposition will not help to avoid duplication. Our proof works by showing that if avoidable duplication occurs then this contradicts the assertion that the projections share a candidate key. We consider a file named FNAME that has fields FX, FY, and FZ such that

FNAME = **proj** FX,FY (FNAME) **join proj** FY,FZ (FNAME)

where FY is a candidate key which is shared by the two projections that constitute this non-loss decomposition of FNAME. In this case *duplication* means that FNAME contains a pair of records such as

FX	FY	FZ
x	y	z
x'	y	z

in which

	y	z

is included more than once. This duplication is impossible because FY is a candidate key and therefore the value y cannot possibly occur in more than one record in FNAME. This completes our proof. Similar reasoning can be used in the case where each of FX,FY,FZ is a collection of fields instead of a single field.

Generally a file can have more than one non-loss decomposition. One of the non-loss decompositions of WHOSUPPLIES consists of the projections **proj** ITEMREFNO,PHONENO (WHOSUPPLIES) and **proj** ITEMREFNO,NAME (WHOSUPPLIES) which share a candidate key, so that replacement of WHOSUPPLIES by this non-loss decomposition will not help to avoid duplication. We have previously considered another non-loss decomposition of WHO-SUPPLIES that *will* help to avoid duplication. In general, if a file has *any* non-loss decomposition in which the projections do not share a candidate key then duplication may or may not occur, and in this case avoidance of the *risk* of duplication is a sensible reason for storing a non-loss decomposition instead of the original file.

3.4. Dangling records

In choosing whether to store a non-loss decomposition instead of an original file we shall also take account of requirements for so-called *dangling* records. We shall first give an example of a dangling record, and then give an abstract definition.

For example let us again consider the file WHOSUPPLIES that we used in Section 3.3.1. Suppose we wish to record that the telephone number of a new supplier named SIMSON is 6632, even though SIMSON has not yet supplied any item. We cannot have a blank entry in a key field because there would be no means of identifying the record. Therefore we cannot record SIMSON's telephone number in WHOSUPPLIES because the ITEMREFNO key field would be blank. We can, however, enter this telephone number into **proj** NAME,PHONENO (WHOSUPPLIES), as follows.

NAME	PHONENO
JACKSON	3692
WILSON	5948
ROBSON	2514
SIMSON	6632

In this the record

SIMSON	6632

is an example of a dangling record.

We now give a general definition of a dangling record. Let R and S be sets of fields of a file FNAME such that

FNAME = **proj** R (FNAME) **join proj** S (FNAME).

For example, FNAME could be our file WHOSUPPLIES, R could be the pair of fields (ITEMREFNO,NAME), and S could be the pair of fields (NAME,PHONENO). A dangling record is a record inserted into **proj** S (FNAME) and not included in any record in **proj** R (FNAME) **join proj** S (FNAME) because no record in **proj** R (FNAME) will concatenate with it. For example no record in

proj ITEMREFNO,NAME (WHOSUPPLIES)

contains the name SIMSON, so SIMSON and his telephone number are left out of the result of the join

proj ITEMREFNO,NAME (WHOSUPPLIES) **join proj**
NAME,PHONENO (WHOSUPPLIES).

After insertion of a dangling record into **proj** S (FNAME), it is no longer exactly a projection of FNAME but it remains predominantly a projection of FNAME, and we shall continue to refer to it by the name **proj** S (FNAME).

It is desirable to be able to record SIMSON's telephone number even if he has supplied no item. In general there are circumstances where dangling records, which are desirable in practice, are made possible by storing a non-loss decomposition instead of the original file. There are other circumstances where non-loss decomposition would not be helpful for dealing with dangling records.

The sharing of a candidate key is again of critical importance. If the projections that constitute a non-loss decomposition of FNAME share a candidate key then this decomposition is not helpful for dealing with dangling records. Suppose for example that we wish to insert into the file CUSTADDRESS (of Section 3.3.2) the name HOBSON of customer number 0643, but not his address. We could easily insert

0643   HOBSON

into **proj** CUSTOMERNO, CUSTNAME (CUSTADDRESS).
Equally well we could insert

0643   HOBSON blank

into the original file CUSTADDRESS. The word *blank* signifies a blank field value, which is legitimate for a non-key field. In this example

0643   HOBSON

is not really a dangling record because it can be inserted, together with a blank, directly into the original file.

Another way of thinking about this is that if we insert

0643   HOBSON

into **proj** CUSTOMERNO,CUSTNAME (CUSTADDRESS) then we can arrange that this is *not* a dangling record by inserting into **proj** CUSTOMERNO,ADDRESS (CUSTADDRESS) the harmless dummy record

0643   blank

which will concatenate with

0643   HOBSON

in the join to give

0643   HOBSON blank

in the file CUSTADDRESS when this is reconstructed by joining the projections. In this case there is no dangling record problem.

We now restate this idea more abstractly to prove that if the projections that constitute a non-loss decomposition of FNAME share a candidate key then this decomposition is not helpful for dealing with dangling records. Let **proj** R (FNAME) and **proj** S (FNAME) be projections which share a candidate key and constitute a non-loss decomposition of FNAME. Let us insert into **proj** S (FNAME) an extra record that we shall denote by s in which no field that is part of the shared candidate key is blank.

We can now also insert into **proj** R (FNAME) a harmless dummy record that we shall denote by r, such that r is identical to s in all fields common to R and S, and is blank in all other fields. Insertion of r into **proj** R (FNAME) is legitimate because, by construction, r includes a candidate key, of which no field is blank. Moreover, insertion of r into **proj** R (FNAME) is harmless because r does not tell us anything that is not already included in s. The significant point is that concatenation with r will bring s into the result of the join

proj R (FNAME) **join proj** S (FNAME)

so that s is not really a dangling record. A dangling record would, by definition, not be included in the result of this join. Thus we have shown that dangling records do not arise if the projections share a candidate key.

We have previously noted that a file may have more than one non-loss decomposition. If, in each of these non-loss decompositions, all projections share a candidate key then there is no advantage, from the viewpoint of dangling records, in storing a non-loss decomposition in place of the original file. If there is any non-loss decomposition in which the projections do not share a candidate key then there is a risk, but not a certainty, of being unable to accommodate dangling records.

3.5. Normalization

3.5.1. *Fifth normal form*

A file is said to be in *fifth normal form* if and only if it has no non-loss decomposition in which the constituent projections do not all share a candidate key. In other words, a file is in fifth normal form if and only if, in each of its non-loss decompositions, all of the projections share a candidate key. A file that has *no* non-loss decompositions is in fifth normal form.

If a file is in fifth normal form then according to our previous reasoning there is *no* advantage, with regard to duplication and dangling records, in replacing the file with a non-loss decomposition.

On the other hand, if a file is *not* in fifth normal form, then we shall avoid all risk of problems with duplication and dangling records if we *do* replace this file with a non-loss decomposition in which the projections do not share a candidate key. If, in this decomposition, the constituent projections themselves are not in fifth normal form, then they should be replaced by non-loss decompositions in which all of the projections are in fifth normal form.

This process of replacement by non-loss decompositions is called *normalization*. The primary aim of normalization is to avoid risk of problems with duplication and dangling records.

3.5.2. Exercises

In each of Exercises 1–6 an original file is specified, together with some non-loss decompositions.

(a) In each exercise, normalize the original file. This may mean replacing the original file by an appropriate one of the given non-loss decompositions. You are merely required to say which of the given non-loss decompositions should replace the original file, unless the original file is already in fifth normal form in which case you should say why you think it is in this form. You can assume that all relevant non-loss decompositions are among those that are given.

(b) For each exercise where the original file is not in fifth normal form, give one example in which normalization reduces duplication and one example in which normalization would allow accommodation of a dangling record that could not be included in the non-normalized file.

1. A detailed map of a park shows individual trees. On the map each tree has a unique identification number. In this exercise the name of the original file is TREEDETAILS. This file contains information about the trees. The field names and some of the file's records are as follows.

TREE NO	SPECIES	HEIGHT	EVERGREEN
1	BEECH	21	NO
2	HOLLY	9	YES
3	BEECH	23	NO
4	ASH	18	NO

First non-loss decomposition

    proj TREENO, SPECIES, HEIGHT (TREEDETAILS),
    proj TREENO, EVERGREEN (TREEDETAILS).

Second non-loss decomposition

    proj TREENO, SPECIES (TREEDETAILS),
    proj TREENO, HEIGHT (TREEDETAILS),
    proj TREENO, EVERGREEN (TREEDETAILS)

Third non-loss decomposition

> **proj** TREENO, SPECIES, HEIGHT (TREEDETAILS),
> **proj** SPECIES, EVERGREEN (TREEDETAILS).

2. The name of the original file is SWEETS. The field names and some of the file's records are as follows.

RECIPE	INGREDIENT	GRAMS	CALS PER GRAM
TOFFEE	SUGAR	450	3.7
TOFFEE	BUTTER	225	7.8
TOFFEE	FLOUR	5	3.5
TOFFEE	TREACLE	20	3.2
FUDGE	SUGAR	450	3.7
FUDGE	BUTTER	225	7.8
FUDGE	CONDENSED MILK	400	4.5

First non-loss decomposition

> **proj** RECIPE, INGREDIENT, GRAMS (SWEETS),
> **proj** INGREDIENT, CALSPERGRAM (SWEETS)

Second non-loss decomposition

> **proj** RECIPE, INGREDIENT, GRAMS (SWEETS),
> **proj** RECIPE, INGREDIENT, CALSPERGRAM (SWEETS)

3. The original file, which is named VISITS, records visits of people to towns. For simplicity, no two people have the same name, and no two towns have the same name. The field names and some of the file's records are as follows.

DATE	NAME	PROFESSION	TOWN	COUNTRY
19920615	JONES	ACCOUNTANT	EFTON	WYLAND
19920615	SMITH	PROGRAMMER	SEETON	EXLAND
19920617	SMITH	PROGRAMMER	AYTON	EXLAND
19920620	SMITH	PROGRAMMER	EFTON	WYLAND
19920620	KNIGHT	ENGINEER	DEETON	ZEDLAND
19920620	YOUNG	ENGINEER	SEETON	EXLAND

First non-loss decomposition

> **proj** DATE, NAME, PROFESSION, TOWN (VISITS),
> **proj** TOWN, COUNTRY (VISITS)

Second non-loss decomposition

> **proj** DATE, NAME, TOWN, COUNTRY (VISITS),
> **proj** NAME, PROFESSION (VISITS)

Third non-loss decomposition

> **proj** DATE, NAME, TOWN (VISITS),
> **proj** TOWN, COUNTRY (VISITS),
> **proj** NAME, PROFESSION (VISITS)

4. The original file, which is named JOURNEYS, records journeys by road between towns. Between any two given towns the same route is always taken, and there is never more than one journey over the same route on any one day. The sixth field is the duration of the journey. The field names and some of the file's records are as follows.

FROM	TO	DISTANCE	DATE	DRIVER	TIME
WINKLEBY	COCKLETON	62	19930305	MARSHALL	3.4
WINKLEBY	COCKLETON	62	19930306	ARNOLD	2.8
COCKLETON	MUSSELGROVE	62	19930306	MARSHALL	4.1

First non-loss decomposition

> **proj** FROM, TO, DATE, DRIVER, TIME (JOURNEYS),
> **proj** FROM, TO, DISTANCE (JOURNEYS)

Second non-loss decomposition

> **proj** FROM, TO, DATE, DRIVER (JOURNEYS),
> **proj** FROM, TO, DATE, TIME (JOURNEYS),
> **proj** FROM, TO, DISTANCE (JOURNEYS)

5. The original file, which is named CHESS, records the names of the players, the winner, and the duration of the chess games. There is never more than one game between the same two players on one day. The field names and some of the file's records are as follows.

DATE	PLAYER1	PLAYER2	WINNER	DURATION
19920502	GRUMBIG	PEEVICH	PEEVICH	3.6
19920502	GRUMBIG	SMITH	SMITH	2.5
19920503	GRUMBIG	PEEVICH	PEEVICH	1.4
19920503	SMITH	PEEVICH	SMITH	5.2

Non-loss decomposition

proj DATE, PLAYER1, PLAYER2, WINNER (CHESS),
proj DATE, PLAYER1, PLAYER2, DURATION (CHESS)

This is the only non-loss decomposition of CHESS that you should consider.

6. The original file, which is named CLAIMS, gives details of insurance claims. No two insurance companies have the same name. There may be more than one claim on the same policy, but there is never more than one claim on the same policy on the same day. A customer may have more than one policy. The following is a list of field names of CLAIMS.

COMPNAME	{name of insurance company}
COMPADDRESS	{address of insurance company}
POLICYNUMBER	
RENEWALDATE	
CLASS	{what kind of cover}
SUMINSURED	
CLAIMDATE	
SUMCLAIMED	
CUSTNUMBER	
CUSTNAME	{name of insured person or firm}
CUSTADDRESS	

First non-loss decomposition

proj COMPNAME, COMPADDRESS, POLICYNUMBER,
    RENEWALDATE, CUSTNUMBER, CLASS, SUMINSURED
    (CLAIMS),
proj POLICYNUMBER, CUSTNAME, CUSTADDRESS,
    CLAIMDATE, SUMCLAIMED (CLAIMS)

Second non-loss decomposition

proj COMPNAME, COMPADDRESS (CLAIMS),
proj CUSTNUMBER, CUSTNAME, CUSTADDRESS (CLAIMS),

proj POLICYNUMBER, COMPNAME, CUSTNUMBER,
RENEWALDATE, CLASS, SUMINSURED (CLAIMS),
proj POLICYNUMBER, CLAIMDATE, SUMCLAIMED (CLAIMS)

3.6. Functional dependence

3.6.1. *Definition of functional dependence*

We have so far assumed that we actually know whether or not a given set of projections constitute a non-loss decomposition. We now give up this assumption and consider how to recognize non-loss decompositions. For this purpose the concept of functional dependence is very helpful.

Let X and Y be sets of (one or more) fields of a file named FNAME. Y is said to be *functionally dependent* on X if and only if there is no possibility that more than one value of Y is associated with any given value of X. Functional dependence of Y on X is a constraint saying that if any two records of FNAME include the same value of X then they will certainly include the same value of Y. This constraint applies not only to the records that are now in FNAME but also to all records that could ever possibly be in FNAME.

For example, if FNAME is the file CUSTADDRESS of Section 3.3.2 and if X = CUSTOMERNO and Y = ADDRESS then Y is functionally dependent on X because CUSTADDRESS is subject to a constraint which says that no two records can ever have the same CUSTOMERNO.

Another example is that in an artificially simple file that contains four records

F1	F2
a	h
b	i
c	j
b	k

we can see that F2 is *not* functionally dependent on F1, because more than one value of F2 is associated with value b of F1. We cannot tell, just by looking at the records in this file, whether F1 is functionally dependent on F2 because we do not know whether this file is subject to a constraint that would prohibit insertion of a new record such as

F1   F2
--   --
c   k

which would associate a second value of F1 with the value k of F2.

If X consists of more than one field, Y is said to be *fully* functionally dependent on X if and only if

(a) Y is functionally dependent on X, and

(b) Y is *not* functionally dependent on any subset X′ of X such that at least one field of X does not belong to X′.

In other words, Y is fully functionally dependent on X if and only if Y is functionally dependent on X and not functionally dependent on any proper subset of X.

For example, in the file ZOOANIMALS of Section 3.2 COUNTRYOFORIGIN is functionally dependent on the pair of fields ZOO, ANIMAL. This is the case because for each pair, e.g.

AYTON   KANGAROO
AYTON   CAMEL

there is exactly one country of origin. It is also the case that COUNTRYOFORIGIN is functionally dependent on ANIMAL alone, i.e. in the simple file ZOOANIMALS each animal has a unique COUNTRYOFORIGIN. Because COUNTRYOFORIGIN is functionally dependent on ANIMAL, it follows that COUNTRYOFORIGIN is *not* fully functionally dependent on the pair of fields ZOO, ANIMAL.

Another simple example file named SIMPLORDERS has the following fields.

SALESORDERNO
ITEMREFNO   {of item ordered}
DESCRIPTION   {of item}
QUANTITYORDERED   {of this item by this order}

The primary key (the only candidate key) of this file consists of the two fields SALESORDERNO and ITEMREFNO. One of these fields alone would not be a candidate key: more than one record may have a given SALESORDERNO, and more than one record may have a given ITEMREFNO. A value of the pair of fields SALE-SORDERNO and ITEMREFNO picks out a unique record and therefore this value of these two fields is associated with a unique value of QUANTITYORDERED. This means that QUANTITY ORDERED is fully functionally dependent on SALESORDERNO and ITEMREFNO. QUANTITY ORDERED is not functionally dependent on SALESORDERNO because records that have the same SALESORDERNO may have different QUANTITYOR-DERED. Similarly, QUANTITYORDERED is not functionally dependent on ITEMREFNO because records that have the same ITEMREFNO may have different QUANTITYORDERED.

DESCRIPTION, however, is functionally dependent on ITEM-REFNO. Therefore DESCRIPTION is not fully functionally depen-dent on the key pair SALESORDERNO, ITEMREFNO.

3.6.2. Heath's theorem

We now introduce Heath's theorem, which relates functional depen-dence to non-loss decomposition. Let H, J, and K be three sets of fields of a file named FNAME such that every field of FNAME belongs to exactly one of these three sets.

Heath's theorem. If K is functionally dependent on J then

FNAME = **proj** H,J (FNAME) **join proj** J,K (FNAME).

In other words, if K is functionally dependent on J then **proj** H,J (FNAME) and **proj** J,K (FNAME) constitute a non-loss decompo-sition of FNAME.

Proof. We shall use the symbols

h and h' to denote possible values of H,
j and j' to denote possible values of J,
k and k' to denote possible values of K.

Each of these values may actually be a composite value consisting of a collection of field values. Our proof commences with the definition of file GNAME:

GNAME = **proj** H,J (FNAME) **join proj** J,K (FNAME).

We consider any record hjk in FNAME. Clearly hj must belong to **proj** H,J (FNAME) and jk must be included in **proj** J,K (FNAME). From the definitions of GNAME and the natural join operation we see that hjk must be a record in GNAME. Therefore every record in FNAME is in GNAME.

We now consider any record h'j'k' in GNAME. From the definition of GNAME it follows that

proj H,J (GNAME)=**proj** H,J (FNAME)

so there must exist a record h'j'k in FNAME. Similarly, since

proj J,K (GNAME)=**proj** J,K (FNAME)

there must exist a record hj'k' in FNAME. K is functionally dependent on J, and the same j' occurs in h'j'k and hj'k' in FNAME. Therefore k = k' and h'j'k = h'j'k'. This means that any record h'j'k' in GNAME is also in FNAME. Since we have previously established the converse of this we have now proved the GNAME= FNAME, thus completing a proof of Heath's theorem.

3.7. Normalization based on functional dependence

3.7.1. *First normal form*

We can use Heath's theorem to find various non-loss decompositions in which the projections do not share a candidate key. We shall systematically study types of non-conformity to fifth normal form, starting with first normal form and then approaching fifth normal form progressively via second normal form, third normal form, and so on.

First normal form provides a clear starting point. A file is said to be in *first normal form* if and only if no record contains more than one value in any single field, and no key field is blank. For example a file named PERFORMSIN that has two fields

ENO   {ensemble number}
MEMBERS   {performer numbers of members}

and contains

ENO	MEMBERS
E1	P5,P8,P9
E2	P3,P5
E3	P9
E4	P1,P4,P7
E5	P5,P9
E6	P1,P7
E7	P3,P5

is *not* in first normal form because, for example, the record for E4 has three PNOs in the MEMBERS field. The music files of Section 2.2. are all in first normal form: every field of every record has exactly one value. A string of characters, such as our example values of ADDRESS in the file CUSTADDRESS, counts as a single value.

3.7.2. Second normal form

As was explained in Section 1.2.3.1, the *primary* key of a file is one of the candidate keys that has been selected to be most commonly used. For example, Typico use CUSTOMER NUMBER as the primary key of the CUSTOMERS file.

A file is said to be in *second normal form* if and only if it is in first normal form and all fields that are not part of the primary key are *fully* functionally dependent on the primary key.

For example the file ZOOANIMALS of Section 3.2 is not in second normal form because COUNTRYOFORIGIN is functionally dependent on ANIMAL and is therefore not fully functionally dependent on the primary key which is the pair of fields ZOO, ANIMAL.

The file WHOSUPPLIES in Section 3.3.1 is in second normal form because NAME and PHONENO are fully functionally dependent on the primary key which is ITEMREFNO.

In Section 3.6.1 the primary key of SIMPLORDERS consists of the two fields SALESORDERNO and ITEMREFNO. Although QUANTITYORDERED is fully functionally dependent on the primary key, SIMPLORDERS is not in second normal form because DESCRIPTION is functionally dependent on ITEM-REFNO.

It is very easy to prove that any file that is not in second normal form is not in fifth normal form. We consider any file FNAME that is not in second normal form. Let K be the set of one or more non-key fields that are not fully functionally dependent on the primary key, and let J be the proper subset of primary key fields upon which K is fully functionally dependent. Let H be the set of all fields of FNAME not in J or K. Because of the functional dependence, Heath's theorem tells us that

FNAME = **proj** H,J (FNAME) **join proj** J,K (FNAME)

These projections do not share a common candidate key, and so FNAME is not in fifth normal form and should therefore be normalized. Normalization consists of replacing the file by the offending non-loss decomposition. For example, ZOOANIMALS should be replaced by the two projections **proj** ZOO,ANIMAL (ZOOANIMALS) and **proj** ANIMAL,COUNTRYOFORIGIN (ZOOANIMALS). The file SIMPLORDERS should be normalized by being replaced by the two projections **proj** SALESORDERNO, ITEMREFNO,QUANTITYORDERED (SIMPLORDERS) and **proj** ITEMREFNO,DESCRIPTION (SIMPLORDERS).

3.7.3. *Third normal form*

A file is said to be in *third normal form* if and only if it is in second normal form and no non-key field is functionally dependent on any other non-key field.

If it is assumed that no two suppliers have the same name, the file WHOSUPPLIES in Section 3.3.1 is not in third normal form because PHONENO is functionally dependent on the non-key field NAME. In Section 3.3.2 CUSTADDRESS is in third normal form; ADDRESS is not functionally dependent on CUSTNAME.

To prove that any file which is not in third normal form is not in fifth normal form, we consider any file FNAME that is not in third normal form. Let K be the set of non-key fields that are functionally dependent on a set J of non-key fields. Let H be the set of fields of FNAME that are not in J or K. Because of the functional dependence, Heath's theorem tells us that

FNAME = **proj** H,J (FNAME) **join proj** J,K (FNAME).

These projections do not share a common candidate key, and so FNAME is not in fifth normal form and should therefore be normalized by being replaced by these projections. For example WHOSUPPLIES in Section 3.3.1 should be normalized by being replaced by **proj** ITEMREFNO,NAME (WHOSUPPLIES) and **proj** NAME,PHONENO (WHOSUPPLIES).

3.7.4. *Boyce–Codd normal form*

Boyce–Codd normal form (BCNF) is the next step after third normal form. A file is said to be in BCNF if and only if every functional dependence is full functional dependence on a candidate key.

The following file, named ANIMALKEEPERS, is an example of a file that is in third normal form but not in BCNF.

ZOO	ANIMAL	KEEPER
AYTON	KANGAROO	PONSONBY
AYTON	CAMEL	PONSONBY
BEETON	EMU	CARUTHERS
BEETON	CAMEL	GIRDLESTONE

The pair of fields ZOO, ANIMAL constitute a candidate key, on which KEEPER is fully functionally dependent. The file ANIMAL-KEEPERS is not in BCNF because the field ZOO, which is part of this candidate key, is functionally dependent on KEEPER, and KEEPER is not a candidate key.

To prove that any file that is not in BCNF is not in fifth normal form, we consider any file FNAME that is not in BCNF. Let K be a set of fields that are functionally dependent on a further set J of fields that do not constitute a candidate key. As usual, let H be the set of fields of FNAME that do not belong to J or K. Because of the functional dependence Heath's theorem tells us that

FNAME = **proj** H,J (FNAME) **join proj** J,K (FNAME).

These projections do not share a common candidate key, and so FNAME is not in fifth normal form and should therefore be normalized by being replaced by these projections. For example, the file ANIMALKEEPERS should be normalized by being replaced by the projections **proj** ANIMAL,KEEPER (ANIMALKEEPERS) and **proj** KEEPER,ZOO (ANIMALKEEPERS).

3.8. Exercises

In each of Exercises 1–5 a file is specified. For each of these files perform the following operations.

(a) List all possible functional dependences. (These can be found by checking whether each field could possibly be functionally dependent on each other field, on each pair of other fields, and so on.)

(b) Assuming that all possible functional dependences are actual functional dependences, normalize the file (i.e. replace the file by projections which are in BCNF).

(c) Give one example in which normalization reduces duplication, and one example in which normalization would allow accommodation of a dangling record that could not be included in the non-normalized file.

1. The field names and file contents are as follows.

HOUSENAME	GARDEN FLOWERS	FLOWERING SEASON
THE GABLES	DAFFODILS	SPRING
THE GABLES	ROSES	SUMMER
COSYCOT	BLUEBELLS	SPRING
COSYCOT	ROSES	SUMMER

2. The field names and file contents are as follows.

ATHLETIC EVENT	WINNER	YEAR OF BIRTH OF WINNER
LONG JUMP	ARMSTRONG	1972
100 METRES SPRINT	MARSHALL	1969
100 METRES HURDLES	MARSHALL	1969
POLE VAULT	WILLIAMS	1969

3. The field names and file contents are as follows.

NAME	DRINK	NUMBER OF GLASSES	COST PER GLASS
ARMSTRONG	WHISKY	3	40
ARMSTRONG	SHERRY	1	30
BECK	WHISKY	1	40
KNIGHT	SHERRY	2	30

4. The field names and file contents are as follows.

CAR OWNER	DATE OF BIRTH	CAR REGISTRATION NUMBER	REGISTRATION DATE
ARMSTRONG	JUN 1960	AHC134T	JUN 1979
ARMSTRONG	JUN 1960	BCY529V	MAY 1980
BECK	MAY 1959	AHD339H	OCT 1972
KNIGHT	JUL 1961	OYY796P	JAN 1976

5. The field names and file contents are as follows. This file gives details of roads and towns through which the roads pass.

ROAD NUMBER	ROAD LENGTH	TOWN	POPULATION
A3	352	ARBY	25632
A3	352	TEETON	62310
A4	219	ARBY	25632
A4	219	ESFIELD	25632

For simplicity assume that no two towns have the same name.

3.9. Fourth normal form

Heath's theorem has to be generalized if it is to help us beyond BCNF. Fourth normal form, which comes between BCNF and fifth normal form, is best defined in terms of a kind of generalized functional dependence which, to save a fairly lengthy explanation, we shall not introduce. The following definition is not as good because it does not tell us how to determine whether a given pair of projections constitute a non-loss decomposition.

A file is said to be in *fourth normal form* if and only if every non-loss decomposition into two projections is such that the two projections share a candidate key.

To construct an example of a file that is in BCNF but not in fourth normal form, let us alter our music PERFORMANCES file so as to record the CNOs of many compositions, rather than just one, for each performance occasion. Further, let us omit the ENO and instead include the PNOs of the performers who actually played on each occasion. The following is *not* in first normal form because the CNOs and PNOs fields contain more than a single value.

DATE	TOWN	COUNTRY	MNO	CNOs	PNOs
19860530	TEETON	TEELAND	M9	{C1,C3,C5}	{P8,P9}
19860615	ARBY	EXLAND	M1	{C3,C4,C6}	{P1,P4,P7}
AND SO ON					

To express this in (at least) first normal form we can take the join of two files that we will call CPART and PPART. The file CPART contains the following.

DATE	TOWN	COUNTRY	CNO
19860530	TEETON	TEELAND	C1
19860530	TEETON	TEELAND	C3
19860530	TEETON	TEELAND	C5
19860615	ARBY	EXLAND	C3
19860615	ARBY	EXLAND	C4
19860615	ARBY	EXLAND	C6
AND SO ON			

This file tells us the CNOs of the compositions performed on each occasion. The file PPART, which also is in first normal form, tells us who the performers were on each occasion. PPART contains the following.

DATE	TOWN	COUNTRY	MNO	PNO
19860530	TEETON	TEELAND	M9	P8
19860530	TEETON	TEELAND	M9	P9
19860615	ARBY	EXLAND	M1	P1
19860615	ARBY	EXLAND	M1	P4
19860615	ARBY	EXLAND	M1	P7
AND SO ON				

Let NEWPERF be the join of CPART with PPART. The join is

actually on the three fields DATE, TOWN, and COUNTRY. NEWPERF is in BCNF: its key fields are DATE, TOWN, COUNTRY, PNO, and CNO. NEWPERF is not in fourth normal form because its projections CPART and PPART constitute a non-loss decomposition. These projections share the fields DATE, TOWN, and COUNTRY which do not constitute a candidate key because any given value of DATE, TOWN, and COUNTRY may occur more than once in NEWPERF.

A file that is not in fourth normal form is not in fifth normal form and should therefore be normalized. For example, NEWPERF should be normalized by being replaced by CPART and PPART.

To ensure that a file is in fourth normal form we need some means of recognizing non-loss decompositions. If, as in the NEWPERF example, the file is defined as, or can obviously be regarded as, a join of two projections, then these two projections constitute a very easily recognizable non-loss decomposition.

Fifth normal form, which was defined in Section 3.5.1, insists that, whatever the number of projections constituting a non-loss de-composition, these must all share a candidate key. Fourth normal form is a special case of this, where the number of projections in the non-loss decomposition is exactly two.

It is difficult to find a convincing example of a practical file that is in fourth normal form but not in fifth normal form. In principle, normalization means ensuring that all files are in fifth normal form. In practice, if we ensure that all files are in BCNF, we are likely to find that they are also in fifth normal form, although it is worth checking as far as we can to make sure of this.

One way to achieve normalization is to start by replacing all files, where necessary, by projections that are in third normal form. Then check that the resulting files are in BCNF: if they are not, then normalize accordingly. Then check that the resulting files are in fourth normal form: in practice non-conformity to fourth normal form may be conspicuous. There is no efficient algorithm for checking whether a file is in fifth normal form.

3.10. Entities and attributes

3.10.1. *Functional dependence of attributes on entities*

To decide what files are required, and what fields should belong to which file, we could start by listing names of all fields as if they belong to a single file. We could then check each field for functional dependence on other sets of fields and use Heath's theorem to arrive eventually at a set of projections in BCNF. For example, we might start from a list of fields like this:

INVOICE NUMBER
INVOICE DATE
SALES ORDER NUMBER
ITEM REFERENCE NUMBER
QUANTITY DELIVERED
DELIVERY CHARGE
TOTAL AMOUNT OF INVOICE
CUSTOMER NUMBER
CUSTOMER NAME
BILLING ADDRESS
CREDIT LIMIT
SALES AREA

This is a modest example: checking for functional dependences within a long list of fields can be laborious.

We now introduce an alternative approach based on the observation that a primary key identifies an entity or a relationship between entities. An entity can either be a *thing*, such as an inventory item, or a *characteristic*, such as a colour. Normally we provide a file for each entity for which we wish to store attributes. In such a file the non-key fields are the attributes of entities identified by the primary key. For example, in Section 3.3.2 CUSTNAME and ADDRESS are attributes of customers who are entities identified by the primary key CUSTOMERNO.

We also provide a file for each relationship between entities such that

(a) we wish to store attributes of that relationship, and/or
(b) the file will be required for linking entity files in joins.

We now illustrate these ideas in terms of the music files.

In the music files, the file named ENSEMBLES records the name, country, and manager, which are attributes of ensembles. Ensembles are entities identified by the primary key ENO. The file named MUSICIANS records the name, date of birth, and country of birth, which are attributes of musicians who are entities identified by the primary key MNO.

The file named PERFORMERS records a relationship between the entities musician (identified by MNO) and INSTRUMENT. The GRADE (AWFUL, ..., GOOD) is an attribute of the relation between musician and instrument. The two fields MNO and INSTRUMENT constitute a candidate key of PERFORMERS. To facilitate cross reference we have provided PERFORMERS with the alternative candidate key PNO, and indeed we use PNO as the primary key.

The file ENSEMBLE MEMBERS records a relationship between performers and ensembles. We found in Chapter 2 that the ENSEM-BLE MEMBERS file is useful despite the fact that it does not record any attribute of the relation between ENO and PNO. In other words, ENSEMBLE MEMBERS has no non-key fields.

INSTRUMENT is an entity, but we do not wish to store any attributes of instruments so there is no INSTRUMENTS file.

We can use these ideas to determine, for the list of fields given at the beginning of the present section, what files are required and which fields should belong to which of these files. We start by recognizing those entities for which we shall wish to store attributes. Two such entities are invoices and customers.

INVOICE NUMBER can obviously be used as a primary key to identify invoices. INVOICE DATE, DELIVERY CHARGE, CUSTOMER NUMBER and TOTAL AMOUNT OF INVOICE are attributes of invoices. The list at the beginning of the present section does not contain any other attributes of invoices, and so we conclude that one of the required files is the following.

<u>INVOICE HEADER</u>   {file name}

INVOICE NUMBER	{primary key}
INVOICE DATE	
CUSTOMER NUMBER	
DELIVERY CHARGE	{a total for all items}
TOTAL AMOUNT OF INVOICE	{total payable}

Customers are entities identified by the primary key CUSTOMER NUMBER. The only attributes of customers included in the list at the beginning of the present section are CUSTOMER NAME,

BILLING ADDRESS, CREDIT LIMIT, and SALES AREA. Thus another one of the required files is as follows.

<u>CUSTOMERS</u>   {file name}

CUSTOMER NUMBER
CUSTOMER NAME
BILLING ADDRESS
CREDIT LIMIT
SALES AREA

If we now look at the remaining fields in the list, QUANTITY DELIVERED appears to be an attribute. Any given item can be included in more than one invoice, and in each case the QUANTITY DELIVERED may be different. QUANTITY DELIVERED is not functionally dependent on ITEM REFERENCE NUMBER, and indeed QUANTITY DELIVERED is not an attribute of an item. Instead, QUANTITY DELIVERED is an attribute of a *relationship* between the two entities invoice and item. Another attribute of this relationship is SALES ORDER NUMBER, which identifies the sales order in which an item was included, resulting in the inclusion of this item in the invoice. Thus we need the following file.

<u>INVOICE DETAIL</u>   {file name}

INVOICE NUMBER
ITEM REFERENCE NUMBER
QUANTITY DELIVERED
SALES ORDER NUMBER

However, we do not need an INVENTORY file in this example because the list of fields at the beginning of the present section does not include attributes of items. In this example the three files identified above include all the listed fields, and no further files are required. It should be noted that our three files are in BCNF and are also in fifth normal form.

If the fields INVOICE NUMBER and CUSTOMER NUMBER had not been included in the original list, we should nevertheless have created them to facilitate cross reference, just as we included the PNO field in the music PERFORMERS file. A little practice enables us to see where useful abbreviation can be achieved by introducing reference numbers, such as PNO, as artificial primary keys.

After we have designed files by analysis of entities, attributes and relationships, we should make two checks:

(a) check that every file is in BCNF (and preferably in fifth normal form), and
(b) check whether the join of all our files includes all the fields that we wish to accommodate.

If either of these checks fails then we must redesign the files to remedy the failure. For example if CUSTOMER NUMBER were omitted from the INVOICE HEADER file then the join of our three files would not include fields such as CUSTOMER NAME, and we should remedy this.

3.10.2. *Examples starting from verbal statements*

In the following very simple example, which starts from a verbal statement, we are required to decide what files are required and which fields belong to which file.

Fixtures example. We are required to give self-explanatory file names and field names for files that record information concerning Bigchester football club fixtures. The information is as follows: match date, name of ground where match will be played, crowd capacity of ground, expected crowd attendance, and distance from Bigchester to the ground.

We tackle this by identifying entities for which we wish to record attributes. These entities are MATCH and GROUND. We shall have one file for each of these entities, with the following fields.

MATCHES   {is file name. Field names are:}

MATCH DATE
NAME OF GROUND
EXPECTED CROWD ATTENDANCE

GROUNDS   {is file name. Field names are:}

NAME OF GROUND
DISTANCE FROM BIGCHESTER TO THIS GROUND
CROWD CAPACITY

It should be noted that the non-key fields of the GROUNDS file are functionally dependent on NAME OF GROUND. If, instead of the two files MATCHES and GROUNDS we had a single file containing the result of MATCHES **join** GROUNDS, this would not be in third normal form.

Library example. We now consider a more elaborate example in which we are required to determine file names and field names for Bigchester City Library. Bigchester City Library consists of a central library and a number of branches in outlying parts of the city. A registered borrower has a unique library ticket number and may borrow from any of these libraries, which all share the same catalogue. Each book is distinguished by a unique international book number (ISBN): different copies of the same book all have the same ISBN. Different editions of the same book have different ISBNs. The library may hold (in one or more branches) several copies of the same edition, and several different editions of a book.

When a book is purchased by Bigchester City Library it is given a unique accession number, which identifies one particular copy of one particular publication. No two books (even in different branches) have the same accession number: different copies that have the same ISBN have different accession numbers. ISBN, title, authors' names, edition (e.g. second), place of publication, publisher, date of publication, number of pages, accession number, shelf number, and branch number must all be recorded for each copy. The branch number identifies a branch of the library, and the shelf number tells us on which shelf the book is kept. The names and addresses of branches and registered borrowers must be stored. All loans and return dates must be recorded.

To determine what files are required we start by identifying those entities for which we shall wish to store attributes. We also identify relationships for which we shall wish to store attributes, or which will be relevant to necessary joins. We shall need a separate file for each such entity and relationship. Specifically, we shall need a separate file for each of the following.

BORROWERS	{entity}
INDIVIDUAL BOOKS	{entity}
LOANS	{relation}
PUBLICATIONS	{catalogue file: entity}
BRANCHES	{entity}

Having identified these, it is quite easy to see which attributes belong to which entity or relationship, as follows.

BORROWERS   {file name. Field names are:}

LIBRARY TICKET NUMBER   {primary key that identifies the
                          borrower}
BORROWER NAME
BORROWER ADDRESS

INDIVIDUAL BOOKS   {file name. Field names are:}

ACCESSION NUMBER   {primary key that identifies the
                        individual book}
ISBN   {useful for obtaining catalogue
                        details}
BRANCH NUMBER
SHELF NUMBER

In this file we achieve abbreviation by including BRANCH NUMBER instead of BRANCH NAME and BRANCH AD-DRESS. We link BRANCH NUMBER with BRANCH NAME and BRANCH ADDRESS by means of the following file.

BRANCHES   {file name. Field names are:}

BRANCH NUMBER   {primary key}
BRANCH NAME
BRANCH ADDRESS

A loan is a relationship between an individual borrower and an individual book. DATE FOR RETURN is an attribute of this relationship. The loans file is as follows.

LOANS   {file name. Field names are:}

LIBRARY TICKET NUMBER   {identifies borrower}
ACCESSION NUMBER   {identifies copy of book}
DATE FOR RETURN

The first two fields constitute the primary key for this file.

More than one copy of a book may have the same ISBN, which is therefore not a candidate key for INDIVIDUAL BOOKS. Attributes such as TITLE and NAMES OF AUTHORS are functionally dependent on ISBN and should therefore not be included in the INDIVIDUAL BOOKS file. Instead such attributes should be included in a catalogue file.

<u>CATALOGUE</u>   {file name. Field names are:}

ISBN	{primary key}
TITLE	{of book}
EDITION	{e.g. second}
NAMES OF AUTHORS	
NAME OF PUBLISHER	
TOWN OF PUBLICATION	
COUNTRY OF PUBLICATION	

Our collection of files is now complete. It should be noted, for example, that an author is an entity, but we do not have an authors' file. This is because there is no requirement to store attributes of authors. We only have files for those entities for which attributes are to be recorded. A publisher is an entity, and if, for example, the town and country of publication were functionally dependent on the publisher (which is generally not the case) then we could sensibly introduce a separate file for publishers.

3.10.3. *Examples starting from files that are not in first normal form*

Instead of starting from a verbal description, we may sometimes wish to start from a collection of files not in first normal form, and thence design a collection of normalized files.

Horse owners example. This example is concerned with racehorses and their owners, starting with two non-normalized files of which some specimen records are as follows.

<u>HORSES</u>   {is file name. Specimen records are:}

HORSE NUMBER	HORSE NAME	COLOUR	HEIGHT	DATEOF BIRTH
H3	TRUNKCALL	BROWN	165	19890630
H5	HOTPOTATO	BLACK	170	19890212
H6	STRAWGOLD	BROWN	164	19881105

This file is at least in first normal form. The file

OWNERS   {is file name. Specimen records are:}

OWNERNAME	ADDRESS	HORSESOWNED
AYSON	CLUMBERWICK	H7,H10,H18
BEESON	WIGHAMSTEAD	H3,H8
GEESON	PLUMHAVEN	H5,H6,H9,H14

is not in first normal form because the HORSESOWNED field contains more than one value in each record. Horses and owners are the only entities for which we need to store attributes, and so we only need to make a change that will achieve normalization of these two files. If no horse has more than one owner (at the current time) then normalization can be accomplished by inserting an OWNER-NUMBER field into both files and deleting the offending HOR-SEOWNED field from the OWNERS file. The normalized files are as follows.

OWNERS   {is file name. Field names are:}

OWNERNUMBER
OWNERNAME
ADDRESS

HORSES   {is file name. Field names are:}

HORSENUMBER
HORSENAME
COLOUR
HEIGHT
DATEOFBIRTH
OWNERNUMBER   {of horse's owner}

Normalization has been achieved by exploiting the fact that each horse has exactly one owner, and so the OWNERNUMBER field is single valued. In the original version of the files we associated horses with owners using the multiple-valued HORSEOWNED field. Multiple values occurred because an owner could own many horses.

Horses, owners, and jockeys example. We now consider an extension to the previous example in which files contain details of jockeys and which jockey has ridden which horse in at least one race. Before normalization there is a JOCKEYS file as follows.

JOCKEYS   {is file name. Some specimen records are:}

JOCKEY NUMBER	JOCKEY NAME	ADDRESS	HORSES RIDDEN
J2	WILSON	WIGGLESWICK	H4,H9,H18
J4	ANDREWS	ALFRISTON	H3,H4
J5	HOBSON	ECCLESFIELD	H3,H4,H9,H10

This is not in first normal form because the field HORSESRIDDEN is not single valued. The HORSES and OWNERS files are normalized, as we explained previously.

If each horse had been ridden by exactly one jockey, we could achieve normalization by deleting the HORSESRIDDEN field from the JOCKEYS file and inserting a JOCKEYNUMBER field into the HORSES file. Unfortunately this will not work when each horse has been ridden by more than one jockey. In this case we can achieve normalization by deleting the HORSESRIDDEN field from the JOCKEYS file and introducing a new file called HASRIDDEN.

HASRIDDEN   {is file name. Some specimen records are:}

JOCKEYNUMBER	HORSENUMBER
J2	H4
J2	H9
J2	H18
J4	H3
J4	H4
J5	H3
J5	H4
J5	H9
J5	H10

The HORSES and OWNERS files remain unchanged. We now have altogether four files, all of them normalized.

To understand why it was necessary to introduce the new file HASRIDDEN, we should appreciate that the HORSESRIDDEN field in the non-normalized JOCKEYS file was recording a relationship between jockeys and horses. Because each jockey had ridden more than one horse and each horse had been ridden by more than one jockey, we could not include this relationship within the JOCKEYS file or HORSES file. The only alternative was to introduce the new file HASRIDDEN to record this relationship in normalized form. We would also have arrived at the four files OWNERS, HORSES, JOCKEYS, and HASRIDDEN by observing that we require attributes of entities OWNERS, HORSES, and JOCKEYS, and also the HASRIDDEN relationship between HORSES and JOCKEYS.

3.11. Exercises

1. This exercise is an extension of the horses, owners, and jockeys example in Section 3.10.3. Delete the file HASRIDDEN and instead insert new files that tell us, for each race, the date, time, location, race name (if any), which horse ridden by which jockey came first, which horse ridden by which jockey came second, and so on. Give self-explanatory file names and field names for the resulting files.

2. A mountaineering club maintains records of climbs. For each climb, the date of beginning and ending the climb, the names and addresses of the climbers, and the name, height, country, and district of the mountain are all recorded. Give self-explanatory file names and field names for normalized files containing this information. From these files, give examples to illustrate how problems of duplication and dangling records can be avoided by normalization.

3. Four family doctors (general practitioners) work together as a coopera-tive partnership. The partnership has files that show the name, sex, date of birth, and home address of every patient. Each time a patient visits a doctor or vice versa, the date, place, symptoms, diagnosis, and prescription (if any) are recorded, along with identification of the patient and the doctor. For each drug that the doctors prescribe they record the drug name, a verbal description of what it is supposed to achieve, its side effects, and in what conditions it should be prescribed. You are required to give self-explanatory file names and field names for files containing the specified information.

4. Bigchester City Council maintains a computer file of names, addresses, and home and office telephone numbers of councillors. The council has

about 40 committees, of which all members are councillors. For example
one committee deals with education, and another with rented accommodation. The Council maintain computer files showing, for each committee, its
present chairperson and members and past chairpeople and members during
the last 10 years, with the dates when each member joined, left, or took the
chair of the committee. Most councillors sit on more than one committee.
The date and place of each committee meeting are recorded in computer
files, along with identification of the members of the council's administrative
staff who took the minutes. The minutes and list of committee members
present at meetings are recorded on paper, and not in computer files. You
are required to specify self-explanatory file names and field names for
computer files for use as mentioned above.

5. The file

CRUISE NUMBER	DEPARTURE DATE	NUMBER OF PASSENGERS
1	840407	380
2	840412	560
3	840529	830
4	840529	790
5	840603	600
6	840630	780
7	840630	400
8	840719	810

contains information about various cruises. The file

SHIP NAME	PASSENGER CAPACITY	CRUISE NUMBERS
CASTLE QUEEN	820	5,6
SEA PRINCESS	460	1,7
MARY ROSE	850	3,8
BRISTOL BELLE	630	2,4

which is not in first-normal form, tells us which ships were used for the
cruises. The file

PORT	HARBOUR CHARGE PER DAY	CRUISE NUMBERS
GIBRALTAR	100	2,3,5,7,8
MARSEILLES	250	2,3,6

ALGIERS	150	2,3,7
ALEXANDRIA	150	1,2,3,5,6
PALERMO	200	4,6,7,8
ATHENS	250	1,3,5,8
ISTANBUL	150	1,4,8

which is not in first-normal form, tells us which cruise visited which port. Give self-explanatory file names and field names for a collection of files in fifth-normal form containing the information shown above.

6. Slippery Fisheries own a number of fishing boats. For each boat they record the name, type, displacement, and date built. For each fishing trip they record the boat, a list of names and addresses of the crew (showing who was skipper, who was bosun etc.), the departure date, the return date, and the total weight of the catch for each kind of fish caught (e.g. cod). A fishing trip may visit more than one fishing ground. For each ground the date entered and left and a rating (good, fair, poor) of the catch are recorded, but the fish are not weighed. Give self-explanatory file names and field names for recording all this information.

7. Willowby's are auctioneers of antiques and works of art. People whose goods are sold by Willowby's are *sellers*. Goods are bought at auctions by *buyers*. When Willowby's receive items from sellers, they decide which sale to place each item in. Willowby's give each item in each sale a *lot number*, which serves as an item reference number for that sale. The same lot number is used for different items in different sales.

For each sale, Willowby's records identify the date, place, time, and speciality, e.g. pre-1900 oil paintings. For each item, Willowby's records identify the sale, lot number, seller, and reserve price, and include a verbal description. Each seller may sell any number of items and each buyer may buy any number of items. Willowby's need to know the names and addresses of all buyers and sellers. One person or one firm may be a buyer and also a seller. After a sale, Willowby's records will show the actual price of each item that was actually sold, as well as identifying the buyer. Give self-explanatory file names and field names for a collection of files in which Willowby's could efficiently store this information.

8. A gramophone record retailer maintains a collection of files that include all the data that are in the music files in Section 2.2. The retailer also retains information about records. Each different record is identified by a unique

label number: copies of the same record are not distinguished from each other. A record may contain performances of more than one composition: for each of these performances the retailer has information like that in the PERFORMANCES music file. For each record the retailer retains the name of the company who produced the record (e.g. EMI) and the name and address of a distributor company from whom the retailer can buy the record. For any given record the distributor and the producing company may or may not be the same. For each record the retailer stores up-to-date retail and wholesale prices, the date of issue of the record, the number of copies sold last year, the number of copies sold so far this year, and the number of copies currently in stock.

Give the file names and field names for any further files that the retailer may require in addition to the music files of Section 2.2. Do not repeat details of the files of Section 2.2 except where you think any change is required.

9. St. Belinda is a fictitious island somewhere near the middle of a large fictitious ocean. Full records have been kept there for at least 300 years.

The records include the name, sex, and dates of birth and death of everyone who has lived on St. Belinda. The names of each person's father and mother are also recorded if known, but for some people one or both parents are not known. The records tell us when each house was built, when it was demolished if it is not still there, its exact address and detailed map reference, and who has lived in it at what dates.

There are, and have been over the centuries, a few firms on St. Belinda, dealing for example in tobacco, sugar cane, and fish. Some people trading under their own name are self-employed and employ no-one. Others are self-employed, trading under their own name, and employ various people at various times. The records tell us who was employed by which firm or individual to do what job, between what dates. Actually the number of different jobs available on St. Belinda, e.g. fisherman, baker, etc., has always been very limited and the records include a verbal description of each job, to explain the job name. Each firm is wholly owned by residents of St. Belinda. Any given firm may be owned by one or more residents, and the records show who owned what share of which firm between what dates. The records also include a verbal description of the business done by each firm, and the dates of commencement and termination of this business.

You are required to assign all this information to a collection of normalized files. Give a self-explanatory name and a list of field names (with explanatory comments if necessary) for each file.

10. Typico sometimes manufacture items instead of purchasing them ready made from suppliers. For this purpose Typico maintain a number of workshops, each capable of performing a specialized part of a manufacturing process. Each product that Typico are able to manufacture is an item in Typico's inventory and has an item reference number, as usual. This number is also used as a product number. For each product number Typico record the date of completion of the most recently manufactured product, what it cost Typico to produce, and how many operations were involved.

An operation is a step in the manufacturing process, and is always carried out in a single workshop in accordance with instructions specified in a single engineering drawing. For each product, for each operation, Typico record the description of the operation, its expected duration, and a drawing number that identifies the associated drawing. For each operation Typico also record the workshop number of the workshop that normally performs the operation.

For each operation Typico record the expected quantity and item reference number of all consumable materials required. Consumable materials are materials such as electric cables that will be used up and will therefore not be available for subsequent re-use. When consumable materials are actually taken from the warehouse for use in an operation, Typico record the item reference number of the consumable materials, the quantity, the workshop number, the employee number of the employee responsible, the time, the date, the operation number, and a work order that we shall explain later. The quantities actually used may not be identical with the expected quantities, e.g. because mistakes may necessitate reworking.

Each workshop contains many tools and facilities. Sometimes a workshop has to borrow further tools from a central tool store in order to carry out an operation. For each type of tool there is a tool type number, and Typico record a verbal description and the total quantity either on loan to a workshop or held in a tool store. Different tools of the same type, e.g. different spanners that have the same dimensions, are distinguished by individual unique tool numbers. For each tool type, Typico record the tool numbers of all tools of this type. For each individual tool, Typico record the date when new.

For each operation, Typico record the tool type and quantity of each tool that is expected to be borrowed. When a tool is actually borrowed, Typico record its unique tool number, the number of the borrowing workshop, the start and end date of the loan, and the work order number. Expected and actual loans may differ.

A work order is analogous to a purchase order, but it goes to Typico's workshops instead of Typico's suppliers. When Typico decide to manufacture an item they created a work order record specifying the product number, the date of creating the order, the requested completion date, and the quantity ordered.

You are required to specify the field names of files that store all this information. These files should permit the answering of a wide variety of queries including, for example, the following.

(a) List the quantity and item reference number of all consumable items that were actually used for work order number 6531.

(b) Do we have (somewhere) all tools required to manufacture product no. 421729?

(c) Where (i.e. workshop number or store) is each tool of type 321? For which operations on which product is this tool required?

4 Persistent programming

4.1. Higher and lower levels of programming

A programming language that allows the programmer to specify an operation without specifying how the operation will actually be carried out is at a *higher level* than a language that requires the programmer to specify the implementation in greater detail. For example, when we write in Pascal

F: = (A + B)*C − D

we are programming at a higher level than in a language that requires us to specify the detailed steps by which the expression will be evaluated, e.g.

G: = A + B; G: = G*C; F: = G − D.

Similarly, when we write in Pascal READ (*X*), where *X* is an integer to be read from a terminal, we are programming at a higher level than in a programming language that requires us to specify the reading of *X* character by character. We may gain more control when we descend to a lower level, but generally at the cost of more complicated programming.

Chapter 2 was at a high level concerned, for example, with selection operations without looking behind the scenes to see in detail how a computer could actually perform a selection operation. In Chapters 5, 6, and 7 we shall consider detailed steps involved in selection and other operations on files, and we shall introduce methods for controlling these steps more explicitly than was possible in Chapter 2. This lower-level programming will sometimes allow greater efficiency than would otherwise be possible, and we shall be able to do practically anything we wish with stored data without limitations such as those mentioned in Sections 2.16 and 2.17.

One of the aims of Chapters 6 and 7 is to enable the reader to see how database programming relates to standard Pascal programming. For this purpose, and for use in the exercises of Chapter 5, a simple non-standard extension to Pascal is introduced in this chapter. We presuppose familiarity with Pascal records and pointers: for an introductory outline see Chapter 9.

4.2. Pascal database declaration

If an ordinary Pascal program sets up a data structure such as a linked list or a table, this structure disappears when execution of the program terminates. We now introduce non-standard extra Pascal facilities that allow specified variables to retain their value after termination of program execution. We shall call these variables, which are not available in standard Pascal, *persistent* variables. By using persistent variables we shall, for example, be able to set up and maintain various indexes that will survive when no program is running.

Persistent variables are declared in a *database declaration*, which looks like the declaration part of an ordinary Pascal program, except that it does not contain declarations of procedures or functions. It may, however, contain declarations of constants and types obeying the rules of standard Pascal. An ordinary Pascal program starts with a program statement, which tells the computer that what follows is a program. A database declaration starts with DBDNAME and then a name given by the programmer, analogous to a program name. A database declaration always ends with the word **finish**.

We shall use DBD as an abbreviation for 'database declaration'. A very simple example of a complete DBD is

```
DBDNAME AP;
const PI = 3.142875;
var RADIUS: INTEGER;
finish
```

More than one program will be able to use the constant PI and the variable RADIUS. A value assigned to RADIUS by one program will survive when execution of this program terminates, and will be available to subsequent programs; we shall illustrate this in the next section. The DBD does not itself assign values to variables declared within it, just as the declaration part of a Pascal program does not assign values to variables.

4.3. Programs that refer to a database declaration

Any program that refers to a database declaration must include, as
the statement following the **program** statement, the statement

invoke name;

in which the name is that of the DBD to which the program refers.
One program may refer to only one DBD, but many programs may
refer to the same DBD. The declarations in the invoked DBD can be
used as if they had been included in the program that invokes the
DBD, except for some differences that we shall explain. Persistent
variables can be used like any other Pascal variables, except that
their values will persist after termination of program execution.

Before using any persistent variable, a program must call a
procedure named STARTTRANSACTION that has a single parameter. This parameter may be either UNRESTRICTED or READ-
ONLY. If a program is going to insert, delete, or change the value of
any persistent variable, the appropriate procedure call is START-
TRANSACTION (UNRESTRICTED). If, on the other hand, a
program is not going to change the value of any persistent variable,
then the appropriate procedure call is STARTTRANSACTION
(READONLY). When a program has satisfactorily finished accessing the persistent variables it must call a procedure named END-
TRANSACTION. Thus all references to persistent variables are
always sandwiched between STARTTRANSACTION and END-
TRANSACTION.

If, between STARTTRANSACTION and ENDTRANSAC-
TION, a program detects that something has gone wrong, it can call
a further procedure ABORTTRANSACTION which effectively
cancels any changes that the program has made to persistent
variables since STARTTRANSACTION, leaving all persistent variables with the value that they had at the time of STARTTRANSAC-
TION. Later we shall explain why STARTTRANSACTION, END-
TRANSACTION, and ABORTTRANSACTION are important.

The following simple example programs use the DBD named AP
that we declared in Section 4.2. The first program merely obtains a
value of RADIUS from the terminal. This program can be used to
initialize the value of RADIUS, and subsequently this same program can be used again to give a new value to RADIUS. This
program is

```
program RUPDATE (INPUT, OUTPUT);
invoke AP; {this tells the computer that this program will refer to DBD
AP}
var
   SELECTOR: CHAR;
begin
   STARTTRANSACTION (UNRESTRICTED);
   WRITELN ('please type the integer value of RADIUS');
   READLN (RADIUS);
   WRITE ('if you are happy with what you have typed type Y   ');
   WRITELN ('else type N');
   READLN (SELECTOR);
   if SELECTOR < > 'Y' then
   begin
      ABORTTRANSACTION;
      WRITELN ('value of RADIUS has not been changed')
   end else
   ENDTRANSACTION
end.
```

The main point of this example is that the value of RADIUS
survives after termination of the program and can subsequently be
used by other programs that invoke the same DBD, for example

```
program ENQUIRE (INPUT, OUTPUT);
invoke AP;
var
   SELECTOR: CHAR;
begin
   STARTTRANSACTION (READONLY);
   repeat
      WRITE ('to get RADIUS type R, CIRCUMFERENCE type C,');
      WRITELN ( ' AREA type A, terminate program type X');
      READLN (SELECTOR);
      if not (SELECTOR in ['R','C','A','X']) then SELECTOR: = 'F';
      case SELECTOR of
      'R': WRITELN ('RADIUS= ', RADIUS);
      'C': WRITELN ('CIRCUMFERENCE= ', 2*PI*RADIUS);
      'A': WRITELN ('AREA= ', PI*sqr (RADIUS));
      'X','F':
      end
   until SELECTOR = 'X';
   ENDTRANSACTION
end.
```

This program straightforwardly uses PI and RADIUS which are available because they are declared in the invoked DBD AP. The value of RADIUS that this program actually uses may have been obtained by previous execution of the program RUPDATE. The program ENQUIRE can be executed many times with the value of RADIUS unchanged. This illustrates how persistent variables can be employed, but this example is too simple to be of practical value. The next example is closer to being useful.

Simple inventory table example. Simplified inventory records are stored in a table that is a persistent variable. We can look up in this table the price, quantity in stock, and supplier number for any specified item. For simplicity we assume that items are identified by ITEMREFNOs in the range 100, . . ., 140, and that each item has exactly one supplier and one price. For this example our database declaration is

```
DBDNAME IX;
type
  REFRANGE = 100 .. 140;
  INVTYPE = record
              QUANTITYINSTOCK: INTEGER;
              PRICEPERUNIT: REAL;
              SUPPLIERNO: 10 .. 99;
              NORECORD: BOOLEAN
            end;
var
  INVTABLE: array [REFRANGE] of INVTYPE;
finish
```

The INVTYPE does not include an ITEMREFNO field because we shall use ITEMREFNO as the subscript of the INVTABLE. (We could have used a similar idea in the indexed invoice table example in Section 9.8.2.) The first program that we shall run using this DBD assigns TRUE to the NORECORD field of every record in the table to signify that the table is initially empty:

```
program INITIALIX (OUTPUT);
invoke IX;
var
  I: REFRANGE;
begin
  STARTTRANSACTION (UNRESTRICTED);
```

```
    for I: = 100 to 140 do
    INVTABLE [I].NORECORD: = TRUE;
    ENDTRANSACTION;
    WRITELN ('initialization completed')
end.
```

This program illustrates the fact that after invoking a DBD a program can use DBD **type** declarations as if they had been declared within the declaration part of the program. For example the program INITIALIX uses the type REFRANGE.

The next program obtains records from the terminal and stores them in the table. We are free to terminate execution of the program when only a few records have been entered into the table. Subsequently we can run this program again to enter further records into the table or to overwrite records that we had previously entered into the table.

```
program ENTERDATA (INPUT, OUTPUT);
invoke IX;
var
    ITEMREFNO: REFRANGE; SELECTOR: CHAR;
begin
    STARTTRANSACTION (UNRESTRICTED);
    repeat
        WRITELN ('if you wish to enter another record type Y else type N');
        READLN (SELECTOR);
        if SELECTOR = 'Y' then
        begin
            WRITE ('type ITEMREFNO, QUANTITYINSTOCK, ');
            WRITELN ('PRICEPERUNIT, SUPPLIERNO');
            READ (ITEMREFNO);
            with INVTABLE [ITEMREFNO] do
            begin
                READLN (QUANTITYINSTOCK, PRICEPERUNIT,
                SUPPLIERNO);
                NORECORD: = FALSE
            end
        end
    until SELECTOR < > 'Y';
    ENDTRANSACTION
end.
```

It would be better to check that the input data have all their fields

within the specified ranges, e.g. ITEMREFNO in 100 . . 140, and we
have omitted such checks only to avoid cluttering up the program.

The next program looks up a given ITEMREFNO and outputs
the associated QUANTITYINSTOCK, PRICEPERUNIT, and
SUPPLIERNO. The use of the NORECORD field can now be seen.

```
program LOOKUPIX (INPUT, OUTPUT);
invoke IX;
var
   ITEMREFNO: REFRANGE;
begin
   STARTTRANSACTION (READONLY);
   WRITELN ('please type ITEMREFNO');
   READLN (ITEMREFNO);
   with INVTABLE [ITEMREFNO] do
   if NORECORD then WRITELN ('no record available in the table')
   else
   begin
     WRITE ('QUANTITY IN STOCK = ', QUANTITYINSTOCK);
     WRITE ('PRICEPERUNIT = ', PRICEPERUNIT: 10:2);
     WRITELN ('SUPPLIER NUMBER = ', SUPPLIERNO)
   end;
   ENDTRANSACTION
end.
```

If we wish to look up more than one ITEMREFNO we can rerun
this program for each ITEMREFNO. Another way of dealing with
this would be to include a **repeat** loop within the program, as we did
in the program ENTERDATA.

4.4. Persistent pointers

Persistent pointers are the same as standard Pascal pointers, except
that if P is a variable of a pointer type declared in a DBD then

(a) we must write CREATE (P) to achieve what would be
achieved by NEW (P) if P were declared in a program instead of in
a DBD, and
(b) we must write DELETE (P) instead of DISPOSE (P).

Whether P is declared in a program or in a DBD, a variable created
by executing CREATE (P) persists after termination of execution of
any program, and indeed persists until deleted by DELETE (P). The

pointer P persists after termination of program execution only if P is declared in a DBD.

To illustrate the use of persistent pointers we shall extend the inventory table example of Section 4.3 to include an index on SUPPLIERNO. We shall use this index to find all the items supplied by any given supplier. (The ideas will be the same as for the indexed invoice table example of Section 9.8.2, except that the index will survive after termination of the program that sets it up and therefore we shall not need to create the entire index each time we wish to use it.) The following DBD is an amended version of the DBD IX that we used previously.

```
DBDNAME JX;
type
  REFRANGE = 100 .. 140;
  SUPPRANGE = 10 .. 99;
  INVTYPE = record
               QUANTITYINSTOCK: INTEGER;
               PRICEPERUNIT: REAL;
               SUPPLIERNO: SUPPRANGE;
               NORECORD: BOOLEAN
            end;
  MEMPTRTYPE = ↑MEMBERTYPE;
  MEMBERTYPE = record
                  ITEMREFNO: REFRANGE;
                  NEXT: MEMPTRTYPE
               end;
var
  INVTABLE: array [REFRANGE] of INVTYPE;
  SUPPINDEX: array [SUPPRANGE] of MEMPTRTYPE;
finish
```

For each supplier, SUPPINDEX points to a linked list of ITEM-REFNOs of all items supplied by this supplier. Initially, before any other program is run, we shall initialize all the index entries to **nil**:

```
program INITJX (OUTPUT);
invoke JX;
var
  I: REFRANGE; J: SUPPRANGE;
begin
  STARTTRANSACTION (UNRESTRICTED);
  for I: = 100 to 140 do INVTABLE[I].NORECORD: = TRUE;
```

```
   for J: = 10 to 99 do SUPPINDEX [I]: = nil;
   ENDTRANSACTION; WRITELN ('initialization completed');
end.
```

The following program enters a single record into INVTABLE and updates the index accordingly. When we wish to enter more than one record we run this program once for each record.

```
program ENTERJX (INPUT, OUTPUT);
invoke JX;
var
   ITEMREFNO: REFRANGE;
   SUPPNO: SUPPRANGE;
   ENTRY: MEMPTRTYPE;
begin
   STARTTRANSACTION (UNRESTRICTED);
   WRITE ('please type ITEMREFNO, QUANTITYINSTOCK,');
   WRITELN ('PRICEPERUNIT, SUPPLIERNO');
   READ (ITEMREFNO);
   with INVTABLE [ITEMREFNO] do
   begin
      READLN (QUANTITYINSTOCK, PRICEPERUNIT,
      SUPPLIERNO);
      SUPPNO: = SUPPLIERNO;
      NORECORD: = FALSE
   end;
   CREATE (ENTRY);
   ENTRY↑.ITEMREFNO: = ITEMREFNO;
   ENTRY↑.NEXT: = SUPPINDEX [SUPPNO];
   SUPPINDEX [SUPPNO]: = ENTRY; {this makes SUPPINDEX
   [SUPPNO] point to the newly created record, which now points to
   the record that was previously first in the list}
ENDTRANSACTION
end.
```

Because MEMPTRTYPE is declared in the DBD, ENTRY is a pointer to a persistent variable whose value survives after termination of execution of ENTERJX. ENTRY itself is not a persistent variable because it is not declared in the DBD, so the value of ENTRY does not survive after termination of execution of ENTERJX. The array element SUPPINDEX [SUPPNO], which points to what ENTRY was pointing to, does survive. Indeed SUPPINDEX is a persistent variable array of pointers to linked lists

of persistent variables, and this entire data structure survives after
termination of execution of the program ENTERJX.

To illustrate the use of the index, the following program reads a
supplier number from the terminal and outputs all the records from
the inventory table for items supplied by this supplier.

```
program SUPPQUERY (INPUT, OUTPUT);
invoke JX;
var
   SUPPNO: SUPPRANGE;
   CURRPTR: MEMPTRTYPE;
begin
   WRITELN ('please type a supplier number');
   READLN (SUPPNO);
   STARTTRANSACTION (READONLY);
   CURRPTR: = SUPPINDEX [SUPPNO];
   if CURRPTR = nil then
   WRITELN ('no items are supplied by supplier ', SUPPNO)
   else
   repeat
      WRITE ('ITEMREFNO= ', CURRPTR↑.ITEMREFNO);
      with INVTABLE [CURRPTR↑.ITEMREFNO] do
      begin
         WRITE('QUANTITYINSTOCK= ',QUANTITYINSTOCK);
         WRITELN ('PRICE PER UNIT= ', PRICEPERUNIT)
      end;
      CURRPTR: = CURRPTR↑.NEXT
   until CURRPTR = nil;
   ENDTRANSACTION
end.
```

To look up any given item reference number in the inventory table
we could use our previous program LOOKUPIX, amended to
invoke JX instead of IX, but otherwise unchanged.

The next example program reads an item reference number from
the terminal and deletes the entry in the inventory table that has this
item reference number. The program also deletes this item reference
number from the supplier index.

```
program DELJX (INPUT, OUTPUT);
invoke JX;
var
   SUPPNO: SUPPRANGE; ITEMREFNO: REFRANGE;
   CURRPTR, PREVPTR: MEMPTRTYPE;
```

```
begin
   STARTTRANSACTION (UNRESTRICTED);
   WRITELN ('type item reference number of record to be deleted');
   READLN (ITEMREFNO);
   SUPPNO: = INVTABLE [ITEMREFNO].SUPPLIERNO;
   INVTABLE [ITEMREFNO].NORECORD: = TRUE; {this effectively
      deletes the record from the table}
   CURRPTR: = SUPPINDEX [SUPPNO];
   if CURRPTR↑.ITEMREFNO = ITEMREFNO then {delete the first
      record from this supplier's linked list in the index}
   SUPPINDEX [SUPPNO]: = CURRPTR↑.NEXT {to make the index
      point to the second record in the linked list}
   else {make CURRPTR point to the record to be deleted}
   begin
      repeat
         PREVPTR: = CURRPTR;
         CURRPTR: = CURRPTR↑.NEXT
      until CURRPTR↑.ITEMREFNO = ITEMREFNO;
      PREVPTR↑.NEXT: = CURRPTR↑.NEXT
   end;
   DELETE (CURRPTR); ENDTRANSACTION
end;
```

Deletion from the index is based on the same method as in the procedure DELETE that is explained with diagrams in Section 9.8.2, except that we now assume that the item reference number sought will certainly be found somewhere in the linked list.

Price history example. In the inventory table example we assumed that each item had exactly one price per unit. We shall now extend the example so that, when the price of an item changes, we shall record the date and the new price, along with the previous prices and the dates when they became effective. Corresponding to each inventory record we shall now have a linked list of price and date data, with the most recent price at the beginning of the list. For a few of the inventory records the data structure might, for example, look like this:

QUANTITY INSTOCK	SUPPLIER NO	LIST	PRICE	DATE	NEXT	PRICE	DATE	NEXT
18	23		12.30	930612		10.90	920109	nil
9	55		9.40	930526		8.95	930201	
			8.50	921001		8.10	920725	nil
75	23		50.00	910701	nil			

This tells us that for the first item the price rose to 12.30 on 12 June 1993, and previously the price had become 10.90 on 9 January 1992. For the second item the linked list contains four prices, and for the third item there is exactly one price. We use linked lists because the number of prices per item is not the same for all items. An alternative idea would be to include in each inventory record an

```
array [1..10] of record
               PRICE: REAL;
               DATE: 880101..980101
          end.
```

to store the prices introduced at various dates. The upper bound 10 of this array is merely an example: if the upper bound is high enough to accommodate the greatest number of different prices, array elements will be wasted in records for items that have had only one or two different prices. This illustrates a general problem of storing variable-length data. In our example we shall use lists rather than arrays because no elements will be unused and wasted, although we shall have to introduce pointers which take up a little memory space; pointers would not be required if we used arrays instead of lists. For simplicity we shall not now have an index of supplier numbers, so that our example is merely an extension of the simple inventory table example to accommodate a variable number of prices. We shall omit the NORECORD field: if the value of the list field is **nil**, this signifies the same as NORECORD = TRUE.

```
DBDNAME KX;
type
   SUPPRANGE = 10..99; REFRANGE = 100..140;
   DPTRTYPE = ↑DPRECTYPE;
   DPRECTYPE = record
                   PRICE: REAL;
                   DATE: 880101..980101;
                   DNEXT:DPTRTYPE
               end;
   INVTYPE = record
                   QUANTITYINSTOCK: INTEGER;
                   SUPPLIERNO: SUPPRANGE;
                   LIST: DPTRTYPE
               end;
var INVTABLE: array [REFRANGE] of INVTYPE;
finish
```

Our initializing program is:

```
program INITKX (OUTPUT);
invoke KX;
var
   I: REFRANGE;
begin
   STARTTRANSACTION (UNRESTRICTED);
   for I: = 100 to 140 do INVTABLE [I].LIST: = nil;
   ENDTRANSACTION
end.
```

In Section 4.3 we used the program ENTERDATA to enter a new record into INVTABLE. If we wished to update one record in the table by altering, for example, the QUANTITYINSTOCK, we could achieve this by using the program ENTERDATA and reading in values for all fields of the record, including those not requiring amendment. To avoid the clumsiness of reading field values that do not require change, and in particular to avoid upsetting the pointer field when an update does not involve a change of price, we now provide separate programs to enter new records and update previous records. The following program enters new records but does not update existing records:

```
program ENTERKX (INPUT, OUTPUT);
invoke KX;
var
   ITEMREFNO: REFRANGE;
   PDENTRY: DPTRTYPE;
begin
   STARTTRANSACTION (UNRESTRICTED);
   WRITELN ('please type ITEMREFNO');
   READLN (ITEMREFNO);
   if INVTABLE [ITEMREFNO].LIST < > nil then
   WRITELN ('program terminating because this is not a new ITEM')
   else
   begin
     CREATE (PDENTRY);
     WRITE ('type QUANTITY IN STOCK, SUPPLIER NO, ');
     WRITELN ('DATE and PRICE');
     with INVTABLE [ITEMREFNO] do
     READ (QUANTITYINSTOCK, SUPPLIERNO);
     with PDENTRY↑ do READLN (DATE, PRICE);
     PDENTRY↑.DNEXT: = nil;
```

```
    INVTABLE [ITEMREFNO].LIST: = PDENTRY
  end;
  ENDTRANSACTION
end.
```

The following separate program updates an existing record. More specifically, this program allows updating of QUANTITYIN-STOCK by overwriting the previous value with a new value. This program also allows insertion of a new price and date at the head of a linked list, not overwriting previous values but preserving them in case they are required.

```
program UPDAKX (INPUT, OUTPUT);
invoke KX;
var
  PDENTRY: DPTRTYPE;
  ITEMREFNO: REFRANGE;
  SELECTOR: CHAR;
begin
  STARTTRANSACTION (UNRESTRICTED);
  WRITELN ('Please type ITEM REF NO');
  READLN (ITEMREFNO);
  if INVTABLE [ITEMREFNO].LIST = nil then
  WRITELN ('program terminating because item unknown')
  else with INVTABLE [ITEMREFNO] do
  begin
    WRITELN ('to update QUANTITY IN STOCK type Y else N');
    READLN (SELECTOR);
    if SELECTOR = 'Y' then
    begin
      WRITELN ('type QUANTITY IN STOCK');
      READLN (QUANTITYINSTOCK)
    end;
    WRITELN ('if you wish to enter new price type Y else type N');
    READLN (SELECTOR);
    if SELECTOR = 'Y' then
    begin
      WRITELN ('type new price and date');
      CREATE (PDENTRY);
      with PDENTRY↑ do READLN (PRICE,DATE);
      PDENTRY↑.DNEXT: = LIST;
      LIST: = PDENTRY
    end
  end;
  ENDTRANSACTION
end.
```

In all these programs we should check that input data items are within their allowed ranges; for example for the program UPDAKX the date must be in the range 880101..980101. We have omitted such checks only to make programs easier to read.

The next program reads an item reference number and date from the terminal and outputs the price that this item had at the specified date.

```
program GETPRICEATDATE (INPUT, OUTPUT);
invoke KX;
var
   PRICEPTR: DPTRTYPE;
   ITEMREFNO: REFRANGE;
   SEEKDATE: 880101..980101;
   FOUND: BOOLEAN;
begin
   STARTTRANSACTION (READONLY);
   WRITELN ('please type the required ITEM REF NO and DATE');
   READLN (ITEMREFNO, SEEKDATE);
   PRICEPTR: = INVTABLE [ITEMREFNO].LIST;
   FOUND: = FALSE;
   while (PRICEPTR < > nil) and not FOUND do
      if PRICEPTR↑.DATE < = SEEKDATE then FOUND: = TRUE
      else PRICEPTR: = PRICEPTR↑.DNEXT;
   if FOUND then
      WRITELN ('price at that date was ', PRICEPTR↑.PRICE:8:2)
   else
      WRITELN ('the item was not in the inventory at that date');
   ENDTRANSACTION
end.
```

This program works along the list that corresponds to the input ITEMREFNO until it comes to the first date that is not later than the input date. It is correct to output the price associated with this date because earlier dates occur later in the list; new dates are inserted at the beginning of the list by the program UPDAKX.

4.5. Further Pascal database facilities

The Pascal database facilities that have been introduced in this chapter are necessary but not sufficient for the purposes of Chapters 6 and 7. To increase the power and the comfort of Pascal database programming we shall introduce further facilities in Section 5.8.

4.6. Exercises

1. This exercise uses the DBD

```
DBDNAME E1;
const
    LENGTH = 24;
type
    RANGE = 1..LENGTH;
    CHARSTRING = packed array [RANGE] of CHAR;
var
    TEXTLINE: CHARSTRING;
finish
```

(a) Write a program to read a sequence of not more than LENGTH characters from the terminal into TEXTLINE. The contents of TEXT-LINE must persist after your program terminates.

(b) Write a separate program to read from the terminal two integers in the range 1..LENGTH. Let these integers be L and U respectively, L being not greater than U. Your program is to output to the terminal, all on one line, the characters TEXTLINE [L], TEXTLINE [$L+1$], ..., TEXTLINE [U].

(c) Try inputting text using the program that you wrote in (a), and then run the program you wrote in (b) to output part of the text. Run the (b) program again several times to output various parts of the text.

2. The matrix

	A	B	C	D	E	F
A	0					
B	12	0				
C	15	6	0			
D	10	30	14	0		
E	8	23	22	40	0	
F	12	6	22	12	45	0

has its rows and columns labelled A..F. These letters represent towns, and the integers in the matrix are distances between pairs of these towns.

(a) Write a DBD for use by the following two programs.

(b) Write a program to read the matrix from your terminal into a two-dimensional array declared in your DBD. The matrix is to contain only the distances, not the characters A..F. The distances must survive after this program terminates, for use by the following program.

(c) Write a program to read a sequence of three letters, each in the range A..F, and output the total distance from the town represented by the first letter to the town represented by the third letter, travelling via the town represented by the middle letter. For example if the input is BED the output is 63, which is the sum of the distance between B and E and the distance between E and D.

3. (a) For use in (b), (c), and (d) write a DBD that includes the array declarations:

var
    DIGITWORDS: **array** [1..40] **of** CHAR;
    WHEREITSTARTS: **array** ['0'..'9'] **of** 1..40;

(b) Write a program to read from the terminal into the array DIGI-TWORDS the string ZEROONETWOTHREEFOURFIVESIXSEVE-NEIGHTNINE. Note that this string consists of the digit names ZERO, ONE, ..., strung together without spaces.

(c) Write a program to read from the terminal into the array WHER-EITSTARTS the 10 integers 1,5,8,11,16,20,24,27,32,37. The meaning of these integers is that ZERO starts at array subscript 1 in DIGITWORDS, ONE starts at array subscript 5 in DIGITWORDS, TWO starts at array subscript 8 of DIGITWORDS, and so on.

(d) Write a program to read a character from the terminal. If this character is a digit your program should output the name of this digit by using the arrays WHEREITSTARTS and DIGITWORDS. For example if the input is 5 the output should be FIVE.

4. This exercise modifies the simple inventory table example of Section 4.3 so that now the inventory records are stored in a linked list instead of an array. The records in the list are sorted on ITEMREFNO. The range of ITEMREFNOs is now 1000..9000, but the linked list may actually contain only a few records. If these few records were stored in an array that had bounds 1000..9000, many of the array elements would be unused, and memory would therefore be wasted. For this exercise you should use the DBD

```
DBDNAME JY:
type
  REFRANGE = 1000..9000;
  INVPTRTYPE = ↑INVTYPE;
  INVTYPE = record
              ITEMREFNO: REFRANGE;
              QUANTITYINSTOCK: INTEGER;
              PRICEPERUNIT: REAL;
              SUPPLIERNO: 10..99;
              NEXTITEM: INVPTRTYPE
            end;
var
  STARTPOINTER: INVPTRTYPE; {this will point to the first record
    in the list}
finish
```

An initializing program is:

```
program INITIALIZEJY (OUTPUT);
invoke JY;
begin
  STARTTRANSACTION (UNRESTRICTED);
  STARTPOINTER: = nil;
  WRITELN ('initialization completed');
  ENDTRANSACTION
end.
```

You are required to:

(a) Write a program that reads one inventory record from the terminal and enters it into the linked list in a position such that the list remains sorted on ITEMREFNO. (Hint: look at the procedure INSERT in Section 9.8.2, and also look at the program ENTERDATA in Section 4.3.)

(b) Write a program that reads an ITEMREFNO from the terminal and outputs the associated QUANTITYINSTOCK, PRICEPERUNIT, and SUPPLIERNO, unless the input ITEMREFNO is not found in the list in which case your program should say so.

5 An introduction to file organization

5.1. Organization for access

In Chapters 1, 2, and 3 we regarded a file as a collection of records persisting in secondary memory when no program is being executed. This was a high level view of a file, because we were not concerned with details of the organization of records in memory. The present chapter is at a lower level and introduces classical methods of organization of records in files to facilitate access under various conditions.

5.2. Sorted order terminology

We shall often encounter collections of records sorted into a non-random sequence. As a preliminary to the introduction of methods of file organization, we now use examples to introduce terminology for specifying sorted order. Our first example is a file named FNAME that has four fields F1, F2, F3, and F4 and contains eight records in the following sequence.

F1	F2	F3	F4
ac	A	62	J
an	A	74	J
bd	C	13	J
ck	A	21	K
de	N	93	K
dw	P	18	K
dx	B	22	J
ea	D	26	J

This file is said to be *sorted on F1*, which means that records are stored in increasing order (here alphabetic order) of F1 field value. *Sorted on F1* is usually assumed to mean *sorted on increasing F1* unless we explicitly say *decreasing*. For example the file

F1	F2	F3	F4
de	N	93	K
an	A	74	J
ac	A	62	J
ea	D	26	J
dx	B	22	J
ck	A	21	K
dw	P	18	K
bd	C	13	J

is *sorted on decreasing F3*.

The field or set of fields that determine the sequence of records is the *sort key*. In the previous examples the sort key consists of just one field, whereas in the following example the two fields F1 and F2 together constitute the sort key.

F1	F2	F3	F4
2	A	62	J
2	C	74	J
2	N	62	J
3	B	62	K
4	C	21	K
4	H	21	K
5	P	74	J
5	X	62	J

This file is said to be *sorted on F2 within F1*. This means that F1 values appear in increasing sequence: for each F1 value the F2 values are in (alphabetically) increasing sequence. F2 varies more rapidly than F1. In this case. F1 is said to be the *major* sort key and F2 is said to be the *minor* sort key. A further example is that for Typico's PENDING INVOICE file DUE DATE is the major sort key and INVOICE DATE is the minor sort key. This file is sorted on INVOICE DATE within SUPPLIER NUMBER within DUE DATE; records that have the same DUE DATE and SUPPLIER NUMBER are sorted in order of increasing INVOICE DATE. In general, any number of *withins* can be concatenated.

5.3. Simple sequential files

5.3.1. *Access to records in simple sequential files*

Simple sequential files provide an obvious starting point for our introductory review of methods of file organization. Standard Pascal files are simple sequential files. In standard Pascal, if we wish data to survive after the termination of execution of a program, we can write this data to a standard Pascal file. A subsequent program that uses this data reads it from the file.

Records in a simple sequential file can only be accessed one after the other: for example, we can only access the nth record by first obtaining records $1, 2, \ldots, n-1$. We must work through these $n-1$ records before we can retrieve information from the nth record. To delete a record we must make a new copy of the file with this record missed out, and to insert a record we must make a new copy of the file with the new record included. To update a record by changing the value of at least one of its fields, we must make a new copy of the file containing the updated record. An introduction to Pascal programming details is given in Chapter 9.

The need to work through $n-1$ records before accessing the nth is sometimes disadvantageous. On the other hand, one of the advantages of simple sequential files is that we can access them by READ and WRITE statements which are similar to those used for reading from, or writing to, a terminal. It is also worth noting that, if a file is physically stored on magnetic tape, then simple sequential organization is natural.

5.3.2. *Batch processing*

Linear search is the technical term for working through a given sequence of values one by one until a sought value is found. If we use linear search to find a given primary key value in a simple sequential file of N records then we can expect to work through $N/2$ records before finding the one we want. That is to say, if we were to conduct many trials, each starting from the beginning of the file and each looking for a randomly selected primary key value, then *on average* we would work through $N/2$ records per trial before finding the sought primary key value.

If we wish to access M records in a simple sequential file of N

records, we usually try *not* to perform linear search, once for each of
the *M* sought records starting each time from the beginning of the
file. *M* repetitions of linear search would probably involve working
through approximately *MN*/2 records, and this would be bad news if
N was large. A more efficient method is to work through the file of *N*
records just once, instead of starting at the beginning for each of the
M sought records. To achieve this efficiency we store the *M* sought
primary key values in a second file which is traditionally called a
transaction file. The file of *N* records which include the ones we want
is traditionally called the *master* file. The transaction file and the
master file must be in the same sorted order. The idea is that we read
the first primary key value from the transaction file and use linear
search to find it in the master file. Then we read the next primary key
value from the transaction file and, carrying on from where we left
off in the master file, use linear search to find this next primary key
value in the master file. We repeat this with successive primary key
values obtained from the transaction file.

Consider, for example, a drastically simplified inventory file
named TOYINVEN that contains 72 records of the type

```
TOYINVREC = record
            ITEMREFNO: STRING4;
            QUANTITYINSTOCK: INTEGER
       end
```

sorted on (increasing) ITEMREFNO. Suppose that we wish to obtain from TOYINVEN the QUANTITYINSTOCK for each of the
10 ITEMREFNOs VF62, DS33, SC84, FS52, TL81, AQ01, HH50,
BC59, RT06, and AH84. Instead of looking these up in TOYIN-
VEN by linear search, starting each time from the beginning, we sort
the 10 ITEMREFNOs into increasing order and store them in a
simple sequential file named TRANSINVEN. TOYINVEN is our
master file, and TRANSINVEN is our transaction file. A program
to find the required QUANTITYINSTOCK values is

```
program BATCHLOOKUP (TOYINVEN, TRANSINVEN, OUTPUT);
type
  STRING4 = packed array [1..4] of CHAR;
  TOYINVREC = record
              ITEMREFNO: STRING4;
              QUANTITYINSTOCK: INTEGER
          end;
```

```
var
   TOYINVEN: file of TOYINVREC;
   TRANSINVEN: TEXT;
   SOUGHTITEMREFNO: STRING4;
   VTOYINVEN: TOYINVREC;
begin
   RESET (TOYINVEN); RESET (TRANSINVEN);
   while not EOF (TRANSINVEN) do
   begin
     READ (TRANSINVEN, SOUGHTITEMREFNO);
     repeat
       READ (TOYINVEN, VTOYINVEN)
     until SOUGHTITEMREFNO = VTOYINVEN.ITEMREFNO;
     with VTOYINVEN do
     WRITELN (ITEMREFNO, ' ', QUANTITYINSTOCK)
     end
end.
```

For simplicity this program does not allow for the possibility that an ITEMREFNO in TRANSINVEN may not be found in TOYIN-VEN. The output of this program is TOYINVEN **join** TRANSIN-VEN. By sorting TRANSINVEN into the same order as TOYIN-VEN we have been able to accomplish this join more efficiently than by starting at the beginning of TRANSINVEN for each ITEM-REFNO in TRANSINVEN.

Batch processing is technical term for searching a master file for records specified by means of a transaction file sorted into the same order as the master file. The example that we have just given illustrates the use of batch processing for looking up records to retrieve information. It is easy to see how batch processing can also be used for updating M records in a master file of N records, or for deleting M records, or for inserting M new records into the master file. The file merging example in Section 9.6 is a batch-processing program that inserts records from a transaction file into a master file to produce a new master file. Exercises 6 and 7 in Section 9.7 are batch-processing exercises.

5.3.3. File block buffer

The Pascal programmer does not need to know how data in a standard sequential file are physically stored on a secondary storage medium such as a disc. Nor does the programmer need to know the detailed steps involved in transferring data between secondary memory and immediate access memory. It is expedient now to go down to a lower level than that of a Pascal programmer and consider how data can actually be transferred.

First we should be clear *why* data is transferred. One reason is that ordinary (non-persistent) Pascal variables are (regarded as being) stored in immediate access memory, and traditionally these variables disappear when program execution terminates. Subsequently the same immediate access memory can be used for storing the variables of another program. If the Pascal programmer wishes to preserve values (of non-persistent variables) after termination of program execution he can arrange to copy them to non-volatile secondary memory. In standard Pascal this copying to secondary memory is accomplished by writing to a standard Pascal sequential file, as we have explained previously.

Besides non-volatility, secondary memory may also have the advantage of costing less (per bit of storage capacity) than immediate access memory. If a program is processing a large quantity of data we may prefer some of these data to be in secondary memory at any given time to avoid the cost of providing enough immediate access memory to contain all the data at once. In this case data are transferred between secondary memory and immediate access memory to help reduce the overall cost of the memory that the data occupies.

Data are usually transferred between secondary memory and immediate access memory at a rate that is so rapid that an ordinary simple central processor unit cannot work fast enough to control the transfer character by character. Instead the character-by-character control is delegated to a special controlling device; the central processor unit simply tells this device how many characters (or more generally bytes) to transfer, where to obtain them from, and where to transfer them to. A sequence of characters (or bytes) transferred in this way is known as a *block*. A block might, for example, consist of 512 characters. It is regarded as the smallest unit of data that can be transferred between secondary memory and immediate access memory. It is important to understand that all transfers of data between secondary memory and immediate access memory are accomplished by transferring one or more blocks.

Depending on the circumstances, a block may contain exactly one record, or part of a record may be stored in one block and another part of this record may be stored in another block. More commonly the number of characters (or bytes) per record is small enough to allow more than one whole record to be stored in one block. In this case records are said to be *packed* into a block.

The number of characters (or bytes) per block may be

(a) fixed physically, or
(b) freely chosen by the programmer.

For discs (a) is simpler than (b) and is therefore more usual. For magnetic tape (b) is more usual. An advantage of (b) is that this allows the programmer to avoid wasting space in a block by making the number of characters (or bytes) per block a multiple of the number of characters (or bytes) per record.

A compromise possibility, having advantages of (a) and (b), is to fix the number of characters (or bytes) per block but allow the programmer to specify that sets of two, four, or eight blocks can optionally be strung together to look like a larger block. A larger block made up in this way is known as a *bucket*. If a record is too big to fit into a single block it may fit into a single bucket, and in this case we may prefer to regard a bucket as the minimum unit of data that can be transferred between secondary memory and immediate access memory. In the present text we shall simply regard a bucket as a large block, and we shall not use the term *bucket*. For simplicity we shall only talk in terms of blocks. We shall assume that the records of a standard Pascal file are packed into blocks of equal size.

When a Pascal program writes to a file of records, the data transfer proceeds physically block by block, not record by record. Behind the scenes the Pascal procedure WRITE has to pack records into blocks; this packing is called *blocking*. Similarly, READ has to unpack records from blocks; this unpacking is called *deblocking*. For use during blocking or deblocking, the declaration of a file causes a *file block buffer* to be created behind the scenes. A file block buffer is a block of immediate access memory that contains the same number of characters (or bytes) as a block of the file in secondary memory. This should not be confused with the file's *file buffer* (see Section 9.6), which is only large enough to contain a single record. A file buffer is visible to a Pascal programmer, but a file block buffer is not. Each file declared in a program has its own file buffer and its own file block buffer which are not shared with other files.

By way of example, let FNAME be a binary file of records and let V be a variable of the same record type. The following loop does not do anything useful, but a more complicated example would be unnecessary.

```
RESET (FNAME);
repeat
  READ (FNAME, V)
until EOF (FNAME)
```

When this loop is executed what goes on behind the scenes is roughly like this:

```
read first block of FNAME from secondary memory to file block buffer;
file buffer: = first record in the file block buffer;
repeat
  V: = file buffer,
  if this was the last record in the file block buffer then
  read the next block of FNAME from secondary memory to file block
  buffer;
  file buffer: = next record from file block buffer
until file buffer contains end-of-file marker.
```

Section 9.6 includes programming examples that show the advantage of reading via the file buffer instead of directly into V. Another reason for using the file buffer is that when it contains the end-of-file marker this should not be assigned to V because it is of the wrong Pascal type.

As a simple example illustrating blocking, consider the following very trivial loop:

```
for COUNT: = 1 to 100 do WRITE (FNAME, V)
```

When this loop is executed what goes on behind the scenes is roughly like this:

```
for COUNT: = 1 to 100 do
begin
  file buffer: = V;
  if there is not sufficient space left in the file block buffer then
  copy the block from the file block buffer to secondary memory;
  pack contents of file buffer into next free space in file block buffer
end.
```

When this loop terminates, the file block buffer may contain a block, perhaps not full, that must subsequently be copied to secondary memory as the final block of FNAME. Furthermore, an end-of-file marker must be inserted after the last record in the file; we shall not give details of this.

The blocking and deblocking routines that we have sketched presuppose that blocks are written to and read from the secondary memory in a known sequence. If the secondary memory is magnetic tape, successive blocks of the file will naturally be successive physical blocks on the tape.

5.3.4. Chained blocks

If a file is stored on disc, successive blocks may possibly be arranged as shown in Fig. 5.1, which represents a single track subdivided into eight blocks. Blocks of our file are numbered 1,2,3,..., and blocks that do not belong to our file are shown hatched. In this case the blocks of our file are said to be *contiguous*, which means that successive blocks are physically next door to each other. If the file has too many blocks to fit on one track, the file can continue as a set of contiguous blocks on the next track (preferably within the same cylinder). A file that has blocks arranged like this is a *contiguous* file.

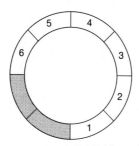

Fig. 5.1. One track subdivided into eight blocks.

In practice, *before* disc blocks are allocated to a file, successive tracks may contain blocks that are already included in other files. For example the occupied blocks might be as shown hatched in Fig. 5.2(a). Figure 5.2(a) only shows four tracks, but other tracks may also contain randomly placed occupied blocks. In this case we may not be able to find a sufficient number of contiguous non-occupied blocks in which to store a contiguous file.

This is one reason why it is quite common *not* to store a sequential file contiguously. Instead a simple sequential file may be stored in blocks that are scattered randomly, although preferably within one cylinder. When allocating blocks to a file, the system simply finds an unoccupied block somewhere and links it into the file. The linking can be achieved by including in each block the address of the next block in sequence. (The address is data that tells the computer where, physically, to find the next block. The address may comprise cylinder number, surface number, and sector number.) The system records somewhere else the address of the first block in the sequence of blocks that are linked or chained together, each pointing to the next. The blocks of a standard Pascal file might, for example, be as shown in Fig. 5.2(b), in which the linking addresses are represented diagrammatically by pointer arrows. This sequential file organization is said to be *chained*.

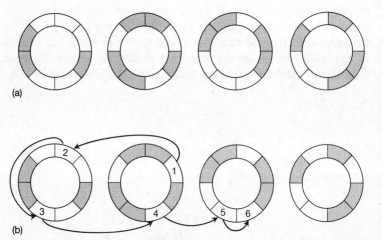

Fig. 5.2. (a) An example of random occupancy of blocks; (b) an example of blocks chained into a sequence.

If a sequential file is to be stored contiguously we have to know in advance the number of blocks required so that we can look for this number of non-occupied free blocks. With a chained file there is no need to know how many blocks are required when we start writing to the file; we can repeatedly append new blocks to the end of the file, and this is an important advantage of chained organization.

5.4. Hit rate and efficiency of access

When a program finds a sought key value in a file this event is called a *hit*. In batch processing a single program is intended to achieve more than one hit in a master file. For a run (i.e. an execution) of such a program we define

$$\text{hit rate} = \frac{\text{number of hits}}{\text{number of records in the file}}$$

An alternative term for hit rate is *activity ratio*. A batch processing run that applies a transaction file of M records to a master file of N records has hit rate M/N unless some of the sought records are not found in the master file. A classical example in which the hit rate is near to unity is payment calculation in payroll processing: every (or almost every) record in the EMPLOYEES file is processed.

When a program accesses just one record somewhere in a file, this is called *random access*. For random access the hit rate is near to zero. A practical example of random access arises when Typico take customers' orders over the telephone and wish to look up items one by one in random order in the inventory file to check that the customer's version of the item reference number agrees with the item reference number and description in the inventory file. If there is any discrepancy Typico prefer to ask the customer about it immediately, before going on to the next item.

Efficiency of random access is inversely proportional to the total time taken to access a random record stored in non-volatile secondary memory. When we examine the factors contributing to the total time taken to access a record we find that the time taken to transfer blocks is usually a strongly dominant factor, that is to say most of the time required for access to a record is actually time required for transferring blocks. Block transfer time comprises seek time, latency, and the time for copying a block that has been found. These factors derive from electromechanical operation of magnetic media. Electromechanical operations tend to be slow compared with the rate at which a computer executes instructions that are stored in immediate access memory. Thus efficiency of access to a record in secondary memory is (roughly) inversely proportional to the number of block transfers required to achieve this access.

Random access to a simple sequential file is generally inefficient, because we have to start at the beginning of the file and transfer successive blocks until we come to the one that contains a sought record. In the following sections we introduce other methods of file organization that are intended to improve the efficiency of random access. These methods, which are not available in standard Pascal, will allow us to access a block without having to transfer all previous blocks.

5.5. Address calculation

5.5.1. *Direct addressing*

In *direct-addressing* file organization we can think of the file as an array of records, such that the subscript of any given record is a function of that record's primary key value. For example the subscript may be the same as the primary key value. We have already used this idea: in the simple inventory table example in Section 4.3, the array of records can be regarded as a direct-addressing file in which the subscript is the primary key value. Compared with a standard Pascal file of inventory records, the advantage is that we can identify the record by a given ITEM-REFNO *without* first obtaining all the preceding records in the file.

If, behind the scenes, the records in the array are packed into contiguous blocks starting at a known address, then given an ITEMREFNO the computer can calculate the address of the block that contains the record identified by this ITEMREFNO, and need transfer only this one block in order to access the record. As a simple illustration, suppose that the array is stored in contiguous blocks numbered 0, 1, . . ., 10, and that records are packed four per block. In this case, to access the record identified by ITEMREFNO = 135, the computer need only access the block whose number is $(135 - 100)$ **div** $4 = 8$. Having accessed this block the computer does not need to unpack the records in turn; instead it can proceed directly to access the fourth record in the block. This is correct because the first record in the block has ITEMREFNO 132, the second has ITEMREFNO 133, and the third has ITEMREFNO 134; the number of the record within the block is $(135-100)$ **mod** $4 + 1$.

In Section 5.3.4 we explained that it may not be practical to find a sufficiently large number of empty contiguous blocks in which to store a file. Instead, available free blocks may be scattered randomly among tracks. In this case we shall store our direct-addressing file in randomly scattered blocks. We shall number these blocks 0, 1, 2, . . . as before, but now we shall set up an index in which we shall be able to look up a given block number and thence find the physical address of the block. For our inventory example the contents of this index might be as follows.

BLOCK NUMBER	PHYSICAL ADDRESS		
	cylinder	surface	sector
0	3	2	4
1	3	1	3
2	2	1	7
3	2	1	3
4	2	1	4
5	2	1	5
6	2	2	3
7	2	2	6
8	2	2	7
9	3	1	7
10	3	2	1

For example we could look up block number 8 in this index and find that the three components of its physical address are

cylinder number = 2
surface number = 2
sector number = 7.

By looking at the physical addresses in this index we can easily see that the blocks are not all contiguous (although a few are contiguous, e.g. blocks 3, 4, and 5).

The index itself is normally stored in at least one block. Given a key value we now require at least two block accesses: one to obtain the index, and another to obtain the block that contains the sought record. By introducing the index we have won the advantage of not requiring contiguous free blocks for the file, but we have incurred the disadvantage of decreased efficiency of access.

We can delete a record from a sequential file by making a new version of the file that simply does not contain the deleted record. It is important that we can delete a record from a direct-addressing file *without* making a new version of the whole file. A direct-addressing file is constructed so that storage space is reserved for every record, including records that have been deleted and records to which no value has yet been assigned. One method of distinguishing bona fide records from records that have been deleted or have no value is to incorporate a boolean field in the record type, as we did in Section 4.3. The boolean field NORECORD has the value FALSE only when a bona fide record is present. To delete a record we simply assign TRUE to NORECORD. A direct addressing file wastes memory if only a few of the records have bona fide values, and in this case it may be more appropriate to use a hash method of file organization.

5.5.2. Hash methods

5.5.3.1. Introduction

In practice we commonly find that the number of possible values of the primary key greatly exceeds the number of values that are actually present in the file at any given time. In this case direct addressing may not be practical because it wastefully provides memory space for records that do not turn up.

For example let us again consider a drastically simplified inventory file named TOYINVEN that has the record type

record
    ITEMREFNO: STRING4;
    QUANTITYINSTOCK: 0..99999
end.

For this file the range of possible values of the primary key ITEMREFNO is AA00, AA01, ..., ZZ99, which comprises $26 \times 26 \times 100$ possible values. If this file actually contains 72 records (having ITEMREFNOs randomly scattered in the range AA00..ZZ99) direct addressing would waste the space for $26 \times 26 \times 100 - 72$ records. We can use a hash method to avoid this waste whilst retaining much of the efficiency of direct addressing.

In a hash method a record is inserted into the first free space in the block whose number is a specified function of the primary key value. This function is known as a *hash* function. The free space may be identified by the boolean field value NORECORD = TRUE. If there is no free space in the block then we insert the record into a block that is known as an *overflow* block (we shall discuss overflow in Section 5.5.2.2).

To illustrate this we have chosen as a hash function for the file TOYINVEN

h (ITEMREFNO) = (the part of the ITEMREFNO that is a two-digit number) **mod** 13

For example $h(AA39) = 39$ **mod** $13 = 0$, and $h(AA62) = 62$ **mod** $13 = 10$. h (ITEMREFNO) is our hash function of ITEMREFNO which is the primary key of the file TOYINVEN. This function has been chosen to yield a value in the range 0 ... 12, thus identifying one of 13 blocks. In this example each block has capacity for a maximum of eight records, so that when the file contains 72 records the available space is about two-thirds full. To facilitate discussion we have labelled the 13 blocks 0, 1, ..., 12. We now show the contents of the blocks after 72 records have been inserted into the file; it may be instructive to check the allocation of a few of these records to blocks by checking that the block number is equal to the hash function of the ITEMREFNO.

0:	AA91	00350	1:	AQ01	00247	2:	FD80	00731
	PK39	00041		AZ27	00065		HS41	00059
	AS65	00184		AH01	00322		FN02	00317
	AA39	00061					AS80	00001
	FS52	00114					FX80	00051

3:	XB03	00315	4:	AC56	00664	5:	AV18	01075
	LX94	00608		YD30	00000		AD31	00059
	DD68	01642		AB82	00196		AB83	00000
	HA16	00579					AC05	01006
	TL81	00034					AP83	00914
	MC55	00082					AE31	07154
							FS44	00321
							RT05	00108

6:	AH84	00621	7:	AL72	00007	8:	FH08	00629
	BA32	00002		MM72	00006		SY73	00094
	MM71	00008		WG33	00016		VR34	00788
	AM19	00034		BC59	00031		RB99	00775
	SX19	00060						
	RT06	00061						
	SC84	00112						

9:	YH61	00070	10:	DT62	00095	11:	FA37	00000
	AC22	00020		AA62	00008		AP76	00015
	MQ09	00014		DD62	00315		DD63	00579
	AJ09	00000		AL62	00085		AP50	00034
				SY75	00008		MT50	00078
				VF62	00315		PA11	00314
				GB75	00338		HH50	00002
							VK89	00456

12:	AF77	00011	V:	XX44	04000
	HL12	00400		PY05	00073
	CE64	00087
	WN77	00019
	PC25	00080

In this example the block labelled V is an overflow block; it contains records for which the hash function value is 5 but there is not room for them in block 5 which is full.

To look up the QUANTITYINSTOCK for a given ITEM-REFNO, we compute h(ITEMREFNO) and then linearly search the block whose number is h(ITEMREFNO) until we find the record whose key value matches the sought ITEMREFNO. When this record is found we output its QUANTITYINSTOCK. For example, to look up the QUANTITYINSTOCK of ITEMREFNO MT50 we compute its hash value, which is 11, and then linearly search block 11 looking for the key value MT50. The required QUANTITY-INSTOCK can be found by accessing only one block; we have retained much of the speed of direct addressing but with far less wasted space. Note that the hash method would not work if primary key values were not included in the records; inclusion of the primary key is essential for hash methods but unnecessary for direct-addressing methods in which the primary key (or a function of it) is used like an array subscript. It is important that, in a hash file, the sequence of records within blocks is generally random and not sorted.

To insert a new record into the file we linearly search the block whose number is the value of h(ITEMREFNO) seeking the first record that has NORECORD = TRUE. We overwrite this record with the newly inserted record. For example, we insert the new record PQ56 00012 in the first free space in the block whose number is h(PQ56) = 4. Block 4 will now contain

AC56   00664
YD30   00000
AB82   00196
PQ56   00012.

If we try to insert a record and find that there is no record that has
NORECORD = TRUE in the block whose number is h(ITEM-
REFNO), then this block is said to have *overflowed*. In Section
5.5.2.2 we shall introduce methods for dealing with this.

To delete a record we linearly search for it in the block whose
number is h(primary key value). If we find it we set NORECORD-
= TRUE; otherwise we look for it in overflow, as will be explained
later. Before any data are entered into the file we set NORECORD-
= TRUE in all records in all blocks.

To update a record by changing its QUANTITYINSTOCK we
look up this record and overwrite the previous QUANTITYIN-
STOCK with the new QUANTITYINSTOCK. No further change is
required.

5.5.2.2.   *Overflow*

Some of the many possible ways of dealing with overflow are as
follows.

(a) *Chained blocks.* When a block overflows, place a pointer in it
to a newly acquired block, preferably within the same cylinder, and
use this newly acquired block exclusively to contain records for
which there is not room in the original block. If this newly acquired
overflow block itself overflows, place a pointer in it to yet another
newly acquired block, preferably within the same cylinder, and so
on. Within the resulting linked list of blocks all the records have the
same hash function value.

(b) *Chained records.* Method (a) has the disadvantage that many
of the overflow blocks may contain only a few records, the remaining space being wasted. To reduce the waste of space, we can place
all overflowing records in the same overflow block, regardless of
which block they have overflowed from. When the overflow block
itself overflows we can accommodate overflowing records in yet
another overflow block, and so on. Within the overflow blocks all
the records that have the same hash function value are included in
one linked list of records. The original block in which an overflowed

record would have been stored if there had been room contains a pointer to the start of the linked list that includes this overflowed record. When we wish to look up a record in the file, we start by linearly searching the block whose number is the hash function of the sought key value. If this key value is not found within this block, we traverse the linked list of overflow records to which this block points and look for the sought key value. This linked list may thread through many overflow blocks.

When we wish to insert a new record for which there is not room in the block whose number is determined by the hash function, we insert it into the first free space in the first overflow block in which there is room, and we link this record into the linked list of records that have this record's hash function value.

Although method (b) may use fewer overflow blocks than method (a), the retrieval of an overflowed record may take longer with method (b) than with method (a). Suppose, for example, that each block has room for eight records, and that we wish to look up the record that is actually the seventh record in an overflow chain (i.e. linked list) of records. In method (a) we shall only have to access the block whose number is the hash function value and then access one overflow block which will contain the seventh record that over-flowed. In method (b), after we have accessed the block whose number is the hash function value, we shall have to traverse a linked list of overflow records. Because overflowing records are entered into shared overflow blocks, it is likely that the seventh record in our linked list will not be located in the first overflow block which may contain records that have various hash function values. Instead, in order to follow the linked list as far as the seventh record, it is likely that we shall have to access more than one overflow block. This illustrates why method (b) may require access to more blocks than is required by method (a). In method (a) records are not chained within blocks.

(c) *Progressive overflow*. This method is the same as method (b), except that records are not chained into linked lists within overflow blocks. When there is not room for a record in the block whose number is the hash function value, we place this record in the first free space in an overflow block that is shared by records which have different hash function values. When we wish to look up a record, we first access the block whose number is the value of the hash function of the key. If the sought key is not found in this block we linearly search through all overflow blocks, looking for the sought key. This search involves looking at records that may have different hash function values, whereas the search in method (b) is quicker because the linking confines it to records that all have the same hash function value. Thus method (c) is slower than method (b). Method (c) has the advantage of requiring less memory, because linking pointers do not have to be stored. Method (c) also has the advantage of simplicity.

5.5.2.3. *Hash functions*

In direct addressing we calculate the block number for a given primary key value, and the number of possible primary key values that would yield the same block number equals the maximum number of records that can be packed into a block. In hashing we calculate a block number for a given primary key value, but the number of possible primary key values that would yield the same block number now exceeds the maximum number of records that can be packed into a block. For our TOYINVEN example the number of possible primary key values that would yield the same value of h(ITEMREFNO) is $26 \times 26 \times (100 \textbf{ div } 13 + 1)$. The factor 26×26 arises because the two letters in the ITEMREFNO are ignored in the calculation of h(ITEMREFNO), so that if we fix the two digits the value of h(ITEMREFNO) will be the same for all possible combinations of the two letters and each of these combinations yields a distinct primary key value.

The choice of a hash function is to some extent arbitrary, and we now consider how to choose a good hash function for any given file. To make a good choice we must know the approximate number of records that the file is likely to contain and how many records can be packed into each block. We use this information to decide how many blocks the file will contain, thus determining the range of the hash function. If we allocate too few blocks to the file, access efficiency will be decreased by overflow. If we allocate too many blocks, access efficiency will be good because there will not be much overflow, but memory capacity will be wasted in blocks that are not full. As a rule of thumb, a good compromise is to aim to have each block about two-thirds full. This is why, knowing that TOYINVEN contains 72 records and that each block has capacity (in our example) for eight records, we allocated 13 blocks to this file. The total capacity of these blocks is $13 \times 8 = 104$ records, and 72 is approximately two-thirds of 104.

A hash function should be chosen so as to satisfy the following conditions as closely as possible.

(a) Its range should be an integer in the range 0..NUMBEROF-BLOCKSAVAILABLE.

(b) It should be quick to compute.

(c) For the set of primary key values that actually occur, each of the possible values of h(keyvalue) should be equally likely. If h(keyvalue) satisfies this condition perfectly then h(keyvalue) is said to *randomize* the key values. Randomization is desirable because it makes all blocks contain approximately the same number of records. If randomization is not achieved, some of the blocks may overflow whilst others contain only a few records and efficiency of access is less than could be achieved with the available amount of memory.

In computing a hash function it may be convenient to regard letters in a key as integers in the range 0..25; thus $A = 0$, $B = 1$, $C = 2$, and so on. For example, using this idea, the numerical value of CB53 is

$(2 \times 26 \times 26 + 1 \times 26) \times 100 + 53.$

By using methods such as this, a key can always be converted into a number. Some popular ideas for hash functions are as follows.

Prime division. We make the number of blocks a prime number and use

h(keyvalue) = keyvalue **mod** NUMBEROFBLOCKS.

The use of a prime number generally yields better randomization than a non-prime number. This is why we chose 13 blocks for the TOYINVEN example.

Using a subset of digits. We can simply use a subset of the digits of a key value as a hash value. For example, if we choose to use the second and fifth digits of a six-digit key as a hash function then, for instance, h(932148) = 34 and h(716559) = 15.

Folding. We can take two (or more) subsets of digits of a key value, put the digits in each subset together in an arbitrary order to make up a number, and use the sum of these numbers as the hash value. Alternatively we may wish to use just the last few digits of this sum as the hash value. If it is assumed that the key has six digits, an example of a hash function of this type is

h (keyvalue) = last two digits of ((fifth digit + second digit) × 7 + third digit + fourth digit).

A hash function of this type is slower to compute than a function that merely uses a subset of digits, but may provide better randomization and may be quicker than prime division.

5.5.2.4. *Non-contiguous implementation*

In discussing hashing we have concentrated on calculating block numbers, and have not yet discussed how to use a block number to find a physical block in secondary memory. This problem is exactly the same as in the case of direct addressing. If the file is stored in contiguous blocks and we know the physical address of the first of these blocks, then we can easily compute the physical address of any block in the file, given its block number. On the other hand, if a sufficient number of contiguous blocks are not available for the file, we can use an index as was explained in Section 5.5.1. The index is usually stored in at least one block, and accessing the file via this index increases by at least one the total number of blocks that must be accessed.

In a case where we insert a new record into a hash file without causing overflow, or in a case where we update or delete a record that is not in overflow, we first determine the address of the appropriate block, then we transfer the block from secondary memory to immediate access memory where we perform the insertion, update or deletion, and finally we copy the block back to secondary memory, overwriting the previous contents of the block. We do not need to copy any other block back to secondary memory.

To insert, delete, or update a record in overflow, we must first transfer at least one block other than the one whose contents will be amended, because we cannot otherwise find the block that we want.

5.5.3. *Unsuitability of hash organization for batch processing*

We can generally find a single record in a hash file by accessing fewer blocks than would be necessary for finding this record by linear search through a simple sequential file. Because hash organization is good for random access, a hash file is sometimes called a *random-access* file or a *direct-access* file. These terms also apply to direct-addressed files; direct addressing can be regarded as a special case of a hash-access method.

For a batch processing run that has hit rate near to unity, a hash file may be slower to use than a simple sequential file. If we require access to records in each of the successive blocks of a sequential file it is quicker to work through these blocks in turn, without taking time doing address calculations, possibly accessing index blocks as explained in Section 5.5.2.4, and possibly accessing overflow blocks. If we are free to choose whether the organization of a given file should be hash or simple sequential, we should take account of expected hit rates: hit rates near zero would suggest hash (or direct addressing), and hit rates near to unity would suggest simple sequential organization.

Another factor that may influence our choice of file organization is whether or not we shall sometimes wish to output the entire contents of the file in sorted order, possibly for use as a hard copy reference document such as a telephone directory. If we often wish to output the contents in sorted order, then this will constitute an advantage of sequential over hash organization, because the records in a hash file are generally not in sorted order. If we only occasionally require the records in sorted order then we can use a sort program to sort them as required, and this occasional requirement for sorting may not influence our choice of file organization.

5.5.4. Exercises

1. A file that says who owns which car has REGISTRATIONNUMBER as the key. For the purposes of this exercise, every registration number consists of a letter, then three digits, and then three letters. Choose a hash function for this file, given that the number of records in the file is expected never to exceed 3000 and that each block has capacity for 10 records. Explain your choice.

2. A file that tells us heights of mountains has record type

record
    MOUNTAINNAME: **packed array** [1..12] **of** CHAR;

```
   COUNTRY: packed array [1..10] of CHAR;
   HEIGHT: REAL
end.
```

The two fields MOUNTAINNAME and COUNTRY together constitute the primary key. Choose a hash function for this file, given that the number of records never exceeds 10000 and that each block has capacity for 32 records. Explain your choice.

3. In Chapter 4, persistent variables are packed behind the scenes into blocks that are deliberately invisible to the Pascal programmer. In this exercise you will use Pascal database facilities to mimic the TOYINVEN hash example of Section 5.5.2.1. Each block will be represented by an array of eight records. Associated with each block is a pointer to a linked list of overflow records, using overflow method (b) of Section 5.5.2.2, except that you will not be concerned with the blocking of overflow records. A **nil** pointer signifies no overflow. You should use the DBD

```
DBDNAME TY;
const
   RECORDSPERBLOCK = 8;
   LASTBLOCKNO = 12;
type
   STRING4 = packed array [1..4] of CHAR;
   OFLOWPTR = ↑OFLOWRECTYPE;
   OFLOWRECTYPE = record
                     ITEMREFNO: STRING4;
                     QUANTITYINSTOCK: 0..99999;
                     NEXTITEM: OFLOWPTR
                  end;
   TOYRECTYPE = record
                     ITEMREFNO: STRING4;
                     QUANTITYINSTOCK: 0..99999;
                     NORECORD: BOOLEAN
                  end;
   BLOCKTYPE = array [1..RECORDSPERBLOCK] of
                     TOYRECTYPE
   HASHRANGE = 0..LASTBLOCKNO;
var
   HASHFILE: array: [HASHRANGE] of
               record
                  BLOCK: BLOCKTYPE;
                  OVERFLOWFIELD: OFLOWPTR
               end;
```

finish.

An initializing program is

```
program TOYINIT (OUTPUT);
invoke TY;
var
   BLOCKNUMBER: 0..LASTBLOCKNO;
   WHICHRECORD: 1..RECORDSPERBLOCK;
begin
   STARTTRANSACTION (UNRESTRICTED);
   for BLOCKNUMBER:=0 to LASTBLOCKNO do
   with HASHFILE [BLOCKNUMBER] do
   begin
      for WHICHRECORD:=1 to RECORDSPERBLOCK do
      BLOCK [WHICHRECORD].NORECORD:=TRUE;
      OVERFLOWFIELD:=nil
   end;
   WRITELN ('initialization completed');
   ENDTRANSACTION
end.
```

As in Section 5.5.2.1 the key ITEMREFNO always comprises two letters followed by two digits. You are to use the hash function

```
function HASH (ITEMREFNO: STRING4): HASHRANGE;
var
   FIRSTDIGIT, SECONDDIGIT: 0..9;
begin
   FIRSTDIGIT:=ORD (ITEMREFNO [3])−ORD ('0');
   SECONDDIGIT:=ORD (ITEMREFNO [4])−ORD ('0');
   HASH:=(FIRSTDIGIT*10+SECONDDIGIT) mod 13
end.
```

(a) Write a program to read a TOYINVEN ITEMREFNO and QUAN-TITYINSTOCK record from the terminal and insert it into the hash file. Keep this program for use in (d).

(b) Write a program to read an ITEMREFNO from the terminal and output the QUANTITYINSTOCK found by looking up this ITEM-REFNO in the hash file. If the file contains no record for this ITEM-REFNO your program should say so.

(c) Write a program to read an ITEMREFNO from the terminal and delete from the hash file the record that contains this ITEMREFNO. If the file contains no record for this ITEMREFNO your program should say so.

(d) Modify your program (a) to check whether the ITEMREFNO read from the terminal is already in the file. If this ITEMREFNO is already in the file then your program should invite you to type Y if you wish the incoming record to overwrite the existing record and N otherwise. Your program should act according to the input character.

Program testing. For (a), (b), (c), and (d) you should test your programs using some of the records from Section 5.5.2.1 together with other records that you simply make up. Initially choose your input records so that overflow will not occur, and check that your programs work properly in this case. Then go on to cause overflow deliberately (by inserting appropriate records) and again check that all your programs work as required.

5.6. Indexed sequential files

5.6.1. Introduction to indexed sequential organization

We have seen that simple sequential file organization may be acceptable if the hit rate is usually high, and hash organization may be appropriate if the hit rate is usually low. If the hit rate is sometimes high and sometimes low, then neither hash nor simple sequential organization will always provide efficient access. To deal with this case we now introduce a further family of methods, known as *indexed sequential* methods. Indexed sequential methods store records in sorted order and allow random access that is generally faster than for a simple sequential file but not as fast as for a hash file.

We shall introduce the simple basic idea of indexed sequential organization by means of an example, again using the very simple file TOYINVEN. In this example the file contains 72 records. Each block has capacity for eight records, but for reasons that we shall explain we initially pack only six records per block. The contents of the blocks are as follows.

1:	AA39	00061	2:	AC22	00020	3:	AH84	00621
	AA62	00008		AC56	00664		AJ09	00000
	AA91	00350		AD31	00059		AL62	00085
	AB82	00196		AE31	07154		AL72	00007
	AB83	00000		AF77	00011		AM19	00034
	AC05	01006		AH01	00322		AP76	00015

4:	AP83	00914	5:	AZ27	00065	6:	DD68	01642
	AQ01	00247		BA32	00002		DT62	00095
	AS65	00184		BC59	00031		FA37	00000
	AS80	00001		CE64	00087		FD80	00731
	AT50	00034		DD62	00315		FH08	00629
	AV18	01075		DD63	00579		FN02	00317

7:	FS44	00321	8:	HS41	00059	9:	MM72	00006
	FS52	00114		HH50	00002		MQ09	00014
	FX80	00051		LE31	00050		MT50	00078
	GB75	00338		LX94	00608		PA11	00314
	HA16	00579		MC55	00082		PC25	00080
	HL12	00400		MM71	00008		PK39	00041

10:	PY05	00073	11:	SY73	00094	12:	WG33	00016
	RB99	00775		SY75	00008		WN77	00019
	RT05	00108		TL81	00034		XB03	00315
	RT06	00061		VF62	00315		XX44	04000
	SC84	00112		VK89	00458		YD30	00000
	SX19	00060		VR34	00788		YH61	00070

It is very important that the records are stored in sorted order. The file has an index that tells us the highest key value in each block and the physical address of each block. The index itself may be a simple sequential file that is packed into blocks. For our example

first block of the index:	AC05	address of block 1
	AH01	address of block 2
	AP76	address of block 3
	AV18	address of block 4
	DD63	address of block 5
	FN02	address of block 6
	HL12	address of block 7
	MM71	address of block 8

second block of the index:	PK39	address of block 9
	SX19	address of block 10
	VR34	address of block 11
	YH61	address of block 12

This tells us that the highest key in block 1 is AC05, the highest key in block 2 is AH01, and so on. Where we have written 'address of block 1' there would be the actual physical address of block 1 (cylinder number, surface number and sector number), and the same is true for other blocks.

Suppose for example that we wish to look up the quantity in stock for the single item reference number FH08. To achieve this random access, we proceed in two stages.

(a) We linearly search the index seeking the first key value that is greater than or equal to the sought key value FH08. This gives us the physical address of the block that contains the sought key. (The sought key cannot be in block 1 because FH08 > AC05. The sought key cannot be in block 2 because FH08 > AH01, and so on. The sought key cannot be in block 5 because FH08 > DD63. Unless missing from the file, the sought key must be in block 6, because FH08 < = FN02.)

(b) We copy the selected block from secondary memory to immediate access memory, and linearly search this block for the sought key value.

In our example the sought key value will be found by accessing only two blocks: one index block and then the sixth data block of the file. This is obviously quicker than linearly searching within six successive blocks of the file as though it were a simple sequential file without an index. The index serves to speed up access when the hit rate is very low. When the hit rate is high we can ignore the index and batch process the records exactly as if they were in a simple sorted sequential file. Compared with hash or simple sequential organization, indexed sequential organization has the advantage that *both* random access and batch processing are practical.

5.6.2. *Insertions and deletions when there is no overflow*

When we insert a single new record into a hash file, we write into secondary memory an updated version of a single block containing the new record, and other blocks need not be accessed at all except perhaps to refer to an index or to deal with overflow. Similarly, because an indexed sequential file is also designed for random access, we arrange that a single new record can be inserted into the file by writing into secondary memory an updated version of a single block, leaving other blocks unchanged except perhaps for overflow and for occasional amendment of the index. We shall now give details of just one indexed sequential method; in fact a family of somewhat different indexed sequential methods exist.

When we initially set up an indexed sequential file we leave some free space within each block. Subsequently, when a new record is inserted it is placed in the position that will preserve the sorted order of the file, and subsequent records within the block shift towards the free space. For example after the new record AS69 00200 is inserted into TOYINVEN as shown above, block 4 will contain

```
AP83    00914
AQ01    00247
AS65    00184
AS69    00200
AS80    00001
AT50    00034
AV18    01075
```

The records for AS80, AT50, and AV18 have shifted towards the free space so that the contents of the block are in sorted order. The index remains unchanged because AV18 is still the highest key value in block 4.

When a record is deleted, subsequent records are shifted towards the beginning of the block to close the gap. For example, after the record TL81 00034 has been deleted, block 11 will contain

```
SY73    00094
SY75    00008
VF62    00315
VK89    00458
VR34    00788
```

The index remains unchanged because VR34 is still the highest key value in block 11.

When the record VR34 00788 is deleted the index entry for block 11 is changed to

VK89   address of block 11

Except in the case of the last block, only deletion, and not insertion, can cause a change in the index. For example the new record SY72 00350 will be inserted as the first record in block 11, and not as the last record in block 10 which would necessitate a change in the index entry for block 10. A record whose key value is greater than the last in the last block will be inserted into the last block, and the index entry for the last block will have to be amended accordingly.

5.6.3. Overflow

When we wish to insert a record into a block in which there is no free space, we do *not* wish the last record of this block to become the first of the next block, the last record of the next block to become the first of the following block, and so on along the file. To avoid this rewriting of subsequent blocks, we provide overflow facilities. Various methods are available for dealing with overflow of indexed sequential files, and we shall outline just one well-known method, which is similar to method (b) in Section 5.5.2.2 except that sorted sequence is preserved.

Associated with each block there is a (possibly empty) linked list of records that have overflowed from this block. A pointer to the beginning of this list is stored in the index, along with the physical address of the block. The index is a file of records that has four fields:

HIGHEST KEY VALUE IN DATA BLOCK
PHYSICAL ADDRESS OF DATA BLOCK
HIGHEST KEY VALUE THAT HAS OVERFLOWED FROM THE
    BLOCK
POINTER TO THE FIRST RECORD IN THE LINKED LIST OF
    RECORDS THAT HAVE OVERFLOWED FROM THIS BLOCK

To illustrate the management of overflow we shall extend the TOYINVEN example of Section 5.6.2 in which each data block has capacity for eight records. Suppose that all data blocks initially contain six records, as at the beginning of Section 5.6.2, except for blocks 9 and 11 which have been filled with eight records as follows:

9:	MM72	00006	11:	SY71	00060
	MQ09	00014		SY73	00094
	MS33	00556		SY75	00008
	MT50	00078		TL81	00034
	MW45	00004		VF62	00315
	PA11	00314		VK89	00458
	PC25	00080		VP16	00082
	PK39	00041		VR34	00788

No data block has yet overflowed. The second block of the index contains the following.

HIGHEST KEY IN DATA BLOCK	ADDRESS OF DATA BLOCK	HIGHEST KEY IN OVERFLOW FROM BLOCK	POINTER TO LIST
PK39	9	PK39	nil
SX19	10	SX19	nil
VR34	11	VR34	nil
YH61	12	YH61	nil

Note that in each of these records the two HIGHEST KEY fields are the same; it is convenient to make these the same when there is no overflow.

We shall now insert MS34 00065 into block 9 and VR33 00006 into block 11. Records are inserted so as to preserve sorted sequence, and in this example the last record in block 9 and the last record in block 11 are shifted out of these blocks into overflow. The contents of blocks 9 and 11 are now as follows.

9:	MM72	00006	11:	SY71	00060
	MQ09	00014		SY73	00094
	MS33	00556		SY75	00008
	MS34	00065		TL81	00034
	MT50	00078		VF62	00315
	MW45	00004		VK89	00458
	PA11	00314		VP16	00082
	PC25	00080		VR33	00006

There are now two overflow records:

PK39   00041 **nil**
VR34   00788 **nil**

Each of these records contains a pointer to the rest of the overflow chain that is associated with its parent data block; at this stage these pointers are **nil** because there are no further overflow records. The second block of the index now contains the following.

HIGHEST KEY IN DATA BLOCK	ADDRESS OF DATA BLOCK	HIGHEST KEY IN OVERFLOW FROM BLOCK	POINTER TO LIST
PC25	9	PK39	to PK39
SX19	10	SX19	nil
VR33	11	VR34	to VR34
YH61	12	YH61	nil

Continuing our example, we shall now insert the following records (in the sequence shown) into our indexed sequential file:

SY08 00416
VQ62 00057
PD95 00006
VR31 00016
MS36 00060
VA70 00011

As a result, data blocks 9 and 11, which are the only ones affected, contain the following.

9:			11:		
	MM72	00006		SY08	00416
	MQ09	00014		SY71	00060
	MS33	00556		SY73	00094
	MS34	00065		SY75	00008
	MS36	00060		TL81	00034
	MT50	00037		VA70	00011
	MW45	00004		VF62	00315
	PA11	00314		VK89	00458

New records have been inserted into these blocks in positions that preserve the sorted order, and this has meant that various records have had to be shifted out into overflow. When we insert a record whose key value is less than the highest in a data block's overflow list, but higher than the highest within that data block, we insert this record directly into this overflow list. For our example the overflow records are now as follows (the linking pointers are shown diagrammatically).

PK39	00041	nil
VR34	00788	nil
VR33	00006	
VQ62	00057	
PD95	00006	
VR31	00016	
PC25	00080	
VP16	00082	

When a record is shifted or inserted into overflow, it is physically placed in the next free space, with linking organized to preserve the sorted order of overflow records. The second block of the index now contains the following.

HIGHEST KEY IN DATA BLOCK	ADDRESS OF DATA BLOCK	HIGHEST KEY IN OVERFLOW FROM BLOCK	POINTER TO LIST
PA11	9	PK39	to PC25
SX19	10	SX19	**nil**
VK89	11	VR34	to VP16
YH61	12	YH61	**nil**

It is easy to see that the records in data block 9 are in sorted order. The index tells us that the list of overflow records from block 9 starts at the record whose key value is PC25. It is worth checking that the overflow records in this list are linked in sorted sequence, and would have been stored in data block 9 if there had been room for them. The index also tells us that the overflow list for block 11 starts at the record whose key value is VP16, and it is easy to check that subsequent records in this list are linked in sorted sequence, ending with the record that was originally the last in block 11.

To insert a record we linearly search the index until we find the first HIGHEST KEY IN OVERFLOW FROM BLOCK that is greater than the key value that is to be inserted. For this block we check whether HIGHEST KEY IN DATA BLOCK is greater than the key value that is to be inserted. If it is greater, we insert the new record into the data block, shifting a displaced record into overflow if necessary and in this case updating the index. Otherwise, if the input key value exceeds the HIGHEST KEY IN DATA BLOCK we insert the input record directly into the overflow list for this block, updating the index only if the input record has become the first record in the list.

To look up the QUANTITYINSTOCK for a given ITEM-REFNO we start by linearly searching the index until we find the first HIGHEST KEY IN OVERFLOW FROM BLOCK that is greater than or equal to the sought key value. For this block we check whether HIGHEST KEY IN DATA BLOCK is greater than or equal to the sought key value: if so, we linearly search the data block; otherwise we traverse the overflow list. We never search *both* a data block *and* an overflow chain; we choose the correct one of these by referring to the two HIGHEST KEY fields for this block in the index.

To delete a record, we start as if we were looking up this record. If the record is found in an overflow list, we delete it by making its predecessor point to its successor and updating the index if the deleted record is the first or last in the list. If the record is found in a data block we delete it and move subsequent records towards the beginning of the block, as in Section 5.6.2, to close the gap that was caused by deletion. If the overflow chain is not empty, we move the first record from the overflow chain back into the data block and update the index accordingly.

To illustrate deletion we shall continue our TOYINVEN example from where we left off. We shall consider deletion of VR33 00006 from the overflow chain of block 11, and deletion of MQ09 00014 from data block 9. As a result of this deletion from block 9, the first overflow record PC25 00080 is moved back into block 9 from block 9's overflow list. Block 9 is now

```
9:   MM72 00006
     MS33  00556
     MS34  00065
     MS36  00060
     MT50  00037
     MW45 00004
     PA11  00314
     PC25  00080
```

The index record for block 9 is changed to

HIGHEST KEY IN DATA BLOCK	ADDRESS OF DATA BLOCK	HIGHEST KEY IN OVERFLOW FROM BLOCK	POINTER TO LIST
PC25	9	PK39	to PD95

The overflow records are now

PK39	00041	nil
VR34	00788	nil
VQ62	00057	→
PD95	00006	→
VR31	00016	→
VP16	00082	→

When a record was deleted from a data block in a hash file in Section 5.5.2.2 we did not bother to shift back into this block one of the records that had overflowed from it. On the other hand, when a record was deleted from a data block of our indexed sequential file, we did shift a record back into this block from overflow. This difference arises because we delete a record from a hash file data block by setting NORECORD = TRUE. Subsequently, when we insert a new record into this block, we insert the new record to overwrite the first record that has NORECORD = TRUE, or if there is no such record we insert the new record into overflow. The vital point is that we can overwrite the first record that has NORE-CORD = TRUE because we do not have to preserve sorted order of records within hash file blocks. This tends to keep hash file data blocks tolerably well filled.

In an indexed sequential file, for efficiency in batch processing, we carefully preserve sorted order. We cannot simply insert incoming new records in random order into free space in data blocks. If we did not shift records back from overflow, deletion would tend to leave free space in data blocks, and inserted records would sometimes unnecessarily be placed in overflow which would entail the disadvantage of traversing overflow lists. Generally a record can be found in a data block without accessing any other data block, but to find an overflow record we may have to traverse a list that threads through several overflow blocks; the longer is the list the more blocks we may have to access to traverse it. For this reason we should pack indexed sequential file data blocks as full as reasonably possible, and minimize the length of overflow lists.

We have described a method of indexed sequential organization in which, as in method (b) in Section 5.5.2.2, overflow records from many different data blocks can be stored in the same overflow block. This sharing of overflow blocks is intended to reduce wasted space. If possible the entire file, including index, data, and overflow blocks, should be stored within a single cylinder. In this case we can go from the index to a data block or to an overflow list without waiting for movement of disc heads.

5.6.4. *Hierarchical indexes for indexed sequential files*

We have so far been concerned with an index that is itself organized as a simple sequential file. We can speed up random access to the index by reorganizing the index as an indexed sequential file. This idea is particularly attractive for a large file that occupies many cylinders. We can access this file by first linearly searching an index that tells us the highest key value in each cylinder. We then access the selected cylinder and obtain from it a block index like that which we used in Section 5.6.2 or 5.6.3, showing the highest key values in blocks in this cylinder. By linear search of this index we find the data block that contains the sought record. For introductory simplicity we shall forget about overflow, and assume that each cylinder contains just four blocks. Figure 5.3 is a simple diagram of the file structure. When the cylinder index is used the total number of blocks that need be accessed to achieve random access to a record in a large file may be substantially less than if the cylinder index were not available.

A general idea is that we may possibly enhance efficiency by using an index that takes us to a more detailed index, which takes us to a yet more detailed index, which takes us to a yet more detailed index, and so on until we reach the actual data. We shall describe a hierarchical structure like this in Section 5.8.

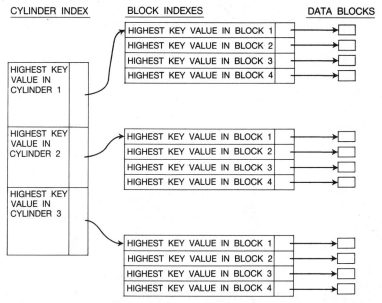

Fig. 5.3. An indexed sequential organization that has a two-level index.

5.6.5. *Exercises*

1. Physical blocks are deliberately invisible to the Pascal programmer. This exercise is concerned with a very simple indexed sequential structure in which a linked list is arbitrarily divided into sections.

(a) For use in (c), (d), and (e), create a text file containing 12 records such as

1 January
2 February
3 March

which tell us the number and name of each month of the year, exactly as in Exercise 1(a) of Section 9.9.

(b) Write a DBD for use in (c), (d), and (e).

(c) Write a program to read the data from your text file into the data structure:

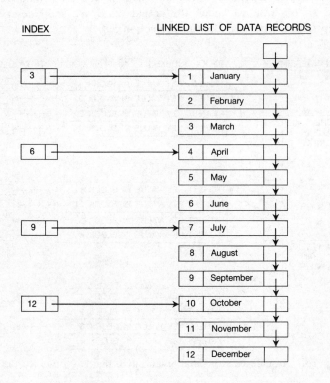

The index can be an array of records (each record comprising month number and a pointer to the first record in that section of the list which ends with this month number). As well as a pointer to the first record in the linked list, you may wish to work with a pointer to the last record; this will facilitate insertion of records at the end of the list.

(d) Write a program to read a month number from the terminal and output the associated month name found by traversing the linked list without using the index. Your program should also output the number of key values with which the input month number was compared before it was found in the linked list.

(e) Write a program to read a month number from the terminal and linearly search the index for the first month number greater than or equal to the input month number. Follow the pointer from the index to the linked list and thence obtain and output the name associated with the input month number. Your program should also output the total number of key values with which the input month number was compared before it was found in the linked list; this number should include key values in the index.

2. (a) In method (b) in Section 5.5.2.2 a pointer to the start of an overflow list is stored in a data block. In the method of Section 5.6.3 a pointer to the start of an overflow list is stored in the index, and not in a data block. Explain this difference.

(b) In the method of Section 5.6.3 we never need search both a data block and that block's overflow list looking for a key value. In the hash overflow method (b) in Section 5.5.2.2 we may sometimes need to search both a data block and also that block's overflow list looking for a key value. Explain why this difference arises.

(c) Explain why records are chained in overflow but not within data blocks in the method of Section 5.6.3.

3. This exercise is concerned with an index that is a linked list of records of the type

record
    HIGHESTKEYINBLOCK: **packed array** [1..4] **of** CHAR;
    POINTERTOBLOCK: BLOCKPTR;
    POINTERTONEXTINDEXRECORD: INDEXPTR
end.

Your DBD will also include

type
    STRING4   = **packed array** [1..4] **of** CHAR;
    BLOCKPTR   = ↑BLOCK;
    TOYINVREC = **record**
                        ITEMREFNO: STRING4;
                        QUANTITYINSTOCK: INTEGER
                    end;
    BLOCK   = **array** [1..6] **of** TOYINVREC

The blocks will be used to contain TOYINVREC records sorted on increasing ITEMREFNO. In the index, records will be linked in sequence of increasing HIGHESTKEYINBLOCK, so the entire structure belongs to the family of indexed sequential structures.

(a) Write a DBD for use in (b), (c), (d), and (e).

(b) Write an initializing program that assigns **nil** to the pointer to the start of the linked list.

(c) Write a program to read a TOYINVEN record from the terminal and insert it into the indexed sequential structure according to the following rules.

(i) If no record has previously been input then CREATE a block, insert the input record into it, and CREATE an index record pointing to this block.

(ii) If possible, insert the new record into an existing block, shifting subsequent records within the block so as to preserve the sorted order. If this results in overflow then CREATE a new block, shift into it three records from the block that has overflowed, CREATE a new index record, and link it into the index so as to preserve the sorted sequence.

(iii) If the key value of the record to be inserted is higher than the highest in the index, CREATE a new block, insert the new record into this block, CREATE a new index record, and link this in as the last in the index.

(d) Write a program to read an ITEMREFNO from the terminal and look it up in the indexed sequential structure to find the QUANTITYIN-STOCK. If found, the QUANTITYINSTOCK should be output. If not found, your program should say so.

(e) Write a program to read an ITEMREFNO from the terminal and delete from the indexed sequential structure the record (if any) that contains this ITEMREFNO. Within a block from which there has been a deletion, subsequent records should be moved down to fill the gap. The index should be updated accordingly. If a block becomes empty it should be DELETED and the index should be amended by deletion of an index record.

5.7. File maintenance

Random access to a hash file is generally quicker if there are few overflow records than if there are many. When there are many overflow records we may wish to overhaul the file as follows. First we copy all the file's records into a simple sequential file. We then erase the hash file and create a new one, initially containing no records. We can give this new file more blocks than we gave its predecessor, and in this case we must change the hash function accordingly. Next we read the records from the sequential file and insert them into the new hash file using the hash function to determine which block each record is placed in. The purpose of this entire operation is to ensure that random access to the revised hash file is generally quicker than to the previous version. This reconstitution operation is an example of file *maintenance*.

If we find that the blocks of a hash file contain only a few records and much space is wasted, we can reconstitute the file with fewer blocks and an appropriately revised hash function; this is another example of file maintenance.

It may also be worthwhile to reconstitute an indexed sequential file of the type described in Section 5.6.3 when the overflow lists become long and thread many blocks, particularly if these blocks are not all in one cylinder. We can copy the records from the file in sorted order into a simple sequential file, then erase the indexed sequential file, and then copy the records back from the simple sequential file into a new indexed sequential file, possibly having a revised number of blocks and certainly leaving a fair amount of free space in each block. This is another example of file maintenance that is intended to enhance subsequent efficiency of access to the file.

In the next section we introduce B-trees which are indexed sequential files having hierarchical indexes managed so that maintenance is unnecessary.

5.8. B-trees

5.8.1. *Tree terminology*

Before introducing B-trees we introduce some technical terms that are commonly applied to trees.

Figure 5.4(a) shows an example of a tree. For present purposes, a tree is a collection of nodes and directed arcs. In Fig. 5.4(a) nodes are represented by boxes and directed arcs are represented by arrows. A *root* node has no arrow pointing to it. A tree has exactly one root node. In Fig. 5.4(a) the nodes are labelled N1, N2, N3, ... for purposes of discussion, and N1 is the root node. A *leaf* node has no arrow pointing away from it; in Fig. 5.4(a) N5, N6, ..., N13 are leaf nodes. The nodes that any given node points to are its *children*. For example, N8, N9, and N10 are children of N3. By definition a leaf node has no children. The node that points to any given node is its *parent*. An essential distinctive property of a tree is that every node, except the root node, has exactly one parent.

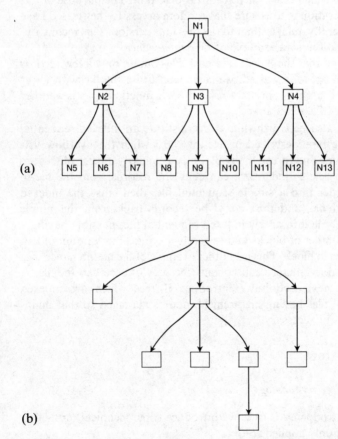

Fig. 5.4. Examples of (a) a balanced tree and (b) an unbalanced tree.

Let NJ and NK be any two nodes such that NK is a child of a child of a child . . . of a child of NJ. In this case we say that NJ is an *ancestor* of NK, and NK is a *descendant* of NJ. For example, in Fig. 5.4(a) N6 is a descendant of N1, and N1 is an ancestor of N8. N3 is also an ancestor of N8, because parents count as ancestors. Moreover, children count as descendants. A tree is said to be *balanced* if and only if every leaf node has exactly the same number of ancestors. Figure 5.4(a) shows an example of a balanced tree, whereas Fig. 5.4(b) shows an example of an unbalanced tree.

5.8.2. B-tree look-up

For simplicity we shall introduce B-trees in terms of an example in which there is only one field per record. This single field is the key and always consists of two letters. The ideas that we shall introduce will work equally well with a more realistic record type comprising many fields.

Figure 5.5 shows a B-tree in which D1, D2, . . ., D7 are data blocks containing data records sorted on the primary key. We use – to represent an absent record (for which NORECORD = TRUE) and we use · to represent a **nil** pointer. Blocks I11, I12 and I13 are index blocks that point to data blocks. These index blocks are pointed to by a further index block I1, which is the root block of this B-tree.

In Section 5.6.3 the index showed the highest key value in each block. In a B-tree it is convenient to make the index show the *lowest* key value in each block. It is important to note this difference. For

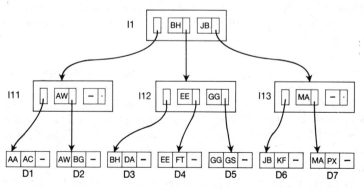

Fig. 5.5. Example of a B-tree.

the first block to which an index points there is no benefit in showing the lowest key value in the first block, because any record that has key value less than the first in the second block should be inserted in the first block, regardless of the current lowest key value in the first block. This is why in a B-tree, such as Fig. 5.5, each index block starts with a pointer that does not have an associated key value. For example, index block I12 starts with a pointer to data block D3, and no key value is associated with this pointer in index block I12. The second record in I12 points to D4 and tells us that the *lowest* key value in D4 is EE. The third record in I12 points to D5 and tells us that the *lowest* key value in D5 is GG. The first record in the root block I1 points to I11 and does not have (because it does not need) an associated key value. The second record in I1 points to I12 and tells us that the lowest key value that I12 points to is BH. The third record in I1 points to I13 and tells us that the lowest key value that I13 points to is JB.

To look up a given key value, we always start by linearly searching the root block until we find the first key value greater than the sought key value or until we reach the end of the block. We then follow the pointer that is contained in the index record immediately before the record where the search stopped. If the search stopped at the end of the block, we follow the last pointer in the block. If the pointer takes us to a further index block, we search it in the same way to select a pointer to follow to a further block. When we arrive at a data block we linearly search it for the sought key value.

Suppose, for example, that the sought key value is FT. We start by comparing this with the second key value in the root block I1. Because FT > BH we proceed to compare the sought key value FT with JB. Because FT < JB the search of I1 stops, and we follow the pointer from I1 to I12. We now search I12 and find that the first key value in I12 greater than the sought key value FT is GG, and so we follow the second pointer from I12 which takes us to D4, wherein we find FT by linear search.

As a further example, suppose that the sought key value is BG. Because BG < BH we follow the pointer from I1 to I11. Our linear search of I11 stops when we reach an absent record. From this we see that we should follow the pointer to D2, wherein we find BG by linear search.

For Fig. 5.5 random access proceeds via two index blocks. The access method that we have described works for a B-tree that has many levels of indexing. Figure 5.6 shows an example of a B-tree that has three levels of indexing.

B-trees belong to the family of indexed sequential structures. The records within data blocks are always in sorted order and can be used like records in a sorted simple sequential file for purposes such as batch processing. The hierarchical index is used for random access, but may be unnecessary for simple sequential access. A B-tree is efficient both for simple sequential access and for random access.

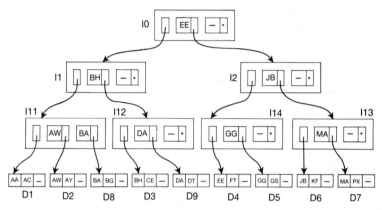

Fig. 5.6. A B-tree with three levels of index.

5.8.3. Characteristic properties of B-trees

We shall not give a general formal definition of a B-tree but we shall say that essential characteristic properties of B-trees are as follows.

(a) Each block has capacity for a maximum of an odd number, exceeding two, of records. In each index block the first record, which lacks a key value, is counted as one of the records in the block. All index blocks have the same capacity, i.e. they all have room for the same number of records. All data blocks have equal capacity, which may differ from the capacity of index blocks.

(b) No block, except the root node index block, may ever be less than half-full.

(c) A B-tree is always balanced.

5.8.4. *The height of a B-tree*

Let the total number of data blocks be D, and to simplify our calculation let us assume that every index block, except the root, contains exactly i records. Let L be the number of levels of the index; for example $L = 2$ for Fig. 5.5. L is the *height* of the tree, not counting the data blocks. The height is of interest because it is the number of index blocks that must be accessed to take us to a required data block, and this is an important factor in the efficiency of random access.

If it is assumed that each index block contains i records, each index block in the level immediately above the data blocks points to i data blocks and so there must be D/i index blocks at this level. Reasoning similarly, we see that the number of index blocks at the next higher level must be $D/(i \times i)$, the number of index blocks at the third level must be $D/(i \times i \times i)$, and so on. The number of index blocks at the root level must be exactly unity, and so

$$D/(i^L) = 1$$

whence

$$L = \log_i d.$$

The height of the tree may be less than this if index blocks actually contain more than the minimum number i of records.

Suppose for example that $D = 100\,000$ and $i = 10$. For random access the number of index blocks accessed will not exceed $\log_{10} 100\,000 = 5$. At the first level there will be not more than $100\,000/i = 10\,000$ index blocks, and if we had to find the appropriate one of these by linear search of the first level then the expected number of index blocks accessed would be $10\,000/2 = 5000$. By using a B-tree with $i = 10$ instead of a single-level indexed sequential file with i records in each index block, we have reduced the expected number of index blocks accessed, and thus reduced the overall total time for access, by a factor of about 1000. This example illustrates the efficiency of B-trees.

Hash organization may allow us to find a sought record by accessing fewer blocks than would be required by B-tree organization, but a B-tree preserves the sorted order of records. When setting up a hash file we need to know approximately the number of records that it will contain. As we shall see, such knowledge is unnecessary for a B-tree, and this is an important advantage.

5.8.5. *Insertion into a B-tree*

To insert a new record into a B-tree we first locate the appropriate data block, just as if we were looking up the record. If there is spare space in the data block, we insert the new record in sequence, moving subsequent records if necessary, as in Section 5.6.2. If there is no room for the insertion, we acquire a new block. We *move* some of the records from the old block to the new block, so that after insertion of the new record the old block and the new block contain an equal number of records. Index records must be updated accordingly.

For example, if we insert BA into the B-tree shown in Fig. 5.5, the only effect is that data block D2 now contains $\boxed{\text{AW} \mid \text{BA} \mid \text{BG}}$. Continuing this example, to insert AY we must acquire a new block because there is not room in D2. We must insert a pointer to the new block D8 in index block I11. The part of the B-tree that has changed is

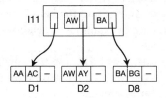

Note that the old block D2 and the new block D8 both contain an equal number of records.

If we now wish to insert CE and DT, there is not space in D3 and so we acquire a new block D9:

There is no room in I12 for a pointer to D9, and so we acquire a new index block I14. There is no room in I1 for a pointer to I14, and so we acquire a further new index block I2. Because the tree is allowed only one root node, we acquire a new root node I0 which points to I1 and I2. After this *propagation* of introduction of new blocks, the tree is as shown in Fig. 5.6.

5.8.6.   Deletion from a B-tree

Using the same routine as that used for look-up, we find the record
that is to be deleted. We delete it and then shift the block's
subsequent records down to close the gap, as in Section 5.6.2. If the
block is now less than half-full, we look for an adjacent child of the
same parent that contains more than the minimum number of
records. If we find such a block we shift records out of it into the
block from which deletion took place so as to even out the numbers
of records in these two blocks as far as possible. The index must be
updated accordingly.

If deletion has left a block with less than the minimum number of
records and if no adjacent child of the same parent contains more
than the minimum number of records, then the block from which
there was a deletion is merged with an adjacent child of the same
parent and a block is relinquished and made available for other use.
Next we delete the index record that points to the deleted block. If
this leaves an index block less than half-full, then we proceed as
described above and so on until no further change is required.

We now give a sequence of examples of deletions, starting with the
B-tree shown in Fig. 5.6.

If we delete AW, this leaves D2 less than half-full, and so we
merge D2 with D8 and relinquish a block, updating I11 accordingly.
The part of the tree that is affected is

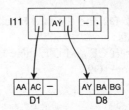

Instead of merging D2 with D8 we could equally well have merged
D1 with D2.

Starting again with the complete B-tree shown in Fig. 5.6, deletion
of BH leads to merging of D3 and D9 into D3, D9 being relinquished. As a result, I12 is less than half-full. I11, which is the only
adjacent child of the same parent, contains more than the minimum
number of records and so we transfer a record from I11 to I12. Note
that I1 must be updated as a result of deletion of BH; this illustrates

the possibility that an ancestor of a parent may have to be modified as the result of deletion. The changed part of the tree is now

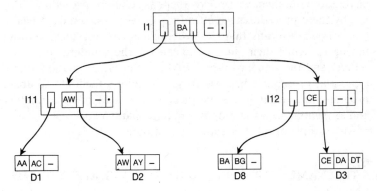

Deletion of JB leads to merging of D6 with D7, which leads to merging of I13 with I14. We must then merge I1 with I2 and relinquish I0, which is no longer required. The resulting B-tree is

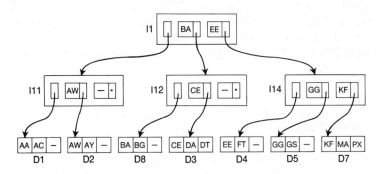

An important advantage of B-trees is that they do not require maintenance, as we have remarked previously. This is because the deletion procedure automatically relinquishes blocks that are no longer required, and the insertion procedure automatically acquires new blocks when necessary.

5.8.7. B-trees types

5.8.7.1. Declarations

We can easily write Pascal procedures to insert, delete, or look up

records in structures such as linked lists or hash files. For B-trees such procedures are more complicated, and to save the programmer having to write them we provide them as standard procedures. For use by these procedures we introduce B-trees as a standard Pascal type: *standard* means that the programmer can use them without having to define them, just as he can use the standard procedure READ and the standard type REAL. We provide standard B-tree types and procedures because these will greatly facilitate database programming, capitalizing the facts that B-trees provide random and sequential access and do not require maintenance.

An example of a B-tree type declaration is

type
 TREENAME = BTREE **of** RECORDTYPENAME **on** FIELDNAME1

This declares TREENAME to be the name of a B-tree type such that the leaf blocks contain records of type RECORDTYPENAME sorted on increasing FIELDNAME1. In this case FIELDNAME1, which must be one of the fields of RECORDTYPENAME, is the sort key of the B-tree. If we wish to declare that the sort key consists of two fields of RECORDTYPENAME, say FIELDNAME1 and FIELDNAME2 with FIELDNAME2 as the minor key (see Section 5.2), we write

type
 TREENAME = BTREE **of** RECORDTYPENAME **on** FIELDNAME2
 within FIELDNAME1

Any number of **withins** can be concatenated: for example if the sort key consists of the N fields FIELDNAME1, FIELDNAME2, ..., FIELDNAMEN, with FIELDNAME1 as the major sort key, we declare

type
 TREENAME = BTREE **of** RECORDTYPENAME **on**
 FIELDNAMEN **within** ... **within** FIELDNAME2 **within**
 FIELDNAME1

The word **descending** can be inserted after **on** or **within** and specifies that the immediately following field name has field values in descending sequence in the B-tree. For example if the records are sorted on decreasing FIELDNAME2 **within** FIELDNAME1 we declare

type
   TREENAME = BTREE **of** RECORDTYPENAME **on descending**
   FIELDNAME2 **within** FIELDNAME1

We shall sometimes refer to the sort key of a B-tree simply as the *key* of that B-tree.

Hitherto we have given examples of B-tree types in which the B-tree leaf blocks contain records. The facility is in fact more general than this: a B-tree can be declared to be **of** any discrete type, for example integer, pointer, character, or subrange type. In this case the B-tree type declaration does not include **on**, and the contents of leaf blocks are always sorted in increasing order. For example we can declare

type
   SUBEX = 100..400;
   TREENAME = BTREE **of** SUBEX;

In this case the leaf blocks will contain not records but integers in the subrange 100..400, in ascending order.

We can declare variables of BTREE types, e.g.

var
   ATREE: TREENAME;
   LOOKATTHESECONDFIELDOFTHISONE: **record**
                     FIRSTFIELD:
                     INTEGER;
                     SECONDFIELD:
                     TREENAME
                 end

Standard procedures that will be introduced in the Section 5.8.8 operate on B-tree variables, i.e. variables whose type is a B-tree type.

5.8.7.2. *Example of DBD that includes a B-tree*

In Section 5.8.8 we shall illustrate the application of the standard procedures using as an example the following very simple DBD:

```
DBDNAME MT;
type
   REFERANGE = 1000..9999;
   INVPTR = ↑INVTYPE;
   INVTYPE = record
                ITEMREFNO: REFRANGE;
                QUANTITYINSTOCK: INTEGER;
                PRICEPERUNIT: REAL;
                SUPPLIERNO: 10..99;
             end;
   INVTREE = BTREE of INVTYPE on ITEMREFNO;
var
   INVENTORY: INVTREE;
finish
```

This declares INVENTORY to be a B-tree persistent variable whose leaf records are of type INVTYPE, sorted on increasing ITEM-REFNO.

5.8.8. B-tree procedures

5.8.8.1. DBSTATUS

We now introduce a collection of procedures that can be used without being declared. All of these procedures are liable to assign a value to a global (non-persistent) variable DBSTATUS which the programmer can use like any other global variable but must not try to declare. DBSTATUS is of the enumerated type (OKAY, NOT-FOUND, DUPLICATE, EMPTY, EXHAUSTED). In other words the possible values of DBSTATUS are OKAY, NOTFOUND, DUPLICATE, EMPTY, and EXHAUSTED. If a program calls one of the following procedures at a time when DBSTATUS < > OKAY the effect will be to execute ABORTTRANSACTION and termi-nate execution of the program.

5.8.8.2. INSERT

To insert a new record into a B-tree we use the procedure call

INSERT (BTREEVARIABLENAME, RECORDVARIABLENAME)

The first parameter specifies which B-tree the record will be inserted into, and the second parameter, which must be of the type that the B-tree is **of**, specifies a variable whose value is to be inserted into a leaf block of the B-tree. The value(s) of the B-tree's key field(s) must be defined in RECORDVARIABLENAME when the procedure INSERT is called.

To illustrate the use of the procedure INSERT, the following program reads an INVTYPE record from the terminal and inserts it into the INVENTORY B-tree declared in Section 5.8.7.2:

```
program INVINSERT (INPUT, OUTPUT);
invoke MT;
var
   INPUTRECORD: INVTYPE;
begin
   STARTTRANSACTION (UNRESTRICTED);
   WRITE ('type ITEMREFNO, QUANTITYINSTOCK, ');
   WRITELN ('PRICEPERUNIT, SUPPLIERNO');
   with INPUTRECORD do
   READLN (ITEMREFNO, QUANTITYINSTOCK,
   PRICEPERUNIT, SUPPLIERNO);
   INSERT (INVENTORY, INPUTRECORD);
   if DBSTATUS = OKAY then ENDTRANSACTION
   else
   begin
      ABORTTRANSACTION; WRITELN ('insertion failed')
   end
end.
```

This program should preferably check that the input field values are within their correct ranges, but as usual we have omitted such checks in order to make the program easier to read.

If the procedure INSERT finds that the inserted key value is already in the tree, it inserts the input record after the most recently inserted record that has the same key value and assigns the value DUPLICATE to DBSTATUS. The sequence of key duplicates in a B-tree is thus the same as the historical order of their insertion.

If the procedure INSERT does not assign DUPLICATE to DBSTATUS, it assigns OKAY.

5.8.8.3. FINDKEY

To look up a given key value in a B-tree we call

FINDKEY (BTREEVARIABLENAME, KEYVALUE, PTRTOLEAF)

in which the second parameter is the given key value, which is a
value of the field that the B-tree is **on**. If the key consists of more
than one field, then KEYVALUE consists of one value per field of
the key, and these values are separated by commas. PTRTOLEAF is
a pointer variable, of the type that points to a record that the B-tree
is **of**. The effect of the procedure call is to assign to PTRTOLEAF a
pointer to the first record in the B-tree that has the key value given
by the second parameter KEYVALUE. If the KEYVALUE is not
found in the B-tree, then the procedure FINDKEY assigns NOT-
FOUND to DBSTATUS. Otherwise DBSTATUS = OKAY.

To illustrate the use of FINDKEY, the following program reads
an ITEMREFNO from the terminal and outputs the QUANTI-
TYINSTOCK of this item:

```
program GETQUANT (INPUT, OUTPUT);
invoke MT;
var
   SOUGHTITEM: REFRANGE;
   ITEMPTR: INVPTR;
begin
   STARTTRANSACTION (READONLY);
   WRITELN ('please type item ref no');
   READLN (SOUGHTITEM);
   FINDKEY (INVENTORY, SOUGHTITEM, ITEMPTR);
   if DBSTATUS = OKAY then
   WRITELN ('QUANTITY IN STOCK = ',
   ITEMPTR↑.QUANTITYINSTOCK);
   ENDTRANSACTION
end.
```

5.8.8.4.   *FINDFIRST and FINDLAST*

The effect of calling FINDFIRST (BTREEVARIABLENAME,
PTRTOLEAF) is to assign to PTRTOLEAF a pointer to the first
record in the B-tree whose name is the first parameter. As in Section
5.8.8.3, PTRTOLEAF is a pointer to a record of the type that the B-
tree is **of**.

The effect of calling FINDLAST (BTREEVARIABLENAME,
PTRTOLEAF) is to assign to PTRTOLEAF a pointer to the last

record in the B-tree. After execution of FINDLAST or FIND-FIRST, if the B-tree was found to be empty then DBSTATU-S = EMPTY, otherwise DBSTATUS = OKAY.

5.8.8.5. *FINDSUCC and FINDPRED*

Before calling FINDSUCC or FINDPRED we assign to PTRTO-LEAF a pointer to a record in the B-tree. The effect of FINDSUCC (BTREEVARIABLENAME, PTRTOLEAF) is to assign to PTRTOLEAF a pointer to the *next* record in the B-tree. The effect of FINDPRED (BTREEVARIABLENAME, PTRTOLEAF) is to assign to PTRTOLEAF a pointer to the record immediately preceding it. After the call of either procedure, if PTRTOLEAF was not pointing to a record in the B-tree, then DBSTATUS = NOT-FOUND. If FINDSUCC was called when there was no successor, or if FINDPRED was called when there was no predecessor, then DBSTATUS = EXHAUSTED. Otherwise DBSTATUS = OKAY.

The following example program outputs all the records from the INVENTORY B-tree in sorted order:

```
program LISTINVEN (OUTPUT);
invoke MT;
var
   ITEMPTR: INVPTR;
begin
   STARTTRANSACTION (READONLY);
   FINDFIRST (INVENTORY, ITEMPTR);
   while DBSTATUS = OKAY do
   begin
      with ITEMPTR↑ do
      WRITELN (ITEMREFNO, QUANTITYINSTOCK,
      PRICEPERUNIT, SUPPLIERNO);
      FINDSUCC (INVENTORY, ITEMPTR)
   end;
   ENDTRANSACTION
end.
```

If this program were amended so that FINDFIRST was changed to FINDLAST, and FINDSUCC was changed to FINDPRED, the effect would be to output the records in the reverse order.

5.8.8.6. *REMOVE*

If we wish to remove a record from a B-tree we call

REMOVE (BTREEVARIABLENAME, PTRTOLEAF)

in which the second parameter is a pointer to the record that is to be deleted. If this record is not found then the procedure assigns NOTFOUND to DBSTATUS. Otherwise, if the record is found and the deletion works satisfactorily, the procedure assigns OKAY to DBSTATUS.

The following program reads an item reference number from the terminal and removes from the INVENTORY B-tree the record that contains this item reference number:

```
program CHOPITEM (INPUT, OUTPUT);
invoke MT;
var
   ITEMPTR: INVPTR;
   CHOPREFNO: REFRANGE;
begin
   STARTTRANSACTION (UNRESTRICTED);
   WRITELN ('please type ITEM REF NO of item to be deleted');
   READLN (CHOPREFNO);
   FINDKEY (INVENTORY, CHOPREFNO, ITEMPTR);
   if DBSTATUS = OKAY then
   begin
      REMOVE (INVENTORY, ITEMPTR);
      WRITELN ('removal completed');
      ENDTRANSACTION
   end else
   begin
      WRITELN ('ITEMREFNO not found');
      ABORTTRANSACTION
   end
end.
```

It is important to understand the distinction between REMOVE and DELETE. REMOVE deletes a record from a B-tree leaf block and amends the B-tree accordingly, possibly by shifting other records within this leaf block and if necessary updating one or more index blocks. DELETE merely deletes a record without updating anything.

5.8.8.7. *Updating a record in a B-tree leaf block*

To minimize the number of 'standard' B-tree procedures, and because we shall use B-trees mainly for implementing indexes rather than for storing data, we have not provided a 'standard' procedure for updating a record in a B-tree leaf block. We can update a record by first FINDing it, making a copy of it, REMOVing the original record from the leaf block, updating the copy (for example by changing the value of a field), and finally INSERTing the updated copy into the B-tree.

5.8.8.8. *Pascal DML*

An ordinary programming language that has been enhanced to operate on persistent variables using procedures such as INSERT and FINDKEY is called a *data manipulation language*, commonly abbreviated to DML. We shall use the name *Pascal DML* for the version of Pascal that has been enhanced as described above for working with persistent variables including B-trees.

DML procedures such as INSERT and FINDKEY are at a lower level than relational algebra expressions. There are systems, which are not exemplified in this text, that allow the programmer to write expressions in a query language such as relational algebra within an ordinary program. These expressions can deliver results that can be processed like any other input to a program. In this case the query language is said to be *embedded* within a *host* language. A query language that is used by itself, in the way that we used relational algebra in Chapter 2, is used as a *stand-alone* query language.

5.8.9. *Exercises*

1. The purpose of this exercise is to consolidate your understanding of B-tree insertion and deletion routines by working them by hand on simple examples.

(a) Insert JC and JD into the B-tree that is shown in Fig. 5.5 and draw a diagram of the resulting B-tree.
(b) Insert JE, JF, and JG into the B-tree that results from (a) and draw a diagram of the resulting B-tree.
(c) Delete BH from the B-tree that results from (b) and draw a diagram of the resulting B-tree.

(d) Delete DA and EE from the B-tree that results from (c) and draw a diagram of the resulting B-tree.

2. In this exercise a B-tree stores details of cars that are currently in a car park. The details are the registration number, the date of entry, and the time of entry. The date consists of month number and day number: for example 902 means 2 September. The DBD for this exercise is

```
DBDNAME PK;
type
    STRING7 = packed array [1..7] of CHAR;
    CARENTRY = record
                    REGNUMBER: STRING7;
                    TIMEIN: 0..2359;
                    DATE: 101..1231
                end;
    PARKTREE = BTREE of CARENTRY on REGNUMBER;
var
    CARSIN: PARKTREE;
finish
```

(a) For use when a car enters the car park, write a program to read a registration number, time, and date from the terminal and enter this information in a new record into CARSIN.

(b) For use when a car leaves the car park, write a program to read a registration number from the terminal and remove this car from CARSIN.

(c) Write a program to read a registration number from the terminal and look it up in CARSIN. If found, your program should output the associated date and time. If not found, your program should say so.

(d) Write a program to output to the terminal all the data records from CARSIN, sorted on registration number.

(e) Write a program to output all the data records from CARSIN to a binary file for use in Exercise 3. Note that this file will be sorted on REGNUMBER.

3. In this exercise you will write a program to read the records from the binary file produced in Exercise 2(e) into a B-tree sorted on time within date. In (b) you will write a program to output this file from the B-tree to the terminal sorted on time within date. For this exercise the DBD is

```
DBDNAME PQ;
type
  STRING7 = packed array [1..7] of CHAR;
  CARENTRY = record
                  REGNUMBER: STRING7;
                  TIMEIN: 0..2359;
                  DATE: 101..1231
              end;
  DATETIMETREE = BTREE of CARENTRY on TIMEIN within
  DATE;
var
  WHENIN: DATETIMETREE;
finish
```

(a) Write a program to read the records from the file produced in Exercise 2(e) into the B-tree WHENIN.

(b) Write a program to output to the terminal the data from WHENIN which will be sorted on TIMEIN within DATE.

4. This exercise extends the inventory example of Section 5.8.8 to include a variable number of prices for each item. For each item we have a collection of records comprising price and date, the date being when the price became effective. For each item this collection of records is stored in a B-tree which is a field of the INVTYPE record. There is no need for a NORECORD field in the INVTYPE record, because an undefined record will have an empty B-tree of prices. For this exercise you are required to use the DBD

```
DBDNAME MX;
type
  REFRANGE = 1000..9999;
  PRICEREC = record
                  PRICE:REAL;
                  DATE: 880101..940101;
              end;
  PRICETREE = BTREE of PRICEREC on DATE;
  INVPTR = ↑INVTYPE;
  INVTYPE = record
                  ITEMREFNO: REFRANGE;
                  QUANTITYINSTOCK: INTEGER;
                  PRICES: PRICETREE;
                  SUPPLIERNO: 10..99;
              end;
```

    INVTREE = BTREE of INVTYPE on ITEMREFNO;
var
    INVENTORY: INVTREE;
finish

(a) Write a program to read a record from a terminal and enter it into the INVENTORY. The fields of this record should be ITEMREFNO, QUANTITYINSTOCK, PRICE, DATE, and SUPPLIERNO.

(b) Write a program to read an ITEMREFNO and a new PRICE and DATE from the terminal. The new PRICE and DATE are to be entered into the PRICES B-tree for this item. If the program finds this tree empty it should say so and terminate, because this means that no record for this item has yet been entered using the program that you wrote in (a).

(c) Write a program to read an ITEMREFNO from the terminal and output the most recent price of this item. Again, if no price has been recorded for this item, your program should say so.

(d) Write a program to read an ITEMREFNO and a date from the terminal and output the price for this item that was in effect at this date.

6 Implementation of selection operations

6.1. Introduction

6.1.1. Selection on the primary key

If V is a value of the primary key field F of a file named FNAME then the selection operation

sel F = V (FNAME)

requires random access to FNAME. To accomplish this random access, fewer blocks need generally be accessed if FNAME is organized as a random-access (e.g. hash) file rather than as a simple sequential file. In this sense we can say that random-access file organization improves efficiency of selection operations on the primary key. For example, in Section 5.2.2.1 the hash organization allows rapid response to a query such as

proj QUANTITYINSTOCK (**sel** ITEMREFNO = 'MQ09'
(TOYINVEN))

In the present chapter we broaden our quest for efficiency of implementation of selection operations: we consider selection conditions that generally involve fields other than the primary key. We improve efficiency and versatility by using indexes.

6.1.2. Owners and members in indexes

An index can be regarded as a file that tells us where to find specified values in another file. For example, part of the index of a book about gardens might be

ALMOND 79, 84
APPLE 78, 95, 107, 125
ASPARAGUS 15, 18, 224
AZALEA 155, 165

In this example the numbers are page numbers: in the book there are references to ASPARAGUS on pages 15, 18, and 224. For the index itself, ASPARAGUS is an example of a primary key value.

In our discussion of indexes we shall use the technical terms *owner* and *member*. Each record in an index consists of a single *owner*, which is the index's primary key value, together with a collection of *members*, which are the entries associated with the owner. In our example, in the first record the owner is ALMOND and the members are 79 and 84. In the second record the owner is APPLE and the members are 78, 95, 107, and 125. In general, any two owners may have different numbers of members.

Within each record in an index the members may be in sorted order: in our example the members are sorted on increasing page number, as is usual in indexes of books. When members are sorted, their order is determined by a sort key associated with these members.

When discussing indexes we shall use the term *data file* to mean the file to which the index refers. In other words, the data file is the file that is indexed.

6.2. Categories of indexes

6.2.1. Primary and secondary indexes

A *primary index* tells us where to find each primary key value. The index in Section 5.6.1 is an example of a primary index. Because a primary key value must be unique, not more than one member may be associated with each owner in a primary index.

A field or set of fields that is not a primary key can be used as a secondary key. A secondary index tells us where to find each secondary key value. A secondary key value may occur in more than one record in the data file, and therefore more than one member may be associated with each owner in a secondary index.

As an example the following very simple file named TOWNA-TIONS tells us in which country various towns belong. TOWN is the primary key, and COUNTRY is a secondary key.

TOWN	COUNTRY
BERNE	SWITZERLAND
BORDEAUX	FRANCE
GENEVA	SWITZERLAND

LIMOGES	FRANCE
LISBON	PORTUGAL
LJUBLJANA	YUGOSLAVIA
OPORTO	PORTUGAL
ROUEN	FRANCE
SARAJEVO	YUGOSLAVIA
TOULOUSE	FRANCE
ZAGREB	YUGOSLAVIA
ZURICH	SWITZERLAND

In general we can find a secondary key value by linear search through a data file. For example, to implement **sel** COUNTRY ='FRANCE' (TOWNATIONS) we can linearly search TOWNA-TIONS looking for COUNTRY = 'FRANCE'. For finding all the towns in a specified country *without* this linear search we can provide a secondary index on COUNTRY (Fig. 6.1). In the secondary index, which is shown on the left of Fig. 6.1, COUNTRYs are owners and pointers are members. COUNTRY, which is a secondary key of the data file, is the primary key of this secondary index. To find all the towns in FRANCE we can look up FRANCE in the secondary index, and thence follow the member pointers in turn to the towns in FRANCE. We do not need to access records for towns that are not in FRANCE. The use of the index speeds up the selection operation by avoiding access to irrelevant data records.

A data file may have more than one secondary index. For example, Typico's CUSTOMERS file, which has CUSTOMER-

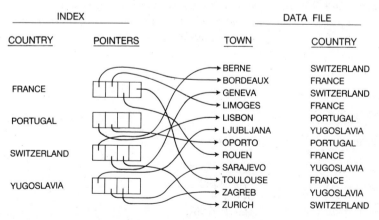

Fig. 6.1. Data file TOWNATIONS with a direct secondary index.

NUMBER as primary key, could sensibly be provided with a secondary index on customer NAME and also with a further secondary index on SALESAREA. Beyond this, it might be worthwhile to provide a third secondary index on SALESPERSONEMPLOYEENUMBER; Typico could use this to find all customers for whom a given employee was responsible.

If we know which selection operations are likely to be performed with what frequency, we can use this knowledge when deciding which fields should have secondary indexes. There is no point in providing a secondary index for a field on which we shall never perform a selection operation.

6.2.2. Sparse and dense indexes

A dense index tells us exactly where to find each member. The COUNTRYs index in Section 6.2.1 is an example of a dense index. A sparse index merely tells us, for each member, the block that contains that member, but does not tell us exactly where to find the member in the block. The index of the indexed sequential file in Section 5.6.1 is an example of a sparse index.

6.2.3. Direct and indirect indexes

An index is said to be *direct* if its members are pointers to, or addresses of, records that contain owner values. For example the COUNTRYs index in Section 6.2.1 is direct because the members are pointers to data records for towns in the owner country.

An index is said to be *indirect* if its members are not pointers but primary key values for data records containing owner values. To illustrate this, here is an indirect index of TOWNATIONS on COUNTRY:

INDEX

COUNTRY	TOWNS
FRANCE	BORDEAUX, LIMOGES, ROUEN, TOULOUSE.

PORTUGAL	LISBON,
	OPORTO.
SWITZERLAND	BERNE, GENEVA
	ZURICH.
YUGOSLAVIA	LJUBLJANA
	SARAJEVO,
	ZAGREB.

DATA FILE

TOWN	COUNTRY
BERNE	SWITZERLAND
BORDEAUX	FRANCE
GENEVA	SWITZERLAND
LIMOGES	FRANCE
LISBON	PORTUGAL
LJUBLJANA	YUGOSLAVIA
OPORTO	PORTUGAL
ROUEN	FRANCE
SARAJEVO	YUGOSLAVIA
TOULOUSE	FRANCE
ZAGREB	YUGOSLAVIA
ZURICH	SWITZERLAND

An advantage of an indirect index is that the members do not have to be updated when records in the data file are physically moved to new addresses. For example, if the GENEVA record is deleted from the TOWNATIONS file and the subsequent data records are physically moved up to fill the gap, members in index records do not have to be updated if the index is indirect. If the index is direct, then pointers to data records for LIMOGES, LISBON, LJUBLJANA, OPORTO, ROUEN, SARAJEVO, TOULOUSE, ZAGREB, and ZURICH will have to be updated to point to new physical addresses.

A disadvantage of an indirect index is that to locate physical records in the data file we have to access the data file using the primary key values obtained from the index. We have to go *from* a primary key value *to* the physical address of a data record containing this primary key value, and this translation generally takes time.

If the data file is organized for direct access, for instance as a hash file, then indirect indexing may be viable. Otherwise indirect indexing may be unacceptably slow because finding primary key values in the data file may involve too much search.

6.3. Implementation of access to members

6.3.1. *Index members stored outside data files*

In the index in Fig. 6.1 COUNTRYs generally have different numbers of associated member pointers. For each owner the associated members can actually be stored in a one-dimensional array, as indicated in Fig. 6.1, where each array has been given four elements in the hope that no owner will have more than four members. If we give each array enough elements to contain the maximum number of members, array elements will be empty and wasted when an owner has less than the maximum number of members. This is a general disadvantage of storing members in arrays.

To accommodate the generally variable numbers of members per owner without wasting much space, we can store the members in linked lists, as shown in Fig. 6.2. Each list contains records that have a pointer-to-next field which was previously unnecessary; introduction of this field is the price we pay for avoiding unused elements in arrays as in Fig. 6.1. Detailed programming of this use of lists is illustrated in the indexed invoice table example in Section 9.8.2.

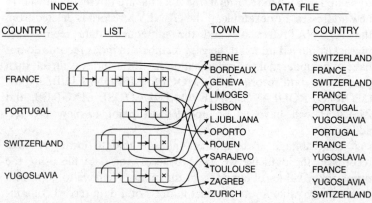

Fig. 6.2. Data file TOWNATIONS with an index implemented by lists.

We can find all the records in the data file that have a given secondary key value by looking up this value in the secondary index and then traversing the list of members owned by this secondary key value. We can use each member to access a record in the data file that contains the given secondary key value. (This is illustrated in the procedure FINDINVOICESOF at the end of Section 9.8.2.) If, for a given owner, we wish to use all or almost all the members in this way, then this use of linked lists is efficient. In other words, the sequential traversal of a linked list is efficient if the hit rate of the traversal is quite close to unity. If the list is short then the question of efficiency is not important anyway.

If an update of a data record changes a secondary key value, we may have to remove a member from association with an owner in a secondary index and instead associate this member with a different owner. Moreover, if we delete a record from the data file we must delete secondary index members that lead to this record. If members are stored in linked lists then we have to traverse a linked list looking for just one member that is to be deleted. In this case the hit rate for traversal of a list of members is low, and we really require random access to one member that is associated with a given owner. To facilitate random access we can store members in B-trees instead of linked lists. Against the advantage of efficient random access we must note the disadvantage that B-trees take up more memory than linked lists. On the other hand, from the point of view of Pascal DML programming, an advantage of this use of B-trees is that we can use procedures such as FINDKEY and REMOVE without having to write them.

When we insert a new record into the data file we should insert new members into secondary indexes, corresponding to the inserted record's secondary key values. For reasons that will become clear in Section 6.4, we usually wish to maintain lists of members in sorted order, which is commonly the sorted order of the data records to which the members lead. In the indexed invoice table example in Section 9.8.2 and in procedure ENTERJX in Section 4.4 new members are inserted at the start of a list, just to simplify programming. Usually we wish to insert a new member into a list in a position that will preserve the prescribed sorted order of the members. If, for each owner, the members are stored in a B-tree as described above, then we can easily insert a new member into the required place in the sequence by using the procedure INSERT, which does not involve traversal of a linked list of members. As in the case of deletion, this use of B-trees will not improve efficiency of access if each owner has only a few members, but the availability of procedures such as INSERT and REMOVE will facilitate programming.

To illustrate the use of B-trees to contain members in secondary indexes, we shall now rework the indexed inventory table example of Section 4.4. The data file will be an inventory file stored in a table organized for direct addressing; the ITEMREFNO will be used as the subscript of this table. The reason for using direct addressing in this example is the extreme simplicity. We shall provide a secondary index on SUPPLIERNO; for simplicity the owners in this index will be accessed by direct addressing. Accordingly the secondary index will be stored in a table that has SUPPLIERNO as subscript. Within the secondary index the members will be subscripts for the inventory table. Our DBD is as follows.

```
DBDNAME MX;
type
    REFRANGE = 100..140;
    SUPPRANGE = 10..99;
    INVTYPE = record
                QUANTITYINSTOCK: INTEGER;
                PRICEPERUNIT: REAL;
                SUPPLIERNO: SUPPRANGE;
                NORECORD: BOOLEAN
            end;
    MEMBERTREE = BTREE of REFRANGE;
var
    INVTABLE: array [REFRANGE] of INVTYPE;
    SUPPINDEX: array [SUPPRANGE] of MEMBERTREE;
finish
```

B-trees are automatically initialized to be EMPTY. We must, however, initialize INVTABLE as in Section 4.4 (where we used the initializing program INITJX). Our initializing program is as follows.

```
program INITMX (OUTPUT);
invoke MX;
var I: REFRANGE;
begin
    STARTTRANSACTION (UNRESTRICTED);
```

```
   for I: = 100 to 140 do INVTABLE[I].NORECORD: = TRUE;
   ENDTRANSACTION; WRITELN ('initialization completed')
end.
```

The following program enters a single record into INVTABLE and updates the index accordingly. The procedure INSERT inserts the new member so that members remain sorted on increasing ITEM-REFNO.

```
program ENTERMX (INPUT, OUTPUT);
invoke MX;
var
   ITEMREFNO: REFRANGE;
   SUPPNO: SUPPRANGE;
begin
   STARTTRANSACTION (UNRESTRICTED);
   WRITE ('please type itemrefno, quantityinstock, ');
   WRITELN ('PRICEPERUNIT, SUPPLIERNO');
   READ (ITEMREFNO);
   with INVTABLE [ITEMREFNO] do
   begin
      READLN (QUANTITYINSTOCK, PRICEPERUNIT,
      SUPPLIERNO);
      SUPPNO: = SUPPLIERNO;
      NORECORD: = FALSE
   end;
   INSERT (SUPPINDEX [SUPPNO], ITEMREFNO);
   if DBSTATUS < > OKAY then
   begin
      WRITELN ('index insertion failed'); ABORTTRANSACTION
   end else ENDTRANSACTION
end.
```

The following program reads a supplier number from the terminal and outputs all the records from the inventory table for items supplied by this supplier. If the input supplier number is S then the output of this program is **sel** SUPPLIERNO = S (INVTABLE).

```
program SUPPQUERY (INPUT, OUTPUT);
invoke MX;
var
   SUPPNO: SUPPRANGE;
   IRNO: REFRANGE;
   MEMPTR: ↑REFRANGE;
```

```
begin
  WRITELN ('please type a supplier number');
  READLN (SUPPNO);
  STARTTRANSACTION (READONLY);
  FINDFIRST (SUPPINDEX [SUPPNO], MEMPTR);
  if DBSTATUS = EMPTY then
  WRITELN ('no items are supplied by this supplier ');
  while DBSTATUS = OKAY do
  begin
    IRNO: = MEMPTR↑; {IRNO is the next ITEM REF NO to be
    processed}
    WRITELN ('ITEMREFNO = ', IRNO);
    with INVTABLE [IRNO] do
      WRITELN ('QUANTITY IN STOCK = ',
      QUANTITYINSTOCK,
        ' PRICE PER UNIT = ', PRICEPERUNIT,
        ' SUPPLIER NUMBER = ', SUPPLIERNO);
    FINDSUCC (SUPPINDEX [SUPPNO], MEMPTR)
  end;
  ENDTRANSACTION
end.
```

The next example program reads an ITEMREFNO from the
terminal and deletes the entry in the inventory table that has this
ITEMREFNO. The program also deletes this ITEMREFNO from
the supplier index.

```
program DELMX (INPUT, OUTPUT);
invoke MX;
var
  SUPPNO: SUPPRANGE; ITEMREFNO: REFRANGE;
  MEMPTR: ↑REFRANGE;
begin
  STARTTRANSACTION (UNRESTRICTED);
  WRITELN ('please type ITEMREFNO of record to be deleted);
  READLN (ITEMREFNO);
  SUPPNO: = INVTABLE [ITEMREFNO].SUPPLIERNO;
  INVTABLE [ITEMREFNO].NORECORD: = TRUE; {deletes record
  from table}
  FINDKEY (SUPPINDEX [SUPPNO], ITEMREFNO, MEMPTR);
  if DBSTATUS < > OKAY then
  begin
    WRITELN ('deletion failed');
    ABORTTRANSACTION
```

end else {remove appropriate member from index}
begin {member to be removed is the one pointed to by MEMPTR}
    REMOVE (SUPPINDEX [SUPPNO], MEMPTR);
    ENDTRANSACTION
end
end.

This program is somewhat easier than its counterpart DELJX in Section 4.4 which worked by traversing a linked list of members.

6.3.2. *Indexing using pointers within data records*

6.3.2.1. *Pointer to owner*

In Section 6.3.1 we were concerned with organizing indexes so as to maximize efficiency and ease of access. We now consider methods for reducing the overall storage area required for a data file and its indexes. By way of introduction we note that in the simple file TOWNATIONS in Section 6.2.1 names of countries are generally repeated several times. For example SWITZERLAND occurs three times in the data file and once in the index. We may be able to reduce the storage requirements of the data file by replacing the field value 'SWITZERLAND' by a pointer to the SWITZERLAND owner in the secondary index, and by replacing the field value 'FRANCE' by a pointer to FRANCE in the secondary index, and so on, so that we have the data structure shown in Fig. 6.3.

To simplify Fig. 6.3 the index is shown with member pointers on the left and owners on the right. In each town data record, instead of storing the name of the country as a text-string, we now store a pointer to the owner index record. If the number of bytes occupied by this pointer is less than the number of bytes required for the longest country name then the replacement of country names by pointers reduces overall requirements for memory capacity. In a very much larger file this reduction could be significant, particularly if the same idea is used for many fields of the data file.

Suppose that we wish to look up LJUBLJANA in Fig. 6.3 to find which country it is in. We find LJUBLJANA in the data file, possibly by linear search. Then we follow the pointer from the LJUBLJANA data record to the index record that contains the owner country name YUGOSLAVIA, which is the required information. Following this pointer takes longer than would have

DATA FILE   INDEX

TOWN   POINTER   MEMBERS   OWNER

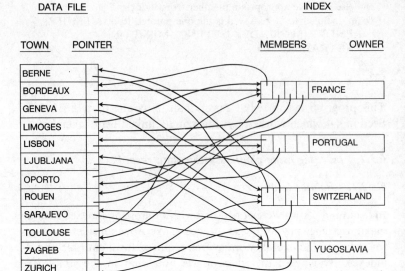

Fig. 6.3. TOWNATIONS file with COUNTRY field replaced by pointer
to owner.

been necessary if the string 'YUGOSLAVIA' were stored in the
LJUBLJANA record in the data file; we have reduced storage
requirements at the cost of increased access time.

At this point we can, in passing, usefully introduce some further
terminology. A data file that contains *only* pointers to index records
is said to be *fully inverted*. A file that has an index on a secondary key
is said to be *inverted on* that secondary key. A file that is inverted on
at least one secondary key is said to be *partially inverted*.

6.3.2.2. *Simple ring structure*

In the towns and countries example there is generally more than one
member pointer associated with each owner country. For example,
four member pointers are associated with FRANCE. We now
introduce an idea which reduces the memory required to store the
index, but further increases the time taken to find the country to
which any given town belongs. The idea is that in the index there is
now not more than one member pointer associated with each

owner. For example there is only one member pointer in the
FRANCE index record. This member pointer points to one town in
FRANCE. In the data record for this French town there is a pointer
to the next French town. In the data record for this next French
town there is a pointer to the next French town, and so on. In the
data record for the last French town there is a pointer to the owner
record in the index, exactly as in Section 6.3.2.1. If we follow the
member pointer from any index record we traverse a sequence of
pointers that leads back to the owner index record. A pointer chain
that goes from an owner via members back to the owner is called a
ring. A ring has exactly one owner, and may have any number of
members. For our example a ring structure is shown in Fig. 6.4.

To find, for example, the country to which LJUBLJANA belongs,
we use LJUBLJANA as the primary key to access the data file.
From the LJUBLJANA record we follow the pointer chain via SARA-
JEVO and ZAGREB to the owner index record where we find the
name YUGOSLAVIA, which is the required information.

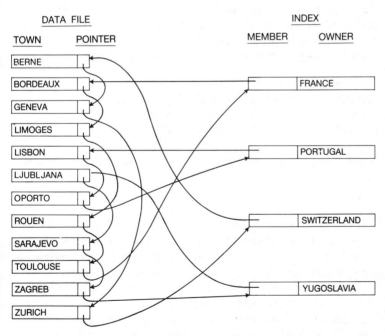

Fig. 6.4. Ring implementation of index on countries.

To find, for example, all French towns, we start by accessing the FRANCE record in the index. Thence we follow the pointer chain via all French towns, outputting their names. Eventually we reach the pointer back to FRANCE which signifies that we have reached the last French town.

Although this ring structure has the advantage that it reduces the storage requirements of the index by reducing the number of member pointers stored in the index, there is a disadvantage that finding the country to which a town belongs generally takes longer than in Fig. 6.3. Storage requirements have been reduced at the cost of increased time for access.

6.3.2.3. *Cellular rings*

If a ring has thousands of members, the time taken to traverse the ring to the owner may be unacceptably long, particularly if the members are in more than one cylinder. To speed up access to the owner, we can subdivide a ring into a collection of separate smaller rings, each having the same owner. If a small ring is entirely contained within a single cylinder it can be traversed without disc head movements. If, for example, each owner has three separate rings, the fields of the secondary index are as follows:

OWNER SECONDARY KEY
POINTER TO FIRST MEMBER OF FIRST RING
POINTER TO FIRST MEMBER OF SECOND RING
POINTER TO FIRST MEMBER OF THIRD RING

If, for example, a record in the data file in the second ring is accessed using the primary key, then we can follow a pointer chain to the owner of this ring without needing to follow pointers via records in the third ring.

If we wish to use the secondary index to find all the members owned by a given secondary key value, we can look up this secondary key value in the secondary index and then traverse the three rings in turn. The total time required for this is almost the same as if all the members belonged to a single large ring. The only disadvantage of subdividing a large ring into smaller ones is that the index record type must now include one pointer field for each ring.

A ring subdivided into smaller rings is called a *cellular* ring.

6.3.2.4. Bidirectional rings

We have so far been concerned with rings in which each component points only to its successor as shown in Fig. 6.5(a). In a *bidirectional* ring, each component points both to its successor and to its predecessor, as shown in Fig. 6.5(b).

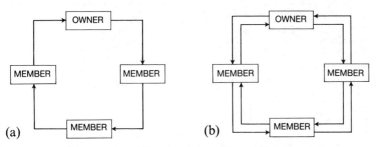

Fig. 6.5. (a) A unidirectional ring; (b) a bidirectional ring.

An advantage of a bidirectional ring is that when we delete a record from the data file we can follow the pointer from this record to the predecessor in the ring. We can then update this predecessor to point to the deleted record's successor. If a ring is not bidirectional, we may have to traverse the ring starting at the owner in order to find a deleted record's predecessor.

A more obvious advantage of a bidirectional ring is that we are free to traverse it in increasing or decreasing order of sort key value. A disadvantage is that the owner and member record types now include two pointer fields for the ring. If a ring is not bidirectional a single pointer field is sufficient.

6.3.2.5. Coral rings

Figure 6.6 is an example of *coral* ring structure. Like a bidirectional ring, a coral ring has two pointer fields per member, but now organized so that we can reach the owner by following pointers via not more than one other member. The advantage is quicker access to the owner from any member. A disadvantage is that programming is more complicated.

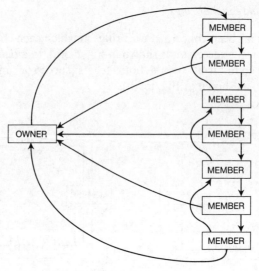

Fig. 6.6. A coral ring.

6.3.2.6. *Multilists*

To introduce a further idea we shall use as an example a file named PEOPLE that tells us the HEIGHT and HAIRCOLOUR of various people, as shown in Fig. 6.7. The primary key is the pair of fields FIRSTNAME, SURNAME. An index on FIRSTNAME is a secondary index because FIRSTNAME is not the complete primary key, but is merely one field of the primary key. This index can be implemented by incorporating member pointers in the data records, as shown in Fig. 6.8. Because FIRSTNAME is part of the primary key we have included a text-string value of the FIRSTNAME field as well as a pointer to next field in each record in Fig. 6.8. Each list of members is terminated by **nil**; there is no need for a pointer to owner, because the text of the owner FIRSTNAME is immediately available in each data record.

We now develop this example by incorporating an index on HAIRCOLOUR, as shown in Fig. 6.9. Because HAIRCOLOUR is not part of the primary key, we have not included text-string HAIRCOLOUR values in data records in Fig. 6.9. Instead we have *replaced* the text-string hair colour by a pointer field, hoping thereby to reduce the total number of bytes required for storing the data file.

FIRSTNAME	SURNAME	HEIGHT	HAIRCOLOUR
ALAN	ARNOLD	164	YELLOW
JOHN	ARNOLD	162	BLACK
MARY	BECK	159	BLACK
JANE	COLLINS	166	BROWN
THOMAS	COLLINS	180	BROWN
JANE	DAVIES	164	RED
WILLIAM	DAVIES	173	BLACK
ALAN	FISHER	159	YELLOW
MARY	FISHER	158	BROWN
ANNE	GREEN	165	BLACK
JOHN	GREEN	172	BROWN
JOHN	KNIGHT	176	WHITE
THOMAS	KNIGHT	181	BLACK
JANE	LINLEY	158	RED
ALAN	MARSHALL	182	BROWN
MARY	MARSHALL	159	BROWN
JANE	REYNOLDS	163	YELLOW
WILLIAM	REYNOLDS	169	BLACK
ANNE	THOMAS	158	BROWN
THOMAS	THOMAS	181	BROWN
JOHN	WILLIAMS	177	BROWN
WILLIAM	WILLIAMS	173	RED
ANNE	YOUNG	169	BROWN
ALAN	YOUNG	171	BLACK

Fig. 6.7.   The file PEOPLE.

For each HAIRCOLOUR value we now have a separate ring in which the last member points to the owner record in the HAIRCO-LOUR index, because this is the only place where the name of the HAIRCOLOUR is actually recorded. If, given a primary key value, we wish to look up someone's HAIRCOLOUR we shall have to use the ring structure to retrieve the HAIRCOLOUR text-string from the HAIRCOLOUR index.

A *multilist* is a data structure in which there is a set of records and a set of lists of these records, such that each record belongs to *more than one* list. Generally each list threads a different set of records. In this context a ring counts as a list, and the PEOPLE file indexed as shown in Fig. 6.9 is therefore an example of a multilist. In this example each data record has two pointer fields and belongs to two lists. In other examples of multilists, each record may belong to a larger number of lists.

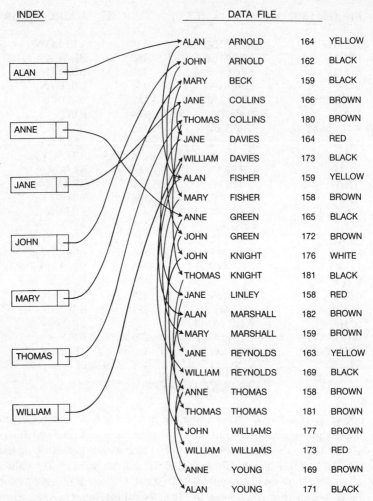

Fig. 6.8. List implementation of a secondary index on FIRSTNAME.

6.4. Implementation of access to owners

In Section 6.3 we only considered the organization of members, not owners. In Section 6.3.2 lists of member pointers were embedded in the data file, whereas in Section 6.3.1 the member pointers were stored separately from the data file. We now consider implementation of access to owners. The method of access to owners is

FIRST NAME DATA FILE HAIRCOLOUR INDEX

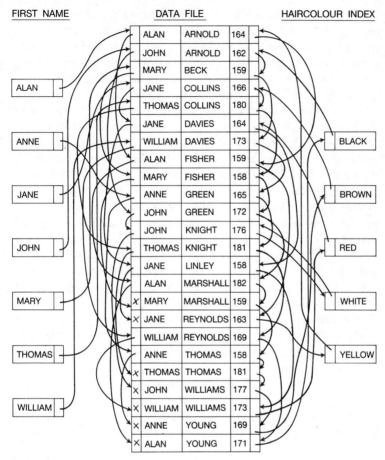

Fig. 6.9. Multilist implementation of indexes on FIRSTNAME and HAIRCOLOUR.

generally independent of the method of organization of members, and can therefore be considered separately.

We commonly require *random* access to an owner in an index. If the number of owners in an index is large then we can organize the index itself as a direct-addressed or hash file that has owners as its primary key values. To simplify programming in Section 9.8.2 and in Section 6.3.1 the indexes were organized for direct-addressed access to owners. If the number of secondary key values that actually turn up is much less than the range of possible secondary key values, then hash organization may be more practical than direct addressing. Another possibility is that the number of owners is small, in which case hash organization may be an unnecessary complication and we may be content instead to store owners in a table and obtain access to any specified owner by linear search.

If the number of owners is large we may prefer to store the owners in a B-tree. Random access may be slower than with hash organization of owners, but B-tree organization has the advantage that we do not need to know the number of distinct owner values at the time of writing the DBD. From the point of view of Pascal DML this use of B-trees has the advantage that we can use the procedures INSERT, FINDKEY, etc., without having to declare them. For the PEOPLE file the number of secondary key values of FIRSTNAME and HAIRCOLOUR is so small that the use of B-trees is not really practical, because the secondary key values could simply be stored in tables for linear search as mentioned above. Nevertheless, we shall now use these two indexes to illustrate the programming required for B-tree organization of owners. In Section 6.3.1 we used B-tree organization only for members. We shall now use B-trees for owners as well as for members, so that our index will be a B-tree of B-trees. Members will be separate from the data file, as in Section 6.3.1, not embedded in multilists as in Section 6.3.2.

For simplicity we shall store the data records of the PEOPLE file in a table, i.e. an array of records. We shall provide secondary indexes on FIRSTNAME and HAIRCOLOUR, in which the members are subscripts of the table. Given a primary key value of FIRSTNAME and SURNAME we could easily look up a person in this table by linear search. If we start with a secondary key value such as a hair colour we can find all the people whose hair is this colour by looking it up in the HAIRCOLOUR index. Similarly we can use the FIRSTNAME index to find all the people who have a given first name. Our DBD is as follows.

```
DBDNAME HA;
type
   SUBSCRIPT = 1..24;
   STRING8 = packed array [1..8] of CHAR;
   PERSON = record
                FIRSTNAME, SURNAME: STRING8;
                HEIGHT: INTEGER;
```

```
                HAIRCOLOUR: STRING8
            end;
    INDEXLEAF = record
                OWNER: STRING8;
                MEMBERS: BTREE of SUBSCRIPT
            end;
    SECONDARYIND = BTREE of INDEXLEAF on OWNER;
var
    TABLE: array [SUBSCRIPT] of PERSON;
    FIRSTNAMEIND, HAIRINDEX: SECONDARYIND;
finish
```

The following program reads a binary version of the file PEOPLE
into the TABLE declared in the DBD. This program also enters
members into the secondary indexes on FIRSTNAME and HAIR-
COLOUR. When, for example, this program encounters the HAIR-
COLOUR RED for the first time, it creates a new INDEXLEAF in
which OWNER = 'RED   '. Our program uses the same procedure UPDATEIND to update the FIRSTNAME index and the
HAIRCOLOUR index.

```
program HAP1 (PEOPLE, OUTPUT);
invoke HA;
var
    I: SUBSCRIPT;
    PEOPLE: file of PERSON;
procedure UPDATEIND (var INDEX: SECONDARYIND; var
SECKEY: STRING8);
var
    LEAFPTR: ↑INDEXLEAF;
begin
    FINDKEY (INDEX, SECKEY, LEAFPTR);
    if DBSTATUS = OKAY then
    begin {this secondary key value has turned up previously so}
        INSERT (LEAFPTR↑.MEMBERS, I); {include subscript I among
        members}
        if DBSTATUS < > OKAY then WRITELN ('insert failed')
    end
    else {this is a new secondary key value, i.e. a new owner}
    begin {to create a new owner entry in the secondary index}
        DBSTATUS: = OKAY;
        CREATE (LEAFPTR); {create a new leaf record}
        LEAFPTR↑.OWNER: = SECKEY;
        INSERT (LEAFPTR↑.MEMBERS, I); {include subscript I among
        members}
```

```
    if DBSTATUS < > OKAY then WRITELN ('first I insert failed')
    else
    begin {to insert the new leaf into the index}
      INSERT (INDEX, LEAFPTR↑);
      if DBSTATUS < > OKAY then WRITELN ('insert LEAF failed')
    end
  end
end {of procedure UPDATEIND};
begin {program body}
  RESET (PEOPLE);
  STARTTRANSACTION (UNRESTRICTED);
  for I: = 1 to 24 do
  begin
    READ (PEOPLE, TABLE [I]);
    UPDATEIND (FIRSTNAMEIND, TABLE [I].FIRSTNAME);
    UPDATEIND (HAIRINDEX, TABLE [I].HAIRCOLOUR)
  end;
  ENDTRANSACTION
end.
```

To illustrate the use of one of these secondary indexes, the following
program reads a hair colour from the terminal and outputs the first
name and surname of all people whose hair is this colour.

```
program HAP2 (INPUT, OUTPUT);
invoke HA;
var
  COLOUR: STRING8;
  LEAFPTR: ↑INDEXLEAF;
  SUBSPTR: ↑SUBSCRIPT;
  S: SUBSCRIPT;
begin
  STARTTRANSACTION (READONLY);
  WRITELN ('please type haircolour consisting of exactly eight ',
  'characters including trailing padding spaces if necessary');
  READLN (COLOUR);
  FINDKEY (HAIRINDEX, COLOUR, LEAFPTR);
  if DBSTATUS < > OKAY then
  WRITELN ('no-one has hair that colour')
  else
  begin {find first member owned by input HAIRCOLOUR value}
    FINDFIRST (LEAFPTR↑.MEMBERS, SUBSPTR);
    while DBSTATUS = OKAY do
    begin
      S: = SUBSPTR↑;
```

```
    with TABLE [S] do WRITELN (FIRSTNAME, SURNAME);
    FINDSUCC (LEAFPTR↑.MEMBERS, SUBSPTR) {find next
    member}
  end
end;
ENDTRANSACTION
end.
```

This program uses the HAIRINDEX secondary index to speed up the evaluation of

proj FIRSTNAME, SURNAME (**sel** HAIRCOLOUR = COLOUR (PEOPLE))

We have not provided an index on SURNAME, so the only way to evaluate, for example

proj FIRSTNAME (**sel** SURNAME = 'MARSHALL' (PEOPLE))

is by linear search of the table, looking for SURNAME = 'MARSHALL'.

6.5. Selection operations on more than one key value
6.5.1. And

We now consider selection that involves **and** conditions. To evaluate an expression such as

proj SURNAME (**sel** (FIRSTNAME = 'JOHN') **and** (HAIRCOLOUR = 'BROWN') (PEOPLE))

we could linearly search PEOPLE looking for FIRSTNAME = 'JOHN' and HAIRCOLOUR = 'BROWN', but this would waste time looking at records that contain neither of these secondary key values. Another idea is to access a secondary index on FIRST-NAME and thence search all the member data records that have FIRSTNAME = 'JOHN', checking each to see whether HAIRCOLOUR = 'BROWN'; in this case we do not waste time looking at data records that do not have FIRSTNAME = 'JOHN'. If member pointers are included within data records as in Section 6.3.2 or if there is no index on HAIRCOLOUR, then this idea is the best available to us.

If, as in Section 6.3.1, member pointers are not included in data records but are instead stored separately, we can access a FIRST-NAME secondary index to obtain a list of member pointers to records that have FIRSTNAME = 'JOHN' and we can also access a HAIRCOLOUR secondary index to obtain a separate list of member pointers to records that have HAIRCOLOUR = 'BROWN'. The *intersection* of these two lists contains pointers to data records that have HAIRCOLOUR = 'BROWN' **and** FIRSTNAME = 'JOHN'. From this intersection we can go straight to these records without wasting time looking at irrelevant records, and if this method is applied to files that contain large numbers of records the total number of blocks accessed may be significantly less than would otherwise be necessary.

To illustrate the programming of the intersection of two sets of members, the following program reads a first name and a hair colour from the terminal and outputs the surname of everyone who has this first name and this hair colour.

```
program HAP3 (INPUT, OUTPUT);
invoke HA;
var
   HPTR, FPTR: ↑SUBSCRIPT;
   HLEAFPTR,FLEAFPTR: ↑INDEXLEAF;
   FIRSTNAME, COLOUR: STRING8;
   H: SUBSCRIPT;
   SOMEONE: BOOLEAN;
begin
   STARTTRANSACTION (READONLY);
   WRITE ('type FIRSTNAME and HAIRCOLOUR ');
   WRITELN ('separated by a single space');
   READ (FIRSTNAME); GET (INPUT); READ (COLOUR);
   FINDKEY (HAIRINDEX, COLOUR, HLEAFPTR);
   SOMEONE: = (DBSTATUS = OKAY); DBSTATUS: = OKAY;
   FINDKEY (FIRSTNAMEIND, FIRSTNAME, FLEAFPTR);
   if (DBSTATUS = OKAY) and SOMEONE then
   begin
      FINDFIRST (HLEAFPTR↑.MEMBERS, HPTR);
      FINDFIRST (FLEAFPTR↑.MEMBERS, FPTR);
      while DBSTATUS = OKAY do
      begin
         H: = HPTR↑;
         if H = FPTR↑ then WRITELN (TABLE [H].SURNAME)
```

```
        else if H > FPTR↑ then
            FINDSUCC (FLEAFPTR↑.MEMBERS, FPTR)
        else FINDSUCC (HLEAFPTR↑.MEMBERS, HPTR)
    end
  end;
  ENDTRANSACTION
end.
```

The first call of FINDKEY looks up the COLOUR in the HAIRIN-
DEX and if found sets HLEAFPTR pointing to the appropriate
INDEXLEAF record. If no-one has this hair colour then the value
FALSE is assigned to SOMEONE. The first call of FINDFIRST
sets HPTR pointing to the first member subscript that is associated
with the owner COLOUR. The second call of FINDFIRST sets
FPTR pointing to the first member subscript that is associated with
owner FIRSTNAME. In the **while** loop, if member subscripts are
the same then the subscripted record in the table belongs to the
intersection and so we output the SURNAME from this record.
Otherwise we FINDSUCC in whichever MEMBERS B-tree the
current subscript is the smaller. We do this because the MEMBERS
B-tree is sorted on increasing subscript, and the FINDSUCC may
yield a new subscript which matches the current subscript in the
other MEMBERS B-tree.

   This example makes use of the sorted order of the MEMBERS B-
trees, and the intersection algorithm would be less efficient if the
MEMBERS B-trees did not all have the same sorted order. Indeed
this example illustrates *why* we have arranged that all the index
MEMBERS have the same sorted order. As well as facilitating
intersection, we facilitate union and other operations by making all
MEMBERS have the same sorted order. If, instead of a BTREE of
records of type

```
record
  OWNER: STRING8;
  MEMBERS: BTREE of SUBSCRIPT
end
```

we were to use as a secondary index a single BTREE of records of
type

record
  OWNER:STRING8;
  MEMBER: SUBSCRIPT
end

Then for each owner, i.e. secondary key value, the member subs-cripts would be inserted in the BTREE in the historical order of their insertion, because this is how the procedure INSERT deals with records that have the same, i.e. duplicate, key values. We would not be able to ensure that for each OWNER the members were sorted on increasing subscript value.

6.5.2. Or

To evaluate an expression such as

proj SURNAME (**sel** (FIRSTNAME = 'JOHN') **or**
(HAIRCOLOUR = 'BROWN') (PEOPLE))

we can linearly search the PEOPLE table looking for records that have FIRSTNAME = 'JOHN' or HAIRCOLOUR = 'BROWN'. If we have FIRSTNAME and HAIRCOLOUR indexes with member pointers stored separately from the data file, in the style of Section 6.3.1, then we may be able to improve efficiency by forming the union of the members associated with JOHN and BROWN in the secondary indexes. This union is a collection of pointers (or subs-cripts) that take us directly to the required data records, and we need not waste time looking at irrelevant records in the data file. If the members are in the same sorted order in the two secondary indexes this simplifies ensuring that no member occurs more than once in the union.

6.6. Indirection

6.6.1. Dense primary indexes

We have previously explained that the organization of the data file, for example as a hash file, can be chosen to provide efficient random access to any given primary key value. We have also explained how the use of dense secondary indexes can speed up selection operations that involve secondary key values. In the present section we consider

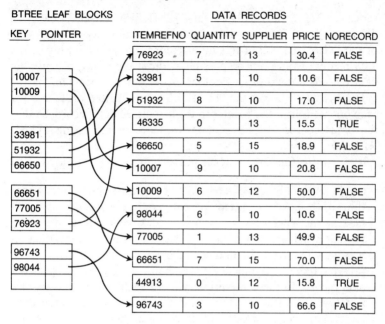

Fig. 6.10. A simplified inventory file with a dense primary index

circumstances in which it is advantageous to provide a dense index
on the primary key, and we begin with a specific example.

This example uses data records of the type INVTYPE that we
used in the simple inventory table example in Section 4.3, except that
REFRANGE is now 10000..99999, and therefore direct addressing
of the inventory table is not practical. In this example, data records
are input from the terminal in random order but are to be accessible
in order of increasing ITEMREFNO value; as in Section 4.3,
ITEMREFNO is the primary key. When a data record is input from
the terminal it is stored in the first free (i.e. NORECORD = TRUE)
space in a data block. At the same time this record's primary key
value and a pointer to (or subscript of) this record are stored in a B-
tree which we use in this example as a primary dense index. The B-
tree is sorted on ITEMREFNO but the data records are stored in
random sequence, as shown in Fig. 6.10. The sequence is random
because, as we have said, an input record is always stored in the next
free space. When a record is deleted its NORECORD field is set to
TRUE and its ITEMREFNO is deleted from the dense primary

index. In Fig. 6.10 the record for ITEMREFNO = 46335 has been deleted and will be overwritten by the next input record, regardless of the ITEMREFNO of this input record. Batch processing of the data records would not be possible without the index, because the data records are stored in random order. Batch processing via the index is easy: we access the ITEMREFNOs in sorted order and for each one we follow the pointer to the associated data record, so that the data records are accessed in sequence of increasing ITEM-REFNO.

The reasons for using a dense primary index are as follows.

(a) In the data blocks of a hash file or a B-tree approximately one-third of the space is wasted. We can reduce the waste of space by making the blocks contain primary index records instead of data records which are now randomly placed elsewhere. This reduction may be effective if the number of bytes per record in the dense primary index is significantly less than the number of bytes per data record. In the dense primary index each record consists of a primary key value together with a pointer to where the data record is stored in a data block in which there may now be no wasted space.

(b) Records in B-tree leaf blocks, or in the data blocks in Section 5.6.2, are liable to move physically in order to preserve sorted sequence within blocks. If the data records in these blocks are the subject of secondary indexes, the members in the secondary indexes will have to be updated when the data records move as a result of insertion or deletion. This updating of indexes is generally not practical, and we can avoid the need for it by using a dense primary index and storing data records separately at addresses where they will not be shifted around physically. Records that are pointed to by indexes are said to be *pinned*, and a very important advantage of using a dense primary index is that it can provide access to pinned records that need not be shifted around in memory. The pinned records remain at fixed (possibly random) addresses in data blocks, and the sorted order can be preserved by shifting index records within B-tree leaf blocks. The shifting of records within the leaf blocks of a B-tree primary index does not necessitate updating of secondary indexes.

In the example shown in Fig. 6.10, we could easily introduce a secondary index on supplier number. In this secondary index the members would be pointers of the same type as in the primary index. Insertion or deletion of data records would not cause physical shifting that would necessitate the updating the secondary indexes, except for the actual records inserted or deleted. If, instead of using a dense index as illustrated in Fig. 6.10, we stored the actual records in the leaf blocks of a B-tree, then a secondary index on supplier number would have to be updated to take account of physical shifting of records, and this would not be practical.

6.6.2. Further indirection

A direct address takes us directly to a sought item, whereas an indirect address takes us to a further address which takes us to a sought item. Indirection may proceed via many stages: for example an address takes us to another address where we find another address which takes us to yet another address and so on, until eventually we reach a sought item.

We have already introduced several examples of indirection. In Section 5.5.1, we saw that if a direct-addressed file is not contiguous then we actually access a data block by obtaining its physical address from an index: looking up the physical address in the index is an example of indirection. A dense primary index provides another example: instead of directly finding the data fields associated with a given primary key value, we find in the index an address that takes us to the data fields.

In many practical database systems, an address obtained from a primary or secondary index is an indirect address that takes us to a direct address which in turn takes us to a sought item. This further indirection allows us to shift data items in memory without updating primary and secondary indexes. We have already introduced dense primary indexes to cope with physical shifting of records within B-tree leaf blocks or within the data blocks of an indexed sequential file. The further indirection which we are now introducing allows occasional physical shifting of actual data records. This physical shifting may be desirable for several reasons.

(a) To minimize the time for access, it is desirable that items which are often accessed consecutively should be physically close together, preferably in the same block, or at least in the same cylinder. In an attempt to achieve this, data items may sometimes be physically relocated.

(b) Hitherto we have worked primarily with fixed-length records, i.e. with record types that require a fixed number of bytes per record. Many practical systems allow variable-length records. For example (not in Pascal) a field of a record may be a text-string of any length, just like a text-file. In this case, when a record is deleted by setting NORECORD = TRUE, the space that is thereby made available may be too large for an incoming input record. If a small input record is placed in a large space, the residual gap may be too small to be useful, so memory will be wasted. To avoid fragmentation problems of this kind, we may wish to move data records together to close up small gaps and instead make gaps that are large enough to contain future input records.

One way of achieving this flexibility is to arrange that the pointers stored as members in primary and secondary indexes are actually integers, which are sometimes called *internal sequence numbers* (ISNs). An ISN is the (direct-addressing) subscript of an index which tells us the physical address that corresponds to each ISN. When data items are physically shifted their addresses in this index are updated, but their ISNs remain unchanged, and therefore there is no need to update primary and secondary indexes.

Another well-known method, which allows access to a data item without first accessing an index block, is to arrange that a database pointer consists of two parts. The first part is the physical address of the block that contains the item, and the second part is an integer that is used for finding the required data item within the block. This integer is used as the (direct-addressing) subscript of an index that is stored within this physical block. For each such integer, this index tells us the byte number within the block where the sought item actually begins. Within the block we can shift items, updating the index accordingly, without having to update database pointers.

Henceforward, as in earlier sections, we shall think of a pointer simply as a kind of address that takes us to a data item, although it is to be understood that in practice this address may entail at least one stage of indirection behind the scenes.

6.7. Exercises

1. This exercise is concerned with an artificially simple file named FEX that has three fields G, H, and K. G is the primary key. The file contains the following.

G	H	K
1	A	Q
9	B	Q
5	B	Q
8	B	P
7	C	Q
3	C	P
4	A	P

(a) Draw a diagram of a data structure in which the data records of FEX are stored physically in the sequence shown, but linked by pointers in sequence of increasing primary key G. The data structure is to include ring-implemented secondary indexes on H and K. Thus each data record is to consist of the primary key field together with three pointer fields.

(b) Draw a diagram of a data structure in which the data records of FEX are stored physically in the sequence shown, and a dense primary index provides access to these records in sequence of increasing primary key G. The data structure is to include secondary indexes on H and K, implemented using member pointers that are not included in the data file FEX. Your diagram should show each of the three indexes as a collection of owners with associated members; further than this, detailed organization of indexes need not be specified.

(c) Explain in words how the data structures in (a) and (b) can each be used to evaluate

proj G (**sel** (H = X) **and** (K = Y) (FEX))

where X and Y are values read from the terminal.

(d) Suppose that FEX now contains 8000 records and that the data structures of (a) and (b) are extended accordingly. In this case review the relative advantages and disadvantages of the data structures of (a) and (b).

2. In this exercise you will program the dense index example of Section 6.6.1, plus a secondary index on SUPPLIERNO, using the DBD:

```
DBDNAME XS;
type
    REFRANGE = 10000..99999; SUPPRANGE = 10..15;
    INVTYPE = record
                    ITEMREFNO: REFRANGE;
```

```
                     QUANTITYINSTOCK: INTEGER;
                     PRICEPERUNIT: REAL;
                     SUPPLIERNO: SUPPRANGE
               end;
  INDEXLEAF = record
                     ITEMREFNO: REFRANGE;
                     POINTER: ↑INVTYPE
               end;
  INDEXTREE = BTREE of INDEXLEAF on ITEMREFNO;
var
  PRIMARYINDEX: INDEXTREE;
  SUPPLIERINDEX: array [SUPPRANGE] of INDEXTREE;
finish
```

For simplicity the SUPPLIERINDEX is accessed using direct addressing.
By including ITEMREFNOs in SUPPLIERINDEX INDEXTREEs, we
enable all inventory records for any given SUPPLIERNO to be retrieved in
sequence of increasing ITEMREFNO.

(a) Using the following program, insert a few records from the terminal
into the dense-indexed inventory file. These records can, for example, be
those shown in Section 6.6.1, or can just be made up.

```
program ENTERINV (INPUT, OUTPUT);
invoke XS;
var
  INVRECPTR: ↑INVTYPE;
  NEWLEAF: INDEXLEAF;
  SNO: SUPPRANGE:
begin
  STARTTRANSACTION (UNRESTRICTED);
  CREATE (INVRECPTR);
  WRITE ('type ITEMREFNO, QUANTITYINSTOCK,  ');
  WRITELN ('PRICEPERUNIT, SUPPLIERNO');
  with INVRECPTR↑ do
  READLN (ITEMREFNO, QUANTITYINSTOCK,
  PRICEPERUNIT, SUPPLIERNO);
  NEWLEAF.ITEMREFNO: = INVRECPTR↑.ITEMREFNO;
  NEWLEAF.POINTER: = INVRECPTR;
  INSERT (PRIMARYINDEX, NEWLEAF);
  if DBSTATUS < > OKAY then
```

```
  begin
    WRITELN ('ITEMREFNO has been inserted previously');
    ABORTTRANSACTION
  end else
  begin
    SNO: = INVRECPTR↑.SUPPLIERNO;
    INSERT (SUPPLIERINDEX [SNO], NEWLEAF);
    if DBSTATUS < > OKAY then
    begin
      WRITELN ('supplier index insert failed');
      ABORTTRANSACTION
    end else ENDTRANSACTION
  end
end.
```

(b) Write a program to output to the terminal all the INVTYPE records that are accessible via the primary index. These records are to be output one per line, sorted on ITEMREFNO.

(c) Let I be an ITEMREFNO. Write a program to read I from the terminal and output to the terminal:

proj QUANTITYINSTOCK (**sel** ITEMREFNO = I (INVENTORY))

where INVENTORY is the collection of records accessible via the primary index. If I is not found in the INVENTORY, your program should say so.

(d) Let S be a SUPPLIERNUMBER. Write a program to read S from the terminal and, using the SUPPLIERINDEX, output to the terminal

proj ITEMREFNO, QUANTITYINSTOCK (**sel** SUPPLIERNO = S (INVENTORY))

(e) Write a program to read S from the terminal and output to the terminal

proj ITEMREFNO (**sel** (SUPPLIERNO = S) **and**
                    (QUANTITYINSTOCK < 8) (INVENTORY))

(f) Write a program to read S from the terminal and output to the terminal

proj ITEMREFNO (**sel** (SUPPLIERNO < > S) **and**
                    (QUANTITYINSTOCK < 8) (INVENTORY))

(g) Write a program to read an ITEMREFNO from the terminal and DELETE from INVENTORY any record that contains this ITEM-REFNO, updating the SUPPLIERINDEX accordingly. If the ITEM-REFNO is not found in the INVENTORY your program should say so.

(h) Write a program to read an ITEMREFNO and QUANTITYIN-STOCK from the terminal. If the ITEMREFNO is not found in the INVENTORY your program should say so. Otherwise your program should change the QUANTITYINSTOCK of this item so as to be equal to the QUANTITYINSTOCK read from the terminal.

3. This exercise is an extension of the PEOPLE example of Section 6.4, using DBD HA.

(a) Let N be a first name and H be a hair colour. Write a program to read N and H from the terminal and output to the terminal

proj SURNAME (**sel** (FIRSTNAME = N) **or** (HAIRCOLOUR = H) (PEOPLE))

(b) Write a program to read N and H from the terminal and output to the terminal

proj SURNAME (**sel** (FIRSTNAME = N) **and not** (HAIRCOLOUR = H) (PEOPLE))

(c) Let L and U be heights. Write a program to read H, L, and U from the terminal and output to the terminal

proj FIRSTNAME, SURNAME (**sel** (HAIRCOLOUR = H) **and** (HEIGHT > L) **and** (HEIGHT < U) (PEOPLE))

7 Implementation of joins

7.1. Hierarchical interfile indexes

To output the join of two artificially simple files FNAME1 and FNAME2

FNAME1

G	H
a	7
b	2
c	9
d	2
e	6
f	9

FNAME2

K	H
p	9
q	6
r	7
s	2
t	9

we could use

```
RESET (FNAME1);
repeat
  READ (FNAME1, FNAME1REC);
  RESET (FNAME2);
  repeat
    READ (FNAME2, FNAME2REC);
    if FNAME1REC.H = FNAME2REC.H then
    WRITELN (FNAME1REC.G, FNAME1REC.H,
      FNAME2REC.K)
  until EOF (FNAME2)
until EOF (FNAME1)
```

If, in a larger example, the two files contain thousands of records, then a nested loop like this will be intolerably slow. If the join is on a field that has the same sorted sequence in both files, e.g.

G	H
d	2
b	2
e	6
a	7
c	9
f	9

K	H
s	2
q	6
r	7
t	9
p	9

then we can improve efficiency by using a batch processing algorithm as in Section 5.3.2. However, it may be impractical to sort the two files into the required sequence.

Another idea is to provide FNAME2 with a secondary index on H. We can then use a routine like the following, to output the join:

```
RESET (FNAME1);
repeat
    READ (FNAME1, FNAME1REC);
    look up FNAME1REC.H in FNAME2 secondary index and hence do
    for each record of FNAME2 that contains this value of H do
        WRITELN (FNAME1REC.G, FNAME1REC.H, FNAME2REC.K)
until EOF (FNAME1)
```

By using the index we avoid wasting time in accessing FNAME2 records whose H value differs from that of the current FNAME1 record. This idea has advantages that we shall explain in Section 7.7. A disadvantage is that time is spent in finding owners in the index. We can avoid this expenditure of time by incorporating the member pointers directly into FNAME, as shown in Fig. 7.1.

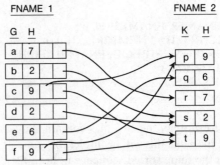

Fig. 7.1. A simple interfile index.

An outline of a routine to output the join is now

```
for each FNAME1 record do
for each member pointer in that record do
begin
    follow the pointer to the FNAME2 record;
    output the K field of this FNAME2 record together with the G and H
    fields of the current FNAME1 record
end
```

In Fig. 7.1 the member pointers are stored separately from the file to which they point, as in Section 6.2.1. Another possibility is that the member pointers are embedded in the file to which they point, as in Section 6.3.2. The essential idea is that with one file's data records we associate pointers to another file's data records. We call this provision of pointers an *interfile index*.

Price history example. We have previously used an interfile index in the price history example in Section 4.4 where each record in a simple inventory file pointed to a linked list of price and date records telling us what price became effective at what date. The data were not stored in files in first normal form in Section 4.4, but can easily be reorganized into first normal form as follows, using two files that we shall name INVENTORY and PRICES:

INVENTORY

ITEMREFNO	QUANTITYINSTOCK	SUPPLIERNO
124	18	23
131	9	55
133	75	23

PRICES

ITEMREFNO	DATE	PRICE
124	930612	12.30
124	920109	10.90
131	930526	9.40
131	930201	8.95
131	921001	8.50
131	920725	8.10
133	910701	50.00

The query 'give the dates of all price changes for items supplied by supplier number 23' can be expressed as

proj DATE (PRICES **join sel** SUPPLIERNO = 23 (INVENTORY))

A simple method of implementing this join by using the normalized files INVENTORY and PRICES would be to search the PRICES file linearly, seeking all ITEMREFNOs that are in **sel** SUPPLIERNO = 23 (INVENTORY). To avoid wasting time looking at PRICES records that do not contain sought ITEMREFNOs we can use an interfile such as that shown in Fig. 7.2. Each INVENTORY record now contains an array of pointers to PRICES records, and we can follow pointers to find the various prices of any given item without searching prices of irrelevant items. In this very small example the time that would otherwise be wasted looking at irrelevant PRICES records would be small, but in a more realistic example involving many thousands of records provision of an interfile index could greatly improve efficiency of implementation of the join.

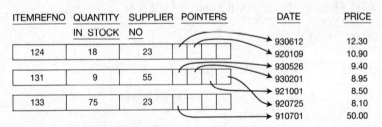

Fig. 7.2. An interfile index associating PRICES records with INVENTORY records.

Hierarchical inventory example. As another example we shall now develop the TOYINVEN example of Sections 5.5.2 and 5.6.1. We shall assume that each item in the TOYINVEN file is made of components that are listed in a further file that we shall name COMPONENTS. A few examples of records in the COMPONENTS file are as follows.

ITEMREFNO	PARTOF	QUANTITYINSTOCK
FT61	AA39	00006
FV04	AA39	00315
KA55	AQ01	00043
KN21	AA39	00031
KX39	AQ01	00050
LA18	BC59	00427

This tells us that the QUANTITYINSTOCK of ITEMREFNO FT61 is 6, the QUANTITYINSTOCK of ITEMREFNO FV04 is 315, and so on. Moreover, FT61, FV04, and KN21 are components of item AA39. KA55 and KX39 are components of item AQ01, and so on. Going a step further, we shall also introduce a file named SUBCOMPONENTS that tells us the ITEMREFNO and QUANTITYINSTOCK of subcomponents of components. A few examples of records in the SUBCOMPONENTS file are as follows.

ITEMREFNO	PARTOF	QUANTITYINSTOCK
PB12	FT61	00050
PB20	FT61	00043
PC81	FV04	00005
PD50	FV04	00100
PE31	FT61	00047

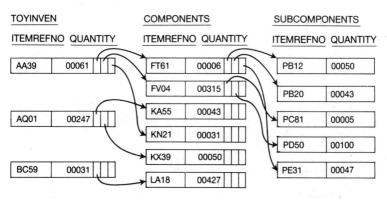

Fig. 7.3. Example of a hierarchical interfile index.

For simplicity we assume that no component is used in the construction of more than one item and that no subcomponent is used in the construction of more than one component. If AA39 is an item in the TOYINVEN file, we shall require at least two join operations to answer a query such as 'list the ITEMREFNO and QUANTITYIN-STOCK of every subcomponent of item AA39'. To speed up the answering of queries such as this, by avoiding the searching of irrelevant records, we can provide an interfile index structure of which Fig. 7.3 shows just a few records and pointers. It is easy to check that the pointers shown in Fig. 7.3 are consistent with the normalized versions of the three files. To find the ITEMREFNO and QUANTITYINSTOCK of every subcomponent of item AA39 we can efficiently use the interfile indexes as in the outline program

find TOYINVEN record that has ITEMREFNO = 'AA39';
for each member COMPONENT pointed to by this TOYINVEN record
do
for each SUBCOMPONENT pointed to by this COMPONENT record
    do WRITELN (SUBCOMPONENT.ITEMREFNO,
    SUBCOMPONENT.QUANTITYINSTOCK).

This hierarchical organization of interfile indexes is a very simple example of hierarchical database organization. In the history of the evolution of database technology, this was one of the first types of database organization to be proved commercially useful.

In Fig. 7.3 the pointers point from items to components to subcomponents, and do not help in answering queries such as 'of which item is PC81 a subcomponent?'. In the price history example we provided pointers from the simple INVENTORY file to the PRICES file. These pointers speed up a join operation for finding the dates associated with any given supplier number, but do not help at all with a join operation for finding all the suppliers who changed any price on a given date. In this sense the pointers only help with queries that go one way: from INVENTORY to PRICES. In Section 7.2 we shall consider two-way navigation.

7.2. Two-way interfile indexes

7.2.1. *Fansets*

Let us consider a file named HORSES, similar to that in Section 3.10.3,

HORSENAME	COLOUR	HEIGHT	DATEOFBIRTH	OWNERNAME
TRUNKCALL	BROWN	165	19890630	BEESON
HOTPOTATO	BLACK	170	19890212	GEESON
STRAWGOLD	BROWN	164	19881105	GEESON
OVERMOON	WHITE	171	19870305	AYSON
MOTORWAY	BLACK	168	19890130	BEESON
BESTMAN	BROWN	165	19880524	BEESON

and a simple filed named OWNERS

OWNERNAME	ADDRESS
AYSON	CLUMBERWICK
BEESON	WIGHAMSTEAD
GEESON	PLUMHAVEN

in which we luxuriously assume that no two owners have the same name and that addresses consist of one word. To speed up the processing of a query such as 'give the colours of horses whose owner's address is wighamstead'

proj COLOUR (HORSES **join sel** ADDRESS = 'WIGHAMSTEAD' (OWNERS))

we shall provide each OWNERS record with member pointers to all the HORSES records that it owns, in the style of Section 7.1. We shall now also provide each horses record with a pointer to owner, in the style of Section 6.3.2.1, to speed up the answering of a query such as 'give the name and address of every owner of a black horse':

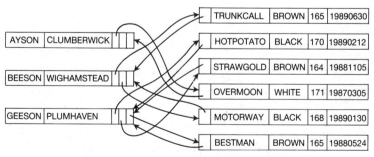

Fig. 7.4. A two-way interfile index structure.

proj OWNERNAME, ADDRESS (OWNERS **join sel**
COLOUR = 'BLACK' (HORSES))

The data structure differs from that in Section 7.1 in that there are
now pointers to owners, as well as pointers to members, as shown in
Fig. 7.4. An outline program to give the name and address of every
owner of a black horse is

for each horse in **sel** COLOUR = 'BLACK' (HORSES) **do**
begin
   follow pointer from horse to OWNER;
   WRITELN (OWNERS.OWNERNAME, OWNERS.ADDRESS)
end

By following the pointer from horse to owner, this program avoids
searching irrelevant owners. Working the other way, an outline
program to find the colour of every horse whose owner's address is
WIGHAMSTEAD is

for each owner whose address is WIGHAMSTEAD **do**
for each member horse to which this owner points **do**
   WRITELN (HORSES.COLOUR)

By following, in turn, pointers from an owner to this owner's horses,
this program avoids wasting time looking at irrelevant horses.

   Instead of storing a set of member pointers in each owner record,
as in Section 6.3.1, we can store the member pointers in the member
records, as in Section 6.3.2.2. For our example a ring structure is
shown in Fig. 7.5. To answer a query such as 'give the name and

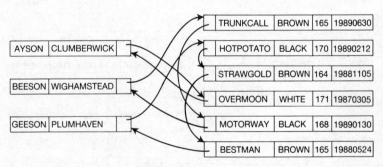

Fig. 7.5.   Ring implementation of a fanset.

address of every owner of a black horse' a ring structure is generally slower than a structure that gives each HORSES record a direct pointer to its owner, because to reach the owner we must now generally traverse a pointer chain via some irrelevant horses. The advantage of this ring structure is that in each record only one pointer is now associated with an owner; the overall total number of pointer fields in the entire structure has been reduced.

The relation between HORSES and OWNERS is many-to-one in our example. One owner can own many horses, but each horse is owned by exactly one owner. Interfile indexes for a many-to-one association of files are so important that special terms have been introduced for them. One of these terms is *set* but in this context *set* does not have its usual mathematical meaning. To avoid confusion with the usual mathematical meaning of the term *set*, the present text uses the alternative technical term *fanset* to mean the same thing. A *fanset* is a many-to-one interfile index structure consisting of owners that point to members and members that point back to their owners. The term *fanset* is used for such a structure whether it is implemented using rings or using member pointers that are not included in the file to which they point. *Fanset* is the general name of this structure, regardless of its implementation. For example, Figs 7.4 and 7.5 show two different implementations of the same fanset.

When we are working with many files linked by different fansets, we may wish to give names to the fansets, just as we give names to files. For example we shall give the name HORSEOWNERS to the fanset that associates HORSES with OWNERS.

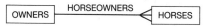

Fig. 7.6. Bachman diagram representing the fanset in Figs. 7.4 and 7.5.

We find it very useful to draw diagrams that show which files are associated by fansets, and show the owner and member files in each fanset. We represent a file by a rectangle containing the name of the file, and we represent a fanset by a line joining the files that it associates. We write the name of the fanset beside the line. We place a claw at the members end of the line, as shown in Fig. 7.6, to indicate which is the member and which is the owner file in the fanset. Other workers use an arrowhead or a circle instead of a claw, but a claw has the advantage that it diagrammatically represents the many-to-one relationship between members and owners. A diagram like this, showing files and fansets, is called a *Bachman diagram*. A Bachman diagram is a short-hand summary of a fanset data structure. For example Fig. 7.6 is a short-hand representation for the fanset shown in Figs 7.4 and 7.5.

7.2.2.   Implementation of many-to-many joins

7.2.2.1.   Without linkers

The following three simple normalized files respectively show CRUISES, PORTS, and VISITS of cruises to ports, as in Exercise 5 in Section 3.11.

CRUISES

CRUISE NUMBER	SHIP NAME	DEPARTURE DATE
1	SEAPRINCESS	840407
2	BRISTOLBELLE	840412
3	MARYROSE	840529
4	BRISTOLBELLE	840529
5	CASTLEQUEEN	840603
6	CASTLEQUEEN	840630
7	SEAPRINCESS	840630
8	MARYROSE	840719

VISITS

CRUISE NUMBER	PORT NAME
2	GIBRALTAR
3	GIBRALTAR
5	GIBRALTAR
7	GIBRALTAR
8	GIBRALTAR
2	MARSEILLES
3	MARSEILLES
6	MARSEILLES

		PORTS	
2	ALGIERS		
3	ALGIERS		
7	ALGIERS	PORT	HARBOUR
1	ALEXANDRIA	NAME	CHARGE
2	ALEXANDRIA		
3	ALEXANDRIA	GIBRALTAR	100
5	ALEXANDRIA	MARSEILLES	250
6	ALEXANDRIA	ALGIERS	150
4	PALERMO	ALEXANDRIA	150
6	PALERMO	PALERMO	200
7	PALERMO	ATHENS	250
8	PALERMO	ISTANBUL	150
1	ATHENS		
3	ATHENS		
5	ATHENS		
8	ATHENS		
1	ISTANBUL		
4	ISTANBUL		
8	ISTANBUL		

From the VISITS file we can see, for example, that CRUISE NUMBER 1 visits ALEXANDRIA, ATHENS, and ISTANBUL. The VISITS file expresses a many-to-many relationship between cruises and ports: each cruise visits many ports, and each port is visited by many cruises.

Two joins are required to answer a query such as 'give the names of all ports visited on any cruise by the MARYROSE'. To speed up the answering of such queries we can provide the CRUISES files with member pointers to PORTS and we can provide the PORTS file with member pointers to CRUISES, as shown in Fig. 7.7. In this structure, the record for CRUISE NUMBER 1 owns, and includes, member pointers to the ports visited by CRUISE NUMBER 1. These member pointers are not stored in the file to which they point. The GIBRALTAR port record owns and includes pointers to all the cruises that visit GIBRALTAR, and we can use this interfile index to find details of these cruises without looking at any cruise that does not visit GIBRALTAR. This interfile index structure is *not* a fanset because it implements a many-to-many association between CRUISES and PORTS, whereas by definition a fanset is a one-to-many interfile index. In Fig. 7.7 the index pointers express the same information as was expressed by the VISITS file, so that this file is no longer required. In fact there is a kind of duplication in this interfile

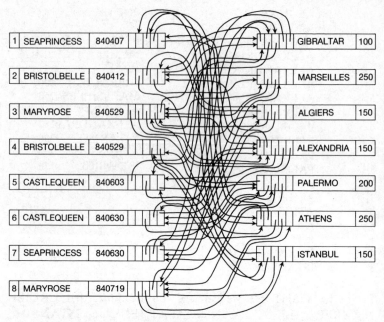

Fig. 7.7. An example of a many-to-many interfile index.

index structure; for example the CRUISE NUMBER 6 record has a member pointer to PALERMO, and the PALERMO record has a separate pointer to CRUISE NUMBER 6.

7.2.2.2. Linkers

In our interfile indexes for the CRUISES and PORTS example of Section 7.2.2.1, the member pointers were not stored in the records to which they point. If we wish to implement these indexes using rings, in order to reduce the overall total number of pointers stored in the system, we have to cope with the fact that each cruise record is owned by more than one port record and that each port record is owned by more than one cruise record. A difficulty arises because in a many-to-many association each member requires a pointer to more than one owner, possibly via an intermediate chain of other members. In this case straightforward ring implementation is impractical because we require more than one pointer per ring per record, and the number of pointers required in each record is variable. In the one-to-many case in Section 7.1 this problem did not arise, because each member had exactly one owner so that ring implementation with one pointer per ring per record was immediately practical.

To implement (two-way) many-to-many interfile indexes using rings, we can always decompose a many-to-many association into two associations, the first one-to-many and the second many-to-one. This involves introducing intermediate records that are called *linkers*. The rings and linkers for the CRUISES and PORTS are shown in Fig. 7.8. Each linker is owned by exactly one cruise and one port; this is why one pointer per record per ring is now sufficient. It is worth checking that these linker records correspond one to one to the records in the normalized VISITS file in Section

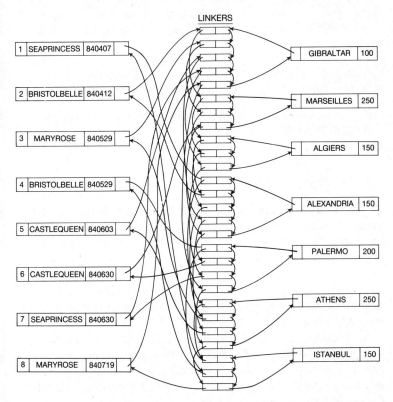

Fig. 7.8. Linkers to implement the many-to-many association between CRUISES and PORTS.

7.2.2.1, and indeed represent exactly the same information. The Bachman diagram shown in Fig. 7.9 is a summary representation of the data structure shown in Fig. 7.8. We are free to give the linkers any name that we please; for example we could name them VISITS instead of LINKERS.

Fig. 7.9. A Bachman diagram for the data structure shown in Fig. 7.8.

As an illustration of the use of linkers to implement joins, the query 'give the names of all ports visited on any cruise by the MARYROSE' could be answered by a program for which an outline is

for each cruise in **sel** SHIPNAME = 'MARYROSE' (CRUISES) **do**
for each linker (found by traversing the ring) owned by this cruise **do**
begin
   find (by traversing a ring) the PORTS record that owns this linker;
   WRITELN (PORTS.PORTNAME)
end.

7.2.2.3. *Linkers that have data fields*

In the example in Section 7.2.2.2 the linker records consist of two pointer fields, one for a ring owned by a CRUISES record and one for a ring owned by a PORTS record. We could easily develop this example so as to include the actual date of each visit of a cruise to a port. We could do this by giving each linker record a third field to store the date of the visit that the linker record represents. This third field would be an example of a data field in a linker record, which is generally a multilist record.

In practice it is common for linker records to have data fields as well as the pointer fields, and we now give an example using drastically simplified sales order detail, sales order header, and inventory records. In this example, normalized versions of the three fils would have the following fields.

INVENTORY	SALESORDERDETAIL	SALESORDERHEADER
ITEMREFNO	SALESORDERNO	SALESORDERNO
QUANTITYINSTOCK	ITEMREFNO	CUSTOMERNO
PRICEPERUNIT	QUANTITYORDERED	DATE
SUPPLIERNO		

Two joins may be required to answer a query such as 'give the CUSTOMERNO of every customer who has placed an order for item reference number 114':

proj CUSTOMER (SALESORDERHEADER **join**
  SALESORDERDETAIL **join sel** ITEMREFNO = 114
  (INVENTORY))

From a relational point of view we could select ITEMREFNO = 114 from SALESORDERDETAIL without using the INVENTORY file. This selection could be speeded up by providing SALESOR-DERDETAIL with a secondary index on ITEMREFNO. A more versatile idea is to replace owners in this index with INVENTORY records. Indeed we shall associate INVENTORY and SALESOR-DERDETAIL records by means of a fanset. Furthermore, to speed up joins of SALESORDERHEADER with SALESORDERDE-TAIL we shall associate these files by means of a second fanset, as indicated in Fig. 7.10. Figure 7.10 is a summary short-hand representation of a structure of records and pointers. Figure 7.11 is a very simple specific example of this structure, showing only a few records. In Fig. 7.11 SALESORDERDETAIL records are now linker records and include multilist pointers instead of ITEMREFNO and SALESORDERNO fields. To answer the query 'give the CUSTOMERNO of every customer who has a sales order for ITEMREFNO 114' an outline of a program is

Fig. 7.10. A Bachman diagram for the data structure shown in Fig. 7.11.

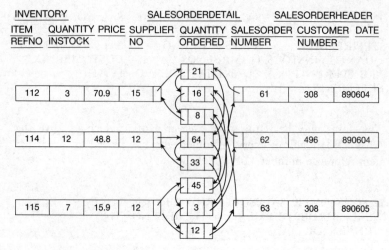

Fig. 7.11. Detailed pointer structure of fansets INCLUDED and
LINESOF.

FIND the INVENTORY record that has ITEMREFNO = 114;
for each SALESORDERDETAIL linker (found by traversing a ring)
   owned by this INVENTORY record **do**
with the SALESORDERHEADER record (found by traversing a ring)
   that owns this SALESORDERDETAIL linker **do**
   WRITELN (CUSTOMERNO)

This program may output the same CUSTOMERNO more than
once. In this and in subsequent examples we shall not worry about
elimination of duplicates. For our detailed example the output of the
program is actually 308. The FIND operation at the start of the
program randomly accesses the INVENTORY file using the primary key value 114; the access method depends on the organization of
the INVENTORY file, which might for example be hash organization.

   The implementation of joins going the other way is similar, as can
be seen in the following outline program to answer the example
query 'give the ITEMREFNO and DESCRIPTION of all items
ordered by CUSTOMER No 308':

for each record in **sel** CUSTOMERNO = 308 (SALESORDERHEADER)
   do
for each SALESORDERDETAIL linker (found by traversing a ring)
   owned by this SALESORDERHEADER record **do**

with the INVENTORY record (found by traversing a ring) that owns this SALESORDERDETAIL linker **do** WRITELN (ITEMREFNO, DESCRIPTION)

If the SALESORDERHEADER file has been provided with a secondary index on CUSTOMERNO then this index can be used to speed up the initial selection operation. Otherwise this selection operation can be done by linear search through SALESORDER-HEADER records seeking CUSTOMERNO = 308.

It is useful to show a secondary index in a Bachman diagram as a fanset owned by (for example) a black dot. If there is indeed a secondary index on CUSTOMERNO then the Bachman diagram shown in Fig. 7.10 should be amended as shown in Fig. 7.12.

Fig. 7.12.   A Bachman diagram showing that SALESORDERHEADER has a secondary index on CUSTOMERNO.

Hitherto we have assumed in our examples that a fanset is implemented by means of rings. An essential characteristic of a fanset is that we *must be able* to implement it using rings with one pointer per record per ring, but we are *not compelled* to implement it that way. Instead we can implement a fanset by storing member pointers in a B-tree field in an owner record and providing each member data record with a pointer to its owner in the fanset. This generally uses more storage space than ring implementation would use, but provides faster access because there is no need to traverse chains of members. Another advantage of using B-trees is that we can use procedures INSERT, FINDKEY, etc.

Using B-tree implementation of fansets, we shall now program the foregoing example in detail, omitting secondary indexes. It is convenient to use B-tree organization for access to the INVEN-TORY file and the SALESORDERHEADER file. If, for example, we were to store INVENTORY records in B-tree leaf blocks, these records would move physically as a result of insertions and de-letions, and the pointer-to-owner pointers in the SALESORDER-DETAIL linkers would have to be updated accordingly which

would not be practical. We use a dense primary index for the
INVENTORY file to avoid this problem of pinning, and we use a
dense primary index for the SALESORDERHEADER file for the
same reason. A DBD is

```
DBDNAME HD;
type
    REFRANGE = 100..140; SONRANGE = 50..99;
    INVPTR = ↑INVTYPE; SOHPTR = ↑SOHTYPE;
    DETAILPOINTER = ↑SODETAIL;
    INVLEAF = record {for primary index of INVENTORY}
                    ITEMREFNO: REFRANGE;
                    POINTER: INVPTR
               end;
    SOHLEAF = record {for primary index of SALESORDERHEADER}
                    SALESORDERNUMBER: SONRANGE;
                    POINTER: SOHPTR
               end;
    SODETAIL = record {linker}
                    INCLUDED: INVPTR; {pointer to owner in
                        INVENTORY}
                    QUANTITYORDERED: INTEGER;
                    LINESOF: SOHPTR {pointer to owner in
                        SALESORDERHEADER}
               end;
    SOMEMBER = BTREE of DETAILPOINTER;
    INVTYPE = record {INVENTORY record type}
                    ITEMREFNO: REFRANGE:
                    QUANTITYINSTOCK: INTEGER;
                    PRICEPERUNIT: REAL;
                    SUPPLIERNO: 10..99;
                    INCLUDED: SOMEMBER {points to linkers that this
                        record owns}
               end;
    SOHTYPE = record {SALESORDERHEADER record type}
                    SALESORDERNUMBER: SONRANGE;
                    CUSTOMERNUMBER: 100..999;
                    DATE: 880101..920101;
                    LINESOF: SOMEMBER {points to linkers that this
                        record owns}
               end;
var
    INVPRIMARY = BTREE of INVLEAF on ITEMREFNO;
    SOHPRIMARY = BTREE of SOHLEAF on
    SALESORDERNUMBER;
finish
```

We have given the names INCLUDED and LINESOF to the two fansets, and we use these names for the fields that implement these fansets. For example the INCLUDED field of an INVENTORY record is a B-tree of member pointers to SALESORDERDETAIL linkers for sales order detail lines for this ITEMREFNO. The INCLUDED field of a linker record is a pointer to the INVEN-TORY record for the item that the sales order detail line specifies.

Before we can use a database structure to answer queries we must of course enter data into the structure. One way of doing this is by reading data directly from the terminal. Another way is by reading from a standard sequential file. The following program reads INVENTORY records from a text file: we have chosen to work with a text file because in this example the programming is simpler than for a binary file.

```
program ENTERINV (INVENTORY, OUTPUT);
invoke HD;
var
  NEWINVPTR: INVPTR;
  NEWLEAF: INVLEAF:
  INVENTORY: TEXT;
begin
  STARTTRANSACTION (UNRESTRICTED);
  RESET (INVENTORY);
  while not EOF (INVENTORY) and (DBSTATUS = OKAY) do
  begin
    CREATE (NEWINVPTR);
    with NEWINVPTR↑ do READLN (INVENTORY, ITEMREFNO,
    QUANTITYINSTOCK, PRICEPERUNIT, SUPPLIERNO);
      NEWLEAF.ITEMREFNO: = NEWINVPTR↑.ITEMREFNO;
      NEWLEAF.POINTER: = NEWINVPTR;
      INSERT (INVPRIMARY, NEWLEAF)
  end;
  if DBSTATUS = OKAY then ENDTRANSACTION else
  begin
    WRITELN ('insert ITEMREFNO ',NEWINVPTR↑.ITEMREFNO,
    'failed');
    ABORTTRANSACTION
  end
end.
```

A program to read SALESORDERHEADER records would be similar to this, and we shall not give details. If SALESORDER-

HEADER records have already been input, the following program reads SALESORDERDETAIL records from a text file and creates a linker corresponding to each order line.

```
program ENTERDETAIL (SALESORDERDETAIL, OUTPUT);
invoke HD;
var
  ITEMREFNO: REFRANGE;
  SALESORDERNUMBER: SONRANGE;
  NEWLINKERPTR: DETAILPTR;
  INVLEAFPTR: ↑INVLEAF;
  SOHLEAFPTR: ↑SOHLEAF;
  ITEMPTR: INVPTR;
  HEADERPTR: SOHPTR;
  NOPROBLEM: BOOLEAN;
  SALESORDERDETAIL: TEXT;
begin
  STARTTRANSACTION (UNRESTRICTED);
  RESET (SALESORDERDETAIL); NOPROBLEM: = TRUE;
  while not EOF (SALESORDERDETAIL) and NOPROBLEM do
  begin
    CREATE (NEWLINKERPTR); {create a new linker record}
    READ (SALESORDERDETAIL, ITEMREFNO,
    SALESORDERNUMBER,
    NEWLINKERPTR↑.QUANTITYORDERED);
    FINDKEY (INVPRIMARY, ITEMREFNO, INVLEAFPTR);
    if DBSTATUS < > OKAY then
    begin
      WRITELN ('ITEMREFNO ', ITEMREFNO, ' not found');
      NOPROBLEM: = FALSE; DBSTATUS: = OKAY
    and else
    begin
      ITEMPTR: = INVLEAFPTR↑.POINTER; {pointer to
      INVENTORY record}
      INSERT (ITEMPTR↑.INCLUDED, NEWLINKERPTR); {insert
      pointer to member}
      NEWLINKERPTR↑.INCLUDED: = ITEMPTR;
    end;
    FINDKEY (SOHPRIMARY, SALESORDERNUMBER,
    SOHLEAFPTR);
    if DBSTATUS < > OKAY then
    begin
      WRITELN ('SALES ORDER NUMBER ',
      SALESORDERNUMBER, ' not found');
      NOPROBLEM: = FALSE; DBSTATUS: = OKAY
```

```
    end else
    begin
      SOHPTR: = SOHLEAFPTR↑.POINTER; {pointer to
      SALESORDERHEADER record}
      INSERT (SOHPTR↑.LINES OF, NEWLINKERPTR); {insert
      pointer to member}
      NEWLINKERPTR↑.LINES OF: = SOHPTR {insert pointer to
      owner}
    end
  end;
  if NOPROBLEM then ENDTRANSACTION else
  ABORTTRANSACTION
end.
```

As an example of a program that uses fansets to implement joins, the following program reads an ITEMREFNO from the terminal and outputs the CUSTOMERNUMBER of every customer for whom there is an order for this item.

```
program WHOORDEREDITEM (INPUT, OUTPUT);
invoke HD;
var
  INVLEAFPTR: ↑INVLEAF;
  MEMBERPTR: DETAILPTR;
  WHICHITEM: REFRANGE;
  ITEMPTR: INVPTR;
begin
  STARTTRANSACTION (READONLY);
  WRITELN ('Please type item reference number');
  READLN (WHICHITEM);
  FINDKEY (INVPRIMARY, WHICHITEM, INVLEAFPTR);
  if DBSTATUS = NOTFOUND then WRITELN ('item not found') else
  begin
    ITEMPTR: = INVLEAFPTR↑.POINTER;
    FINDFIRST (ITEMPTR↑.INCLUDED, MEMBERPTR);
    if DBSTATUS = NOTFOUND then
      WRITELN ('there are no orders for this item')
    else
    repeat
      WRITELN
      (MEMBERPTR↑.LINESOF↑.CUSTOMERNUMBER);
      FINDSUCC (ITEMPTR↑.INCLUDED, MEMBERPTR)
    until DBSTATUS < >OKAY
  end;
  ENDTRANSACTION
end.
```

For simplicity this program does not eliminate duplicate output customer numbers, nor does the next program eliminate duplicates. The next program, which reads a customer number from the terminal and outputs the ITEMREFNO and descriptions of all items ordered by this customer, is more complicated because CUSTOMERNUMBER is a secondary key and we have not provided a secondary index.

```
program ITEMSORDEREDBYCUS (INPUT, OUTPUT);
invoke HD;
var
   SOHLEAFPTR: ↑SOHLEAF; HEADERPTR: SOHPTR;
   MEMBERPTR: DETAILPTR;
   WHICHCUST: 100..999 {CUSTOMERNUMBER range}
begin
   STARTTRANSACTION (READONLY);
   WRITELN ('type customer number'); READLN (WHICHCUST);
   FINDFIRST (SOHPRIMARY, SOHLEAFPTR);
   if DBSTATUS = NOTFOUND then WRITELN ('there are no orders')
   else
   repeat
     if
     SOHLEAFPTR↑.POINTER↑.CUSTOMERNUMBER = WHICHCUST
     then
     begin
       HEADERPTR: = SOHLEAFPTR↑.POINTER;
       FINDFIRST (HEADERPTR↑.LINESOF, MEMBERPTR);
       if DBSTATUS = OKAY then
       repeat
         with MEMBERPTR↑.INCLUDED↑ do
         WRITELN (ITEMREFNO, DESCRIPTION);
         FINDSUCC (HEADERPTR↑.LINESOF, MEMBERPTR)
       until DBSTATUS < > OKAY; DBSTATUS: = OKAY;
     end;
     FINDSUCC (SOHPRIMARY, SOHLEAFPTR);
   until DBSTATUS < > OKAY;
   ENDTRANSACTION
end.
```

7.2.2.4. *Fanset implementation of the music database*

As an example of a database structure incorporating many fansets, we now introduce a simple implementation of the music database of Section 2.2. In this implementation we give the MUSICIANS file an index on MNAME, the COMPOSITIONS file an index in TITLE, and the ENSEMBLES file an index on ENAME. There is no means of accessing the data except via these indexes. Figure 7.13 is a Bachman diagram for this structure. This structure assumes, as in Section 2.2, that each PERFORMANCES record gives details of the performance of exactly one composition. Owing to this assumption, each PERFORMANCES record has exactly one COMPOSITIONS owner in the PERFORMED fanset. Note that ENSEMBLE-MEMBERS is a linker, and that PERFORMANCES is a three-way linker.

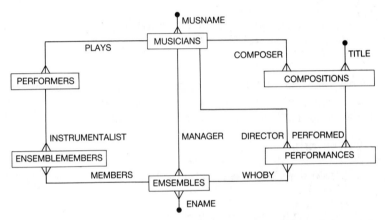

Fig. 7.13. Bachman diagram for a fanset implementation of the music database.

The following is an outline of a program to answer to the query 'give the names of all performers in THE CEES' which assumes, for simplicity, that there is only one ensemble named THE CEES.

find ENSEMBLES record that has ENAME = 'THE CEES';
for each ENSEMBLE MEMBERS record owned in fanset MEMBERS by this ENSEMBLES record **do**
begin
    find the owner PERFORMERS record in the INSTRUMENTALIST fanset;
    find the MUSICIANS record that owns this PERFORMERS record in the PLAYS fanset;
    WRITELN (MUSICIANS.MNAME)
end.

This example uses three fansets to speed up three joins, and the same is true of the next example, which answers the query 'give the names of all ensembles that have performed any composition by AYEFSKY', assuming for simplicity that there is only one musician named AYEFSKY.

```
find MUSICIANS record that has MNAME = 'AYEFSKY';
for each COMPOSITIONS record owned in COMPOSER fanset by this
MUSICIANS record do
for each PERFORMANCES record owned in PERFORMED fanset by
this COMPOSITIONS record do
begin
   find owner in WHOBY fanset for this PERFORMANCES record;
   WRITELN (ENSEMBLES.ENAME)
end.
```

The following is a DBD for this database structure. As before, we use the name of a fanset for the field that is a pointer to owner and for the field that is a B-tree of pointers to member.

```
DBNAME MU;
type
   STRING12 = packed array [1..12] of CHAR;
   DATETYPE = 15000101..19991231;
   TOMUSICIANS = ↑MUSICIANS;
   TOPERFORMERS = ↑PERFORMERS;
   TOENSEMBLEMEMBERS = ↑ENSEMBLEMEMBERS;
   TOENSEMBLES = ↑ENSEMBLES;
   TOCOMPOSITIONS = ↑COMPOSITIONS;
   TOPERFORMANCES = ↑PERFORMANCES;
   MUSICIANSLEAF = record
                    MNAME: STRING12;
                    POINTER: TOMUSICIANS
                 end;
   COMPOSITIONSLEAF = record
                    TITLE: STRING12;
                    POINTER: TOCOMPOSITIONS
                 end;
   ENSEMBLESLEAF = record
                    ENAME: STRING12;
                    POINTER: TOENSEMBLES
                 end;
   MUSICIANS = record
                    MNAME: STRING12;
```

```
                    BDATE: DATETYPE;
                    BCOUNTRY: STRING12;
                    PLAYS: BTREE of TOPERFORMERS;
                    MANAGER: BTREE of TOENSEMBLES;
                    DIRECTOR: BTREE of TOPERFORMANCES
                end;
PERFORMERS = record
                    INSTRUMENT, GRADE: STRING12;
                    PLAYS: TOMUSICIANS;
                    INSTRUMENTALIST: BTREE of
                    TOENSEMBLEMEMBERS
                end;
ENSEMBLEMEMBERS = record
                    INSTRUMENTALIST:
                    TOPERFORMERS;
                    MEMBERS: TOENSEMBLES
                end;
ENSEMBLES = record
                    ENAME, ECOUNTRY: STRING12;
                    MANAGER: TOMUSICIANS;
                    MEMBERS: BTREE of
                    TOENSEMBLEMEMBERS;
                    WHOBY: BTREE of TOPERFORMANCES
                end;
COMPOSITIONS = record
                    TITLE: STRING12;
                    CDATE: DATETYPE;
                    COMPOSER: TOMUSICIANS;
                    PERFORMED: BTREE of
                    TOPERFORMANCES
                end;
PERFORMANCES = record
                    PDATE: DATETYPE;
                    TOWN, COUNTRY: STRING12;
                    DIRECTOR: TOMUSICIANS;
                    PERFORMED: TOCOMPOSITIONS;
                    WHOBY: TOENSEMBLES
                end;
var
    MUSNAMEINDEX = BTREE of MUSLEAF on MNAME;
    TITLEINDEX = BTREE of COMPOSITIONLEAF on TITLE;
    ENSEMBLEINDEX = BTREE of ENSEMBLESLEAF on ENAME;
finish.
```

The three indexes are in fact secondary indexes, because MNAME,

TITLE, and ENAME are not unique. We can, if required, distinguish between musicians who have the same name by accessing the index using FINDKEY (MUSNAMEINDEX, MNAME, MUSLEAFPTR) and then using FINDSUCC (MUSNAMEINDEX, MUSLEAFPTR) to check other fields of MUSICIANS records that have the same MNAME.

The programming of reading data into this database is more complicated than in our previous example, and we shall not give details. We shall now assume that the database has already been *loaded*, which means that it has had data inserted into it. The following program outputs the names of all musicians who play in an ensemble named THE CEES, assuming for simplicity that only one ensemble has this name:

```
program PLAYSINCEES (OUTPUT);
invoke MU;
var
   ENSEMBLESLEAFPTR: ↑ENSEMBLESLEAF;
   ENSEMBLESPTR: TOENSEMBLES;
   MEMBERSPTR: TOENSEMBLEMEMBERS:
begin
   STARTTRANSACTION (READONLY);
   FINDKEY (ENSEMBLEINDEX, 'THE CEES ',
   ENSEMBLESLEAFPTR);
   if DBSTATUS < > OKAY then WRIETLN ('not found') else
   begin
      ENSEMBLESPTR: = ENSEMBLESLEAFPTR↑.POINTER;
      FINDFIRST (ENSEMBLESPTR↑.MEMBERS, MEMBERSPTR);
      repeat
         WRITELN
         (MEMBERSPTR↑.INSTRUMENTALIST↑.PLAYS↑.MNAME);
         FINDSUCC (ENSEMBLESPTR↑.MEMBERS, MEMBERSPTR)
      until DBSTATUS < > OKAY
   end;
   ENDTRANSACTION
end.
```

The following program outputs the names of all ensembles who have played any composition composed by AYEFSKY, assuming for simplicity that there is only one musician called AYEFSKY:

```
program HASPLAYEDAYEFSKY (OUTPUT);
invoke MU;
```

```
var
  MUSICIANSLEAFPTR: ↑MUSICIANSLEAF:
  MUSICIANSPTR: TOMUSICIANS;
  COMPOSITIONSPTR: TOCOMPOSITIONS:
  PERFORMANCESPTR: TOPERFORMANCES;
begin
  STARTTRANSACTION (READONLY):
  FINDKEY (MUSNAMEINDEX, 'AYEFSKY ',
  MUSICIANSLEAFPTR);
  if DBSTATUS < > OKAY then WRITELN ('AYEFSKY not found')
  else
  begin
    MUSICIANSPTR: = MUSICIANSLEAFPTR↑.POINTER:
    FINDFIRST (MUSICIANSPTR↑.COMPOSER,
    COMPOSITIONSPTR);
    while DBSTATUS = OKAY do
    begin
      FINDFIRST (COMPOSITIONSPTR↑.PERFORMED,
      PERFORMANCESPTR);
      while DBSTATUS = OKAY do
      begin
        WRITELN (PERFORMANCESPTR↑.WHOBY↑.ENAME);
        FINDSUCC (COMPOSITIONSPTR↑.PERFORMED,
        PERFORMANCESPTR)
      end;
      DBSTATUS: = OKAY;
      FINDSUCC (MUSICIANSPTR↑.COMPOSER,
      COMPOSITIONSPTR)
    end;
  end;
  ENDTRANSACTION
end.
```

This program may output the same ensemble name more than once. From the point of view of programming, a simple way of eliminating duplicate output names is not to output them directly, but instead to insert them into a B-tree if they are not already in it. FINDKEY tells us whether a given name is already in the B-tree. At the end of the program we can output the names from the B-tree in sorted order, with no duplicates.

7.3. Exercises

1. (a) For the fixtures example in Section 3.10.2, draw a Bachman diagram

showing a fanset for implementing joins of the files MATCHES and
GROUNDS.

(b) Write an outline of a program that uses this fanset to answer the
query 'what is the distance from Bigchester to the ground of the match on
date 19890317?'.

(c) Write an outline of a program that uses this fanset to answer the
query 'on what dates are there matches at grounds that have crowd
capacities that exceed 50000?'.

2. (a) For the horses, owners, and jockeys example at the end of Section
3.10.3, draw a Bachman diagram showing fansets associating owners with
horses, as in Section 7.2.1, and also associating horses with jockeys via a
linker HASRIDDEN.

(b) Write an outline of a program using this database to answer the query
'give the names of owners of all horses that have been ridden by jockey
HOBSON'. In this and in subsequent exercises do not worry about
elimination of duplicates in the output.

(c) Write an outline of a program using this database to answer the query
'give the names of all jockeys who have ridden any horse owned by
GEESON'.

3. (a) For the library example in Section 3.10.2, draw a Bachman diagram
for a database using fansets.

(b) Write an outline of a program to read a library ticket number from
the terminal, to identify a borrower, and output for each book on loan to
this borrower the title, author, and the name of the branch from which the
book was borrowed.

(c) Write an outline of a program to read an author name and book title
from the terminal and output the name and library ticket number of every
borrower to whom a book having this author name and title is on loan.

4. (a) For Exercise 3 in Section 3.8, draw a Bachman diagram for a
database using fansets.

(b) Write a DBD for this database.

(c) Write a Pascal DML program to load the data from Exercise 3 in
Section 3.8 via your terminal into the database.

(d) Write a Pascal DML program using this database to read a name
from the terminal and, for all drinks had by this person, output the name
of the drink and the cost per glass. In this exercise and in (e) assume that
no two people have the same name.

(e) Write a Pascal DML program to read a name from the terminal and output the total cost of all drinks taken by the person who has this name.

5. Using the music database **DBD MU** of Section 7.2.2.4, write Pascal DML programs to perform the following functions.

(a) Output the title and composition date of each composition by AYEFSKY. Along with the title, your program should also output the total number of performances of this composition.

(b) Output the name and country of every ensemble that includes at least three performers.

(c) Output the name of the manager of every ensemble that includes at least three performers.

(d) Output the name of every ensemble in which at least one of the performers has composed at least one composition.

(e) Output the name of every ensemble that includes a saxophone and a clarinet.

(f) Output the name of every musician who has no compositions.

(g) Output the name of every musician who has composed at least one composition or directed at least one performance (or both).

(h) Output the name of every musician who has directed a performance of at least one of his own compositions.

(i) Output the composition title and the name of the composer of every composition of which there is exactly one performance.

(j) Output the name of every ensemble that has performed all the compositions of AYEFSKY.

(k) Output the title of every composition for an ensemble that includes a saxophone.

7.4. CODASYL DBTG

7.4.1. *Introduction*

Indexes, fansets, and direct-access (e.g. hash) methods provide *access paths* that can speed up selection and join operations. When we introduced relational algebra in Chapter 2 we were concerned only with composing correct expressions to answer queries, and not at all with access paths that might improve efficiency. We shall use the term *relational database* to mean a collection of files for which the access paths are invisible to the programmer: the music files in Section 2.2 constitute an example of a relational database, and the

Typico files in Chapter 1 constitute another example. Practical relational databases have query languages that can be used without knowledge of access paths, and relational algebra is a very simple example of such a language.

In the sense explained in Section 4.1 we can regard a relational query language, such as relational algebra, as being at a higher level than Pascal DML because in Pascal DML we are explicitly concerned with access paths which are invisible in relational algebra. Pascal DML is, however, at a considerably higher level than a language that does not have in-built procedures such as INSERT and FINDKEY. The internal working of such procedures is deliberately invisible to the Pascal DML programmer. A language in which such working was visible to the programmer would be at a lower level than Pascal DML.

Pascal DML can be used to answer queries that can be expressed in relational algebra, and indeed many of the exercises in Section 6.7 were concerned with translating relational algebra expressions into Pascal DML, just as a Pascal program might be translated into a sequence of primitive instructions as in Section 4.1. One reason why we may wish to write directly in Pascal DML is to gain control of the detailed answering of a query, hoping thereby to achieve greater efficiency than would be attained if we delegated to the system the detailed implementation of an expression in a relational query language. Another reason is that we can use the full capabilities of Pascal in answering queries, thus overcoming limitations such as those mentioned in Section 2.17. In Section 7.3, Exercises 4(e), 5(a), 5(b), and 5(c) were examples of queries that could be answered in Pascal DML but not in relational algebra. If, to answer such queries, we upgrade the capabilities of a relational query language, we may compound the difficulty of learning to use it.

Pascal DML is a deliberately simple member of a family of DMLs. A more sophisticated and commercially important example is that developed by CODASYL. CODASYL is an acronym for *C*onference on *D*ata *Sy*stem *L*anguages. One of the early achievements of CODASYL was the production of COBOL, which is an important commercial programming language. Subsequently CODASYL set up a database task group, known as DBTG, which in 1971 produced an influential report prescribing database facilities. Subsequent reports recommended various amendments and enhancements, resulting in a family of database systems known generically as CODASYL DBMS. DBMS stands for database management system.

A CODASYL DBMS uses fansets. A very important difference between CODASYL DML and Pascal DML is that CODASYL does not expect the programmer to program explicitly with pointers. Avoidance of explicit pointers is intended to make programming easier and somewhat closer to natural English. Instead of explicit pointers, CODASYL systems use *currency indicators* which are pointers that the programmer does not handle explicitly. A currency indicator indicates which record is currently being processed. In Pascal DML when we have programmed the use of fansets we have sometimes associated a pointer with a record type, and we have sometimes associated a pointer with a fanset. For example in the program ENTERDETAIL in Section 7.2.2.3 we associated the pointer ITEMPTR with the INVENTORY file and used this pointer to point to the INVENTORY record that was currently being processed. ITEMPTR is like a currency indicator because its value tells us which INVENTORY record is currently being processed. Similarly, in the program WHOORDEREDITEM in Section 7.2.2.3 the pointer MEMBERPTR shows which is the current member in the fanset INCLUDED. In CODASYL DBMS the system automatically provides a separate currency indicator for each record type and for each fanset.

7.4.2. CODASYL schemas

7.4.2.1. DDL

We declare a CODASYL database by writing a *schema*, which is analogous to a Pascal DBD. A schema looks like an elaboration of the declaration part of a COBOL program, just as a Pascal DBD looks like the declaration part of a Pascal program. The language in which a schema is written is known as a *data description language*, commonly abbreviated to DDL. A serviceable introduction to CODASYL DDL and DML would take at least a hundred pages, and the reader is referred to specialist texts. We shall merely note some points of principle, and we shall defer until Section 8.5 the introduction of the idea of a subschema.

7.4.2.2.   Record-type declarations.

A CODASYL schema declares record types and fansets in which
pointer fields are not visible to the programmer. A record type
declaration resembles a Pascal record type declaration, but also
gives further details. An important detail is the *location* mode, which
may be CALC, or VIA, or DIRECT. We can think of the records of
a given type as constituting a file: the *location mode* specifies the kind
of organization of this file.

   Location mode CALC means that the file is a direct access file,
typically a hash file. If the location mode is CALC the programmer
is obliged to specify the key fields, and whether duplicate key values
are allowed or not allowed. (The term CALC comes from *address
CALCulation*.)

   Location mode VIA means that the file will only be accessible via
fansets, and the name of one such fanset must be specified. For
example in Section 7.2.2.4 PERFORMERS records are accessible
VIA the fanset PLAYS.

   Location mode DIRECT means that access will be via a pointer
stored in a specified location. This pointer is not regarded as a
pointer, but instead as a *database key*, which practically amounts to
the same thing.

7.4.2.3.   Fanset-type declarations.

In a Pascal DBD a fanset is not explicitly declared like a record type.
A CODASYL schema differs in that each fanset is declared as a type
that has a name and also has an ORDER, an OWNER, and at least
one MEMBER record type.

   The ORDER of a fanset is the order in which members would be
found by FINDFIRST, FINDSUCC, FINDSUCC, ... in an
equivalent Pascal system. The programmer can specify whether the
members are sorted on a sort key, or whether the order is determined
in some other way. Members that have the same sort-key value are
known as *duplicates*. If the programmer specifies a sort-key, he must
also specify whether duplicates are allowed and, if so, whether newly
inserted duplicates should be inserted before or after existing
duplicates. If the programmer does not specify a sort key he must
instead specify whether newly inserted members are to be inserted at
the beginning or end of the fanset, or before or after the *current*

member of the fanset. Here *current* means 'pointed at by the fanset's currency indicator'.

In Pascal DML, if we use FINDKEY to find a key value in a member of a fanset, the key value can be regarded as a *search key*. In a CODASYL schema we can give a fanset a search key and a sort key that are not the same.

The OWNER of a fanset may either be SYSTEM or a specified record type. If the owner is SYSTEM this means that the fanset will be used as an index, like the TITLE index in Section 7.2.2.4. A fanset declaration may specify by what means an OWNER record will be found when used by DML procedures. As well as specifying the OWNER of each fanset, the schema also specifies at least one MEMBER record type, which is the record type of the fanset's members.

A MEMBER can be declared to be either MANDATORY or OPTIONAL. MANDATORY means that once a MEMBER has been inserted into a fanset it cannot be removed by a DML program. OPTIONAL means that it can be removed.

A MEMBER can also be declared to be either AUTOMATIC or MANUAL. AUTOMATIC means that when a new MEMBER record is CREATED it will automatically be inserted into the fanset. MANUAL means that insertion is not automatic, and can instead be done, if and when required, by a DML program.

An essential characteristic of a fanset is that we must be able to implement it by means of rings, but there are CODASYL systems which actually implement fansets by means of B-trees, as in Pascal DML. A schema writer is not free to choose between rings and B-trees, and indeed the choice between rings and B-trees is invisible in CODASYL DDL and DML.

7.4.2.4. *How to design a CODASYL database.*

Like a Pascal DBD, a CODASYL schema is an expression of the design of a database. A design process whereby we arrive at a CODASYL schema is fairly similar to that whereby we produce a Pascal DBD using fansets, as in Section 7.2.2.3 or 7.2.2.4. An outline of a typical design process is as follows.

(a) Start by designing normalized files as in Section 3.11. Check that these files contain all the required information. Draw a

Bachman diagram showing only the files, initially without fansets.
(b) In the Bachman diagram, write CALC beside every file to
which random access is likely to be required.
(c) Introduce fansets to implement commonly required joins, and
show these in the Bachman diagram.
(d) Introduce secondary indexes for all secondary keys to which
access will frequently be required, and show these indexes in the
Bachman diagram.
(e) Working from the Bachman diagram and from knowledge of
fields of files designed in (a), write a detailed schema or Pascal
DBD.

By way of example we shall now design a database to record
details concerning advertisements. Marketing companies sign contracts with advertising agencies to produce advertisements and
arrange publication in journals (including newspapers). Advertising
agencies subcontract the graphical design of advertisements to
individual artists. The database contains names and addresses of
artists, agencies, journal publishers, and companies who are marketing the products that are advertised. For contracts between companies and agencies, and between agencies and artists, the date of
signing the contract, the date of completion of the work, and details
of the work are recorded. For contracts between companies and
agencies these details include the item reference number and description of the product, category of the market (e.g. consumer, commercial electronic, commercial transport, etc.), and the payment agreed.
For contracts between agencies and artists the details include the
contract number of the contract between the agency and the
company, the physical dimensions of the published advertisement,
the colours available, a code indicating the required style of the
graphic design, and the artist's fee.

Each advertisement may be published one or more times in one or
more journals. Each such publication is a *placement*. The journal,
date, and cost of each placement are recorded, along with the names
of the journals, their frequency of publication, and the names of
their publishers. A publisher may publish more than one journal.

From an analysis in terms of entities, relations and attributes we
see that the following collection of files would be plausible for a
relational database. For each file we give a list of field names that are
intended to be self-explanatory.

COMPANY	AGENCY	ARTIST	PUBLISHER
COMPNO	AGENO	ARTNO	PUBNO
COMPNAME	AGENAME	ARTNAME	PUBNAME
COMPADDRESS	AGEADDRESS	ARTADDRESS	PUBADDRESS

PRODUCT

ITEMREFNO {assumed unique}
COMPNO {of marketing company}
DESCRIPTION
MARKETCATEGORY {e.g.
  consumer}

JOURNAL

JOURNALNO
JOURNALNAME
PUBNO {to identify publisher}
FREQUENCY {of publication}

AGENCYCONTRACT

AGENTCONTRACTNO
ITEMREFNO
CONTRACTDATE
COMPLETIONDATE
AGENO
AMOUNTPAYABLETOAGENCY

ARTISTCONTRACT

ARTCONTRACTNO
AGENTCONTRACTNO
CONTRACTDATE
COMPLETIONDATE
DIMENSIONS
COLOURS
STYLE
ARTNO
FEE

ADVERTISEMENT

ADVERTNO
ARTCONTRACTNO

PLACEMENT

ADVERTNO
JOURNALNO
DATE
COST

We can now draw a Bachman diagram for this by drawing one rectangle for each file and by showing a fanset linking each pair of files that have a common field on which there are likely to be joins. We can see which way round each fanset should be by checking whether it is a one-to-many or a many-to-one association. For example, one publisher generally publishes many journals, and one artist generally has many contracts. One artist contract may result in more than one advertisement, which may have more then one placement. In the Bachman diagram shown in Fig. 7.14 we have included a fanset from PRODUCT to ADVERTISEMENT in the expectation that we shall frequently wish to access all the advertisements for a given product. In our relational database this access would involve joining PRODUCT with AGENCYCONTRACT with ARTISTCONTRACT with ADVERTISEMENT. If we tried to shorten this route by including an ITEMREFNO field in the ADVERTISEMENT file, this file would not be third normal form because ITEMREFNO would be functionally dependent on the non-key field ARTCONTRACTNO, although in practice this might not matter. DESCRIPTION is not a candidate key of the PRODUCT file, because more than one product may have the same DESCRIPTION, e.g. MICROWAVE OVEN. To access advertisements for all products that have the same DESCRIPTION we could provide the PRODUCT file with a secondary index on DESCRIPTION. Alternatively, instead of providing this index, we can make PRODUCT a hash file with DESCRIPTION as the hash key and be prepared for duplicate values of the DESCRIPTION field. This is what we have done in Fig. 7.14, which is why the PRODUCT file is marked CALC. We have also made JOURNAL, as well as PUBLISHER, a CALC file because often we shall wish to access a JOURNAL record without first accessing the journal's PUBLISHER.

PLACEMENT is very clearly a VIA file because we shall always access it via ADVERTISEMENT or via JOURNAL. We might conceivably wish to access ARTISTCONTRACT directly, but this

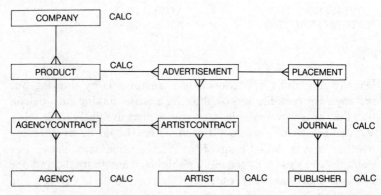

Fig. 7.14. Bachman diagram for advertisement database.

would require knowledge of a primary key value. In a CODASYL version of the database the ARTISTCONTRACT file does not need an ARTCONTRACTNO primary key field. If this field is missing then direct access does not make sense, which is why ARTISTCON-TRACT is not shown as CALC in Fig. 7.14. Consideration of provision of secondary indexes is left as an exercise for the reader.

7.4.3. *CODASYL DML*

CODASYL DML includes procedures analogous to CREATE, DELETE, REMOVE, INSERT, and FIND in Pascal DML, and has further facilities as well. We shall not give syntactic details, which are apt to be elaborate.

The effect of a FIND is Pascal DML is to assign a pointer value to a pointer variable. In CODASYL DML the effect of a FIND is to assign a pointer value to one or more of the currency indicators that are associated with record and fanset types. For instance in a CODASYL version of the INVENTORY example of Section 7.2.2.3, an effect of FINDing an INVENTORY record is to make the INVENTORY currency indicator point to this record. Another effect of this FIND is to make the currency indicator of the INCLUDES fanset point to this same record. A third effect is to make a currency indicator that is named *current-of-run-unit* point to this same record. Current-of-run-unit points to the record, whatever its type, that was found most recently.

If the next FIND in a DML program finds a SALESORDERDE-TAIL linker record the effects are as follows:

(a) the currency indicator for the SALESORDERDETAIL re-cord type points to the SALESORDERDETAIL record that has been found;
(b) the currency indicator for the INCLUDES fanset points to the SALESORDERDETAIL record that has been found;
(c) the current-of-run-unit points to the SALESORDERDETAIL record that has been found.

The currency indicator for the INVENTORY record type remains unchanged, still pointing to the INVENTORY record that was last found. The general idea is that for each record type, the currency indicator points to the record of that type which was most recently found. For each fanset, the currency indicator points to the record,

whether owner or member, most recently found in that fanset. The
current-of-run-unit is updated by every FIND operation, regardless
of the type of the operand, whereas the currency indicator for a
fanset or for a record type is not affected by any FIND operation
that is applied to another type.

In Pascal DML assignments to and from persistent variables are
written using ordinary Pascal assignment statements. CODASYL
DML differs in that it only allows access to persistent variables via
special non-persistent variables known as *user work area* variables,
which the programmer does not have to declare. For each record
type in the schema there is a user work area variable of that type,
and the name of this variable is automatically the same as the name
of its type. If the DML programmer uses FIND to find an
INVENTORY record in the database, he can subsequently use the
DML procedure GET to assign to the INVENTORY user work
area variable the value of the database inventory record to which the
INVENTORY currency indicator points. After this the programmer
can, if he wishes, output the value of the INVENTORY user work
area variable to the terminal. The only way of transferring inventory
records from the database to the terminal is via the INVENTORY
user work area variable. Similarly, the only way of transferring data
from the terminal into an INVENTORY record in the database is
via the INVENTORY user work area variable.

By way of example we now give in English, not in CODASYL
DML syntax, an outline of a CODASYL DML program to answer
the query "find the name and address of every company that is
marketing a product described as 'CIGAR '", using the Fig. 7.14
database. We give the name COMPANYPRODUCTS to the fanset
that associates COMPANY with PRODUCT. An outline program
is as follows.

PRODUCT.DESCRIPTION: = 'CIGAR '; {for the record type
    PRODUCT there is a user work area variable that also has the name
    PRODUCT. The initial assignment statement assigns 'CIGAR ' to the
    DESCRIPTION field of this record variable for use in the first FIND
    statement.}
FIND RECORD PRODUCT; {using hash access, this FIND finds the
    first PRODUCT record in the database which has
    DESCRIPTION = 'CIGAR '. Some effects of this FIND are that this
    record is pointed at by the PRODUCT currency indicator, the fanset
    COMPANYPRODUCTS currency indicator, and the current-of-run-
    unit.}

while DBSTATUS = OKAY **do** {not OKAY means none left}
begin
    FIND OWNER IN COMPANYPRODUCTS OF CURRENT OF
        RECORD PRODUCT; {apart from the semicolon, this statement is
        in strict CODASYL DML and illustrates the deliberate resemblance
        to natural English. This statement makes the owner COMPANY
        record become (i.e. be pointed at by) the current-of-run-unit for use
        in the following GET statement. This FIND also makes this
        COMPANY record current of COMPANYPRODUCTS, i.e. pointed
        at by the currency indicator which is associated with the fanset
        COMPANYPRODUCTS.}
    GET COMPNAME, COMPADDRESS; {this copies from the database
        the COMPNAME and COMPADDRESS fields from the
        COMPANY record which is pointed to by the current-of-run-unit.
        These field values are copied into the COMPANY user work area
        variable record.}
    WRITELN (COMPANY.COMPNAME,
        COMPANY.COMPADDRESS);
    FIND NEXT DUPLICATE WITHIN RECORD PRODUCT {this
        statement is in strict CODASYL DML. A result is that the currency
        indicator for PRODUCT points to the next record in the
        PRODUCT file that has DESCRIPTION = 'CIGAR '. If there is no
        such record then a value other than OKAY is assigned to
        DBSTATUS.}
end.

A general impression is that CODASYL DML is at a higher level
than Pascal DML and is more like natural English, but the rules that
the programmer must obey are very much more complicated and the
number of errors that the system can detect is very much greater.
Once mastered, CODASYL DML may be more concise and more
easily readable than Pascal DML.

7.5. TOTAL

Complication is a disadvantage of CODASYL DBMS, and various
simpler systems can be found in commercial use. TOTAL is an
important example of a simpler system that uses fansets.

    In a CODASYL DBMS a file can be declared to be a hash file, and
the DML programmer can use CODASYL DML FIND to find a
record in this file, given a key value. In Pascal DML there is no such
provision for hash files, and if the programmer chooses to set these
up for himself he may wish to write his own FIND and INSERT

procedures for application to hash files. The result will be two families of procedures such as FIND and INSERT: one for hash files, and one that can be used for traversing and using fansets. This is what we find ready made in TOTAL. Both families of procedures are simplified in TOTAL by insisting that each file is either an owner file or a member file, but no file is both an owner and a member. Owner files are hash files in which no two key values may be the same, and member files are accessible only via fansets implemented by rings. Because the access mechanisms for hash files and fansets are very different, one family of procedures such as FIND is applicable only to owner files, and the other family of such procedures is applicable only to member files.

Fig. 7.15. A CODASYL Bachman diagram.

In the Bachman diagram shown in Fig. 7.15 SALES ORDER HEADER is a member of a fanset owned by CUSTOMERS: one customer has many SALES ORDERs. SALES ORDER HEADER is also the owner of a fanset that has SALES ORDER DETAIL records as members: many SALES ORDER DETAIL records correspond to one SALES ORDER HEADER record. SALES ORDER HEADER violates the rule that no record can be both an owner and a member. For use with TOTAL we can change the structure as shown in Fig. 7.16. A manoeuvre like this can always be made. As a further example, Fig. 7.17 is a Bachman diagram for the music database of Section 7.2.2.4, revised for TOTAL implementation and with a linker to allow more than one composition to be performed on one occasion. MNO, PNO, ENO, and CNO are the same as in Section 2.2. MUSICIAN NAME can be regarded as a hash-organized index of unique names. The MUSICIAN NAME TO NUMBER linker allows more than one MNO to correspond to one musician name, and the DML programmer can only investigate these duplicates via the linker. Again because duplicate key values

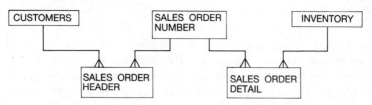

Fig. 7.16. A TOTAL version of the database shown in Fig. 7.15.

are not allowed in owner files in TOTAL, the file COMPOSITION TITLE contains each title only once. The TITLE TO COMPOSITION linker links each title to all the CNO and DATE OF COMPOSITION records that have this title. PERFORMANCE NUMBER is included in the database as an owner because PERFORMANCE DATE and PLACE is not allowed to own PERFORMED.

A disadvantage of TOTAL is that to answer a query, for example to find the names of all musicians who play in any ensemble named THE CEES, it may be necessary to proceed via a larger number of fansets than would be necessary in a CODASYL DBMS.

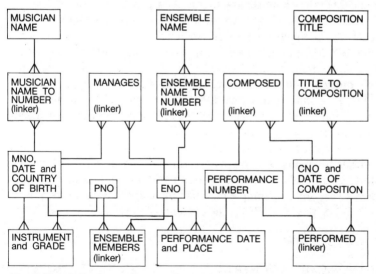

Fig. 7.17. A Bachman diagram for TOTAL implementation of the music database.

7.6. ADABAS

In Section 6.5 we saw that if the member pointers of secondary indexes are not included in the files to which they point, but are stored separately, then **and** or **or** in selection operations can be implemented by intersection and union operations on collections of members. The resulting member pointers take us directly to the required data records, and no time is wasted in accessing data records that turn out to be unwanted.

If data records contain many fields, we may be able to pack only a few data records per block. In this case, accessing unwanted data records may imply accessing blocks that contain no wanted data records, thus degrading the efficiency of the DBMS. Index records only contain keys and pointers, and we can therefore expect to be able to pack more index records per block than data records per block. If we implement **and** and **or** operations by performing intersections and unions of collections of member pointers, before accessing any data block, we may thereby reduce the overall number of blocks that must be accessed to answer a given query, thus improving efficiency.

ADABAS is a DBMS in which indexes, including interfile indexes, are deliberately kept separate from data files to improve efficiency. In this respect ADABAS is radically different from CODASYL and TOTAL, in which pointers associated with fansets are (or at least may be) stored in data files so that fanset acess paths require access to data records. Because the access paths of ADABAS are deliberately outside data records, rings and fansets are not appropriate to ADABAS. Indeed, in Pascal DML there is no need to be restricted to ring implementation, and we have used fansets only to provide an introduction to CODASYL and TOTAL.

When there is no requirement for ring implementation the interfile indexes for many-to-many associations do not require linkers. To illustrate interfile indexes that are separate from data files we now give a very simple example in which there are two data files named STOWNS and SPEOPLE. The contents of these files are as follows.

STOWNS data file			SPEOPLE data file		
TOWNNAME	COUNTRY		PERSONNAME	PROFESSION	
R1: AYTON	EXLAND		S1: WILBY	PROGRAMME}	
R2: SEETON	EXLAND		S2: KNIGHT	ENGINEER	

R3:	DEETON	ZEDLAND		S3:	SMITH	PROGRAMMER
R4:	EFTON	WYLAND		S4:	JONES	ACCOUNTANT
R5:	GEETON	ZEDLAND		S5:	YOUNG	ENGINEER

The file STOWNS tells us to which country each town belongs; for simplicity we assume that no two towns have the same name. SPEOPLE tells us the profession of each PERSON, and for simplicity we assume that no two people have the same name. In the STOWNS file, R1,...,R5 are *not* actually stored in the file, but are instead subscripts of a table in which pointers to data records are stored. Subscript R1 leads to the AYTON record, R2 leads to the SEETON record, and so on. Similarly, subscript S1 leads to the WILBY record, S2 leads to the KNIGHT record, and so on. These subscripts are the members in the following secondary indexes:

COUNTRY secondary index		PROFESSION secondary index	
OWNER	MEMBERS	OWNER	MEMBERS
EXLAND	R1,R2	ACCOUNTANT	S4
WYLAND	R4	ENGINEER	S2,S5
ZEDLAND	R3,R5	PROGRAMMER	S1,S3

We also require dense primary indexes:

TOWNS primary index		PEOPLE primary index	
OWNER	MEMBER	OWNER	MEMBER
AYTON	R1	JONES	S4
DEETON	R3	KNIGHT	S2
EFTON	R4	SMITH	S3
GEETON	R5	WILBY	S1
SEETON	R2	YOUNG	S5

As in Section 6.6.1, the data files contain records in random sequence, whereas the primary indexes are sorted on the primary key. Data records can be inserted and deleted without having to shift other data records in order to preserve a sorted sequence.

The following interfile indexes tell us who has visited which town, and which town has been visited by which people. Note that there is a many-to-many association between towns and people. For example, SEETON has been visited by more than one person, and SMITH has visited more than one town.

TOWNBYPEOPLE interfile index		PEOPLETOTOWN interfile index	
OWNER	MEMBERS	OWNER	MEMBERS
R1	S3	S1	R2
R2	S,S3	S2	R3,R5
R3	S2	S3	R1,R4,R5
R4	S3,S4	S4	R4
R5	S2,S3	S5	R2

The contents of one of these indexes can be entirely deduced from the contents of the other; this redundancy is typical of interfile indexes. Section 7.2.2.1 gives another example of this redundancy.

To find who has visited SEETON we look up SEETON in the TOWNS primary index and find the member R2. We look up R2, as owner, in the TOWNSBYPEOPLE interfile index and hence find that WILBY and YOUNG have visited SEETON.

An interfile index such as PEOPLETOTOWN has pointers S1, S2,... instead of PEOPLE names as owners because this allows union and intersection operations to be done on indexes before any data file is accessed. To illustrate this, suppose we wish to find the names of all ENGINEERS who have visited at least one town in ZEDLAND. We look up ZEDLAND in the country secondary index and find R3 and R5. We look up R3 in TOWNSBYPEOPLE and find S2, and we look up R5 in TOWNSBYPEOPLE and find S2,S3. The union {S2,S3} of the set {S2} of members owned by R3 and the set {S2,S3} owned by R5 consists of pointers to all the people who have visited at least one town in ZEDLAND. We now look up ENGINEER in the PROFESSION secondary index and find {S2,S5}. To find all the people who are ENGINEERs *and* have visited at least one town in ZEDLAND we intersect {S2,S5} with the previous union {S2,S3}. The result of this intersection is {S2} so we access the data record S2 and find that the result of the query is KNIGHT. It is very important that this name has been obtained without accessing any unwanted data record. If the TOWNSBY-PEOPLE interfile index had TOWNNAME as key we would have needed to access the data records for towns in ZEDLAND to obtain the names of these towns in order to look them up in the interfile index. These STOWNS records would have been unwanted in the sense that they do not contain information that directly answers the query.

We now program this example in detail, storing STOWNS and SPEOPLE records in tables (and omitting one stage of indirection). Our DBD is as follows.

```
DBDNAME VT;
type
  PESUBSCRIPT = 1..100; {subscript range for SPEOPLE}
  TNSUBSCRIPT = 1..50; {subscript range for STOWNS}
  STRING12 = packed array [1..12] of CHAR;
  PERSON = record
              PERSONNAME, PROFESSION: STRING12
          end;
  TOWN = record
              TOWNNAME, COUNTRY: STRING12
          end;
  PERSONLEAF = record
                  PERSONNAME: STRING12;
                  WHO: PESUBSCRIPT
               end;
  TOWNLEAF = record
                  TOWNNAME: STRING12;
                  WHICH: TNSUBSCRIPT
             end;
  PERSONMEMBERS = BTREE of PESUBSCRIPT;
  TOWNMEMBERS = BTREE of TNSUBSCRIPT;
  COUNTRYLEAF = record
                  COUNTRY: STRING12;
                  MEMBERS: TOWNMEMBERS
                end;
  PROFESSIONLEAF = record
                  PROFESSION: STRING12;
                  MEMBERS: PERSONMEMBERS
                   end;
  TPLEAF = record
              WHICH: TNSUBSCRIPT;
              MEMBERS: PERSONMEMBERS
           end;
  PTLEAF = record
              WHO: PESUBSCRIPT;
              MEMBERS: TOWNMEMBERS
           end;
var
  STOWNS: array [TNSUBSCRIPT] of TOWN;
  SPEOPLE: array [PESUBSCRIPT] of PERSON;
  TOWNPRIMARY: BTREE of TOWNLEAF on TOWNNAME;
```

PERSONPRIMARY: BTREE **of** PERSONLEAF **on**
PERSONNAME;
COUNTRYSECONDARY: BTREE **of** COUNTRYLEAF **on**
COUNTRY;
PROFESSIONSECONDARY: BTREE **of** PROFESSIONLEAF **on**
PROFESSION;
TOWNSBYPEOPLE: BTREE **of** TPLEAF **on** TNSUBSCRIPT;
PEOPLETOTOWNS: BTREE **of** PTLEAF **on** PESUBSCRIPT;
finish

For use in answering a query, we now provide intersection and
union procedures. The intersection procedure inserts into B-tree C
the leaf records that are in B-tree A and also in B-tree B. The
principle of the algorithm is the same as in program HAP3 in
Section 6.5.1.

```
procedure INTERSECT (var A,B,C: PERSONMEMBERS);
var
  APTR, BPTR: ↑PESUBSCRIPT;
begin
  FINDFIRST (A,APTR);
  if DBSTATUS = OKAY then
  begin
    FINDFIRST (B,PBTR);
    while DBSTATUS = OKAY do
    begin
      if APTR↑ = BPTR↑ then
      begin
        INSERT (C, APTR↑); FINDSUCC (A,APTR)
      end
      else
      if APTR↑ < BPTR↑ then FINDSUCC (A,APTR)
      else FINDSUCC (B,BPTR)
    end
  end; DBSTATUS = OKAY
end;
```

This works through successive leaves of A and B. If leaves are equal,
one of them is inserted into C; otherwise we FINDSUCC in
whichever B-tree has the smaller leaf value, thus giving it a chance to
catch up with the other B-tree. The following union procedure
merges the leaves of A and B into C, and the algorithm is similar in
principle to the batch-processing routine used in the file-merging
example in Section 9.6. By making the insertion into C conditional

on BPTR↑ < > APTR↑ we ensure that no two identical leaves are inserted into C. Otherwise leaves belonging to the intersection would be inserted in duplicate into C.

```
procedure UNION (var A,B,C: PERSONMEMBERS);
var
  APTR, BPTR: ↑PESUBSCRIPT;
  YESA, YESB: BOOLEAN;
procedure SOMELEFT (var YES: BOOLEAN);
begin
  YES: = (DBSTATUS = OKAY); DBSTATUS: = OKAY
end;
begin {body of procedure UNION}
  FINDFIRST (A,APTR); SOMELEFT (YESA);
  FINDFIRST (B,BPTR); SOMELEFT (YESB);
  while YESA and YESB do
  begin
    if BPTR↑ < APTR↑ then
    begin
      INSERT (C, BPTR↑);
      FINDSUCC (B, BPTR↑); SOMELEFT (YESB)
    end else
    begin
      if BPTR↑ > APTR↑ then INSERT (C, APTR↑);
      FINDSUCC (A, APTR↑); SOMELEFT (YESA)
    end
  end
  if YESA then
  repeat
    INSERT (C, APTR↑); FINDSUCC (A,APTR)
  until DBSTATUS < > OKAY;
  if YESB then
  repeat
    INSERT (C, BPTR↑); FINDSUCC (B,BPTR)
  until DBSTATUS < > OKAY
end;
```

The procedure SOMELEFT is used to indicate whether there are still some B-tree leaves to be processed. The procedure UNION inserts into C whichever of BPTR↑ or APTR↑ is the smallest, unless these are equal. FINDSUCC is applied to the B-tree that has the smaller leaf value, so that the merged sequence preserves the sorted order.

Using these procedures the following Pascal DML program reads

the name of a country and of a profession from the terminal, and
outputs the names of all people of this profession who have visited at
least one town in this country. We assume that the database has
already been loaded with data.

```
program PROFESSIONALVISITORS (INPUT, OUTPUT);
invoke VT;
var
  WHICHPROFESSION, WHATCOUNTRY: STRING12;
  COUNTRYLEAFPTR: ↑COUNTRYLEAF;
  PROFESSIONLEAFPTR: ↑PROFESSIONLEAF;
  POINTERTOTNSUBS: ↑TNSUBSCRIPT;
  POINTERTOPESUBS: ↑PESUBSCRIPT;
  WHOWENT, PROFWHOWENT: PERSONMEMBERS;
procedure UNION (var A,B,C: PERSONMEMBERS);
  begin {declaration omitted: see preceding text} end;
procedure INTERSECTION (var A,B,C: PERSONMEMBERS);
  begin {declaration omitted: see preceding text} end;
begin {program body}
  WRITELN ('type 12-character name of profession and country');
  READ (WHICHPROFESSION); GET (INPUT);
  READ (WHATCOUNTRY);
  STARTTRANSACTION (READONLY);
  FINDKEY (COUNTERSECONDARY, WHATCOUNTRY,
  COUNTRYLEAFPTR);
  if DBSTATUS < > OKAY then WRITELN ('no data for this country')
  else
  begin
    FINDFIRST (COUNTRYLEAFPTR↑.MEMBERS,
    POINTERTOTNSUBS);
    while DBSTATUS = OKAY do
    begin
      FINDKEY (TOWNBYPEOPLE, POINTERTOTNSUBS↑,
      TPLEAFPTR);
      if DBSTATUS = OKAY then
      UNION (TPLEAFPTR↑.MEMBERS, WHOWENT,
      WHOWENT)
      else DBSTATUS: = OKAY;
      FINDSUCC (COUNTRYLEAFPTR↑.MEMBERS,
      POINTERTOTNSUBS)
    end; DBSTATUS: = OKAY;
    FINDKEY (PROFESSIONSECONDARY, WHICHPROFESSION,
    PROFESSIONLEAFPTR);
    if DBSTATUS < > OKAY then
```

```
    WRITELN ('none for this profession')
    else
    begin
       INTERSECT (PROFESSIONLEAFPTR↑.MEMBERS,
       WHOWENT, PROFWHOWENT);
       FINDFIRST (PROFWHOWENT, POINTERTOPESUBS);
       while DBSTATUS = OKAY do
       begin
          WRITELN (SPEOPLE
          [POINTERTOPESUBS↑].PERSONNAME);
          FINDSUCC (PROFWHOWENT, POINTERTOPESUBS);
       end
    end
  end; ENDTRANSACTION
end.
```

This program works in the manner that we explained for an example in which engineers visited towns in ZEDLAND. The B-trees WHOWENT and PROFWHOWENT are initially empty. The first **while** loop uses the UNION procedure to build up in WHOWENT a collection of pointers to the PERSON records of all the people who have visited WHATCOUNTRY. The second FINDKEY obtains from the PROFESSIONSECONDARY index member pointers to the PERSON records of all people of WHICHPROFESSION. The INTERSECT procedure assigns to PROFWHOWENT pointers to all the people of WHICHPROFESSION who have visited any town in WHATCOUNTRY. The final **while** loop could have been combined with the INTERSECT procedure, but has been made separate for purposes of logical clarity.

ADABAS has query language facilities that enable the answering of queries without detailed programming like that illustrated above, and indeed without detailed knowledge of the index structures.

7.7 Implementation of joins using secondary indexes

We have considered speeding up joins by using various kinds of interfile indexes. This has the disadvantage that we have to know in advance which files we shall wish to join. When we used relational algebra to answer queries in Chapter 2, we were free to join any pair of files having at least one common field. Our view of data was purely *relational*, i.e. we thought of the files simply as collections of records and we were not concerned with access paths. We did not have to rely on all required joins having been correctly anticipated at the time of writing a DBD.

To preserve this freedom we can use secondary indexes instead of interfile indexes to speed up joins. We shall illustrate this using a very simple SALESORDERHEADER file that has fields SALE-SORDERNUMBER, CUSTOMERNUMBER, and DATE. We shall also use a simplified CUSTOMERS file that has fields CUSTO-MERNUMBER, NAME, CREDITLIMIT. Each of these files is a hash file, and we provide a secondary index for each non-key field. To evaluate

proj SALESORDERNUMBER (SALESORDERHEADER **join sel**
NAME = 'HOBSON' (CUSTOMERS))

we can use the NAME secondary index to obtain **sel** NAME = 'HOBSON' (CUSTOMERS), and for each of these selected records we can look up the CUSTOMERNUMBER in the CUS-TOMERNUMBER secondary index of the SALESORDER-HEADER file. The records that we thereby find are the SALESOR-DERHEADER records that would be concatenated in the join, and they contain the SALESORDERNUMBERs that we want. We do not access any unwanted SALESORDERHEADER records.

This method tends to be slower than methods that use interfile indexes because of the time taken to access each owner secondary key value in the secondary index. In our example the time taken to look up each customer number from **sel** NAME = 'HOBSON' (CUSTOMERS) in the SALESORDERHEADER secondary index on CUSTOMERNUMBER may be longer than the time that would be taken to find SALESORDERHEADER members in fansets owned by the selected customers.

In the sense explained in Section 6.2.3 fansets are direct indexes, whereas the method that we have introduced in the present section is an indirect indexing method because it involves looking up key values instead of directly following pointers.

7.8. Exercises

1. (a) Draw a Bachman diagram of a CODASYL database structure for
   the people visiting towns example in Section 7.6. This diagram will be the

same as it would be for a Pascal DBD using fansets for the same database.
(b) Write an outline of a DML program using this database to answer the query 'give the names of all people who have visited any town in ZEDLAND'. Do not worry about eliminating duplicates.

2. Perform the following functions for Exercise 1 in Section 3.11.

(a) Draw a Bachman diagram of a CODASYL database structure. Beside each file in the Bachman diagram, write CALC if the file should be a hash file and write VIA if the file should be accessible only via at least one fanset.
(b) Draw a Bachman diagram of a TOTAL database structure. Write an outline of a DML program using this database to answer the query 'give the names of the owners of all horses who have been ridden by jockey HOBSON'.

3. A restaurant maintains a collection of data including, for each dish, a name (e.g. ROASTBEEF) and a list of ingredients. For each ingredient the files show the quantity of the ingredient required in each recipe and the units (e.g. kilograms or litres) in which the quantity is measured. An ingredient is generally used in more than one recipe, and for each ingredient the restaurant records the quantity in stock, the units in which the quantity is measured, and the purchase price per unit. For each date, separately for lunch and dinner, the restaurant records the total number of customers, the number of customers who had each dish on the menu, and the price of each dish. The menu, which is simply a list of dishes, is generally not the same for any two meals.

(a) Draw a Bachman diagram for a CODASYL implementation of this database, indicating which files should be CALC.
(b) For each file, give self-explanatory names for all fields of each record type.
(c) Write an outline of a DML program to answer the query 'give the date, and say whether lunch and/or dinner, when the menu included any dish that had PAPRIKA as one of its ingredients'.

4. Perform the following functions for Exercise 6 in Section 3.11.

(a) Draw a Bachman diagram for a CODASYL database. Beside each file indicate whether it is a CALC or a VIA file.
(b) Draw a Bachman diagram for a TOTAL database.

5. (a) For Exercise 2 in Section 3.11 describe in detail the types of all owner and member fields of interfile indexes for an ADABAS database.
(b) Explain in English how to use ADABAS indexes to answer the query 'give the names of all mountains that have been climbed by HOBSON'. For simplicity assume that no two climbers have the same name.

6. Explain in English how to use secondary indexes as in Section 7.7 to answer the query 'give the name of all mountains that have been climbed by Hobson' using the files designed in Exercise 2 in Section 3.11.

7. Draw a Bachman diagram for a CODASYL database for Typico, incorporating all the information specified in Chapter 1.

8. Using the DBD VT of Section 7.6, write Pascal DML programs to

(a) output the name of every town that has been visited by at least one engineer and at least one programmer, and
(b) output the name of every programmer who has visited any town in EXLAND or WYLAND (or both).

8 Administrative issues

8.1. Integrity control

8.1.1. Type checking

As far as possible the data in a database should of course be valid, accurate, and consistent. *Integrity* preservation facilities are intended to protect a database against updates or insertions involving data that could not possibly be valid.

Type checking is an example of an integrity preservation facility. *Type checking* means checking that a value is within a declared range of admissible values. For example, if CUSTOMER NUMBER is declared to be of the subrange type 100000..999999 then an attempt to assign the value 203 to CUSTOMER NUMBER will be prohibited by the system. As another example, if a CUSTOMER is in a SALESAREA that can only be one of SE, SW, LN, EA, EM, WM, WA, NE, NW, SL, then assignment of 'PARIS' to SALESAREA will not be allowed by the system.

8.1.2. Constraints on changes of value

If Typico are sure that in their SALES ORDER DETAIL file a QUANTITY NOT YET DELIVERED can never increase, any increase should be prohibited, thus guarding against a class of possible mistakes. In Pascal DML an integrity check such as this would have to be programmed explicitly. A more sophisticated DBMS may provide facilities for declaration of constraints on changes of value.

As another example of this kind of constraint, if Typico are confident that a QUANTITY IN WAREHOUSE field value in the INVENTORY file will never increase, at the time of a single update, by more than QUANTITY TO ORDER, then any increase that exceeds this limit should be prohibited by the DBMS.

8.1.3. Duplicate key values

In a CODSAYL DBMS schema the programmer can specify whether or not duplicate key values will be allowed in a direct-access (e.g. hash) file (that has location mode CALC). The programmer can also specify whether or not duplicate search keys or sort keys will be allowed in a fanset. When the programmer has specified in the schema that duplicates are not allowed, the DBMS will not allow a DML program to insert a duplicate, thus avoiding what would presumably be a mistaken update of the database. For example, no two records in Typico's INVENTORY file should have the same ITEM REFERENCE NUMBER.

In Pascal DML the procedure INSERT assigns the value DUPLICATE to DBSTATUS when a duplicate is inserted. Subsequently the program will fail unless the DML programmer assigns OKAY to DBSTATUS. By bringing duplicates to the attention of the programmer, the system defends the database against accidental insertion of illegal duplicates.

8.1.4. Constraints involving more than one field

In Typico's EMPLOYEES file, the value of INCOME TAX FOR THIS YEAR TO DATE must not be less than INCOME TAX FOR THIS MONTH. This is an example of a constraint involving more than one field.

A more extreme example is that the sum of balances of all accounts must be zero in a double-entry book-keeping system. This is an integrity constraint that has proved to be valuable in manual accounting, and can be incorporated into a database system by explicit programming rather than by declaration in the DBD or schema.

Another kind of constraint is concerned with foreign keys. In Typico's CUSTOMERS file the primary key is CUSTOMER NUMBER. CUSTOMER NUMBER is a *foreign key* in the SALES ORDER HEADER file, because it is the primary key of some *other* file. Similarly, ITEMREFNO is a foreign key in Typico's INVOICE DETAIL file. There are database systems which insist that if a record includes a foreign key value, then this must be an actual primary key value currently existing somewhere in the database. This constraint prohibits sales orders for non-existent items.

8.1.5. Pre-input constraints

8.1.5.1. Data validation

Errors may be introduced into data before the data are entered into a database. We now introduce two classical methods for detecting errors in data *outside* a database.

8.1.5.2. Batch totals

Suppose, for example, that a customer sends Typico a purchase order that has 100 detail lines. Suppose that this order is initially in manuscript and is subsequently typed. One way to guard against typing errors is to sum, for example, the values of the QUANTITY field in the 100 detail lines. If the sum of these values in the typed version is not the same as in the manuscript version then there is presumably at least one typing error in a QUANTITY field value. A total of the values of a field is an example of a *batch total*. We have previously mentioned, in Section 1.5.2.1, the idea of using a batch total as an integrity constraint.

As well as totalling genuinely numeric fields such as QUANTITY and UNIT PRICE, we can also total fields such as CUSTOMER NUMBER. A resulting total is called a *hash total* because it is meaningful only for checking for errors.

Moreover, it is often useful to check that the *number* of records is the same before and after a process such as typing. This number is an example of a *batch count*.

8.1.5.3. Check digits

Suppose, for example, that CUSTOMER NUMBER always consists of exactly five digits, which we shall denote by $d_5 d_4 d_3 d_2 d_1$. We could check the sum

$$\sum_{i=1}^{i=5} d_i$$

for errors in copying these five digits. A related idea is to append a sixth digit d_0 to the five-digit number, where d_0 is given by

$$d_0 = 11 - \{(\sum_{i=1}^{i=5} d_i) \bmod 11\}$$

The extra digit d_0 is a *check* digit. Whenever we wish to check for an error in copying the number $d_5 d_4 d_3 d_2 d_1 d_0$ we check whether

$$(\sum_{i=0}^{i=5} d_i) \bmod 11 = 0,$$

and if this equation does not hold then there is an error, e.g. the number 249639 has been wrongly copied as 247639.

This technique does not detect accidental *permutation* of digits, e.g. 249639 copied wrongly as 294639. To remedy this we can use a slightly more elaborate check digit calculation

$$d_0 = 11 - \{(\sum_{i=1}^{i=5} w_i d_i) \bmod 11\}$$

where, typically, $w_1 = 2$, $w_2 = 3$, $w_3 = 4$, $w_4 = 5$, $w_5 = 6$. These values are called *weights*. By using different weights for different digits we ensure that the sum

$$\sum_{i=0}^{i=5} w_i d_i$$

changes when digits are permuted. If we find that

$$(\sum_{i=0}^{i=5} w_i d_i) \bmod 11 <> 0,$$

where $w_0 = 1$, then a substitution error such as $249639 \rightarrow 247639$ or a permutation error such as $249639 \rightarrow 294639$ has occurred.

We have introduced this method for five-digit numbers by way of example. The method is readily extended to any number of digits. International Standard Book Numbers (ISBNs) include check digits, wherein x represents 10.

8.2. Recovery from failure

8.2.1. *Types of failure*

The data in a database may be of vital importance to a company. A fault such as mechanical failure of a disc system must not be allowed to result in irreparable loss of data. A complete database management system (DBMS) provides facilities for recovering the data after any kind of error or physical disaster has occurred.

A hardware failure, such as disc failure owing to heads ploughing into the recording surface, is a *system failure*. The term *system failure* is also applied to programming errors or malfunctions (e.g. deadlock) in behind-the-scenes software that has not been written by user programmers such as DML programmers.

If a DML program detects failure of an integrity check or if a DML program itself fails owing to a programming error such as assigning a Boolean value to an integer variable, this kind of failure is a *transaction failure*.

8.2.2. *Transaction failure*

A database *transaction* is a section of program being executed: this section is sandwiched between STARTTRANSACTION and ENDTRANSACTION (or possibly ABORTTRANSACTION). Between STARTTRANSACTION and ENDTRANSACTION the programmer writes a section of program that he wishes to have executed as if it were the *only* transaction accessing the database during the period of execution.

Failure of a database transaction may be more damaging than failure of a non-DML Pascal program. When a non-DML Pascal program fails, for example because of an attempt to divide by zero, any output that the program may have written to standard Pascal files may be incomplete and possibly useless. Output produced by a failed program should generally be regarded as corrupt. If, after the cause of failure has been remedied, a program is rerun, it will rewrite its output files completely, and if the program terminates successfully then the previous failure will have done no harm because the previously corrupted contents will have been entirely overwritten by the new contents of output files.

One of the respects in which a database differs from a standard

Pascal file is that miscellaneous records can be updated without rewriting the entire database. If a transaction fails and its updates are not undone, the database may be left containing incorrect data that may soon be accessed by other transactions which may render further data incorrect, and so on. For example, if a transaction is creating INVOICE DETAIL and a picking list for Typico's warehouse, and fails after inserting an item into INVOICE DETAIL and before increasing QUANTITY ALLOCATED correspondingly in the INVENTORY file, then the database contains inconsistent data. This inconsistency must, if possible, be removed by undoing the failed transaction's updates.

ENDTRANSACTION tells the DBMS, among other things, that the programmer believes that any update which has been done by the transaction is now complete and consistent. If a DML program fails after ENDTRANSACTION there is no need to undo the transaction's updates.

8.2.3. Before-images

One way of undoing a transaction's updates is by using before-images. A simplified explanation is as follows.

In a database, records are physically packed into blocks (which are deliberately invisible to the Pascal database programmer). When a record is to be updated, the block containing that record is copied from secondary memory to a buffer in immediate access memory. From there, before being updated, the block can be copied into a *before-image file*. A *before-image* of a block is a copy of its pre-update contents. After copying the before-image to the before-image file, the DBMS can update a record in the version of the block that is still in the buffer in immediate access memory. Subsequently the updated block is copied back into secondary memory, to the same physical address whence it came, overwriting the pre-update contents of the block in the physical database. The before-image of the superseded block is stored in the before-image file at a different physical address in secondary memory and is not overwritten.

The DBMS keeps the before-images of all blocks that have been updated during the execution of transactions that have not yet terminated. A transaction's updates can be undone by overwriting their blocks with their before-images, so as to make the database contents the same as at the time of the transaction's START-

TRANSACTION. This method is called *roll back*. If all records are known to be fixed length then we can use before-images of individual records instead of complete blocks.

If a transaction fails but is not rolled back, or if some other failure invalidates the database, we may be able to use the before-image file to roll back all incomplete transactions that were updating the database. This method of *recovery* cannot cope with physically damaged discs because the damage generally spoils blocks for which there is no before-image.

8.2.4. Commitment

Another way of protecting a database against failure of individual transactions is to prevent actual physical update of the database until the time of ENDTRANSACTION. Before this time, updated records are not copied into the database to overwrite original contents. Instead, updated records are written to a separate file of *after-images*.

When a transaction accesses a record it first seeks this record among the after-images that it has produced. If found, this will be used as the up-to-date version of the record. Otherwise the DBMS will attempt to find the record in the actual physical database.

In a system that uses after-images, the procedure END-TRANSACTION *commits* the physical database by updating it with the transaction's after-images. The procedure ABORT-TRANSACTION prevents this update and the physical database remains in the state that it was in at the time of START-TRANSACTION.

This approach tends to be slower than the approach using before-images, because a DML FIND may involve access *both* to an after-image file *and* to the physical database. If before-imaging is used instead, the before-image file will be written to at the time of an update but need not always be accessed at the time of mere retrieval of data.

8.2.5. Dumping

As a precaution against a disaster such as fire or physical malfunction of discs, it is usual to copy the contents of a database onto magnetic tape or onto a duplicate disc installation, preferably housed in a separate building. This precaution is known as *dumping*. As well as dumping databases it is usual to dump non-database files such as standard Pascal files. The frequency of dumping is typically not more than once per day, nor less than once per week.

If a disaster causes loss of standard Pascal files, a user programmer may be able to obtain a dumped version of a file and rerun updating programs to recover the lost version. Database recovery is less straightforward if many users' transactions have updated the database since it was last dumped. One transaction may use data that was updated by a previous transaction, and probably no single user knows the whole story. This means that users generally cannot be expected to accomplish recovery under their own steam. Instead an after-image file can be used as will be briefly explained in the following section.

8.2.6. Roll forward

To provide a means of recovery, a DBMS can copy a transaction's after-images to a file that is physically separate from the database and not subject to the same risks. As well as the actual after-images, this file contains identification of updating transactions. Such a file is sometimes called a database *journal*. Starting from a dumped version of a database we can use after-images from this file as updates to recover a lost version of the database. This recovery process is known as *roll forward* from a dumped version.

After-images may be filed for possible use in roll-forward recovery even if the method of Section 8.2.3, not Section 8.2.4, is used for protection against failure of individual transactions.

8.3. Concurrency control

8.3.1. Introduction to concurrency

We now consider the problems of allowing many DML programs to access the same database concurrently, i.e. *at the same time*. Most major commercial DBMS allow concurrent access.

A *multi-access* operating system is one that allows many users, typically at terminals, to use a computer at the same time. The system is intended to give the impression that each user is the only user of the computer at that time. A simple way of achieving this is to give each transaction (or task) in turn a brief time slot (e.g. 20 ms), during which the central processor unit (CPU) executes that transaction, whilst others wait their turn.

Another reason for switching control of a CPU from one transaction (or task) to another is to prevent the CPU from doing nothing useful whilst waiting for something to happen somewhere else. For example, if a transaction requires access to a block that has not yet been copied from disc to immediate access memory, the CPU may idly wait for the block to be copied and then resume execution of the transaction. To prevent such wasting of a CPU's time, a *multi-programming* operating system arranges that, when one transaction is held up, another takes over to do useful work whilst the CPU would otherwise be idle. If this second transaction is held up, a third may take over control of the CPU, and so on. There could, for example, be a total of five active transactions (or tasks), one executing, and the other four either held up or ready and waiting for a CPU time slot.

In a multi-access or multi-programming system, execution of a transaction is liable to be suspended at unpredictable times and to be resumed after other transactions have had control of the CPU. From the programmer's point of view it looks *as if* other people's transactions (or tasks) are running at the same time as his. In other words, it looks as if many transactions are running *concurrently*. If a computer system has more than one CPU, transactions can actually run concurrently. In either case, whether actual or due to multi-programming, concurrency must not allow one transaction to spoil another's work.

We generally wish to prevent a transaction from reading data that is at the same time being updated by another transaction. For example, suppose a transaction finds that for all lines of a sales order the QUANTITY IN WAREHOUSE minus QUANTITY ALLOCATED exceeds the QUANTITY ORDERED, and therefore outputs a message to say that a shipment could be made. This message may be invalidated if a concurrent transaction increases the QUANTITY ALLOCATED for some of the items in the order.

We also wish to prevent two transactions from updating the same data concurrently. To understand what can go wrong, we must appreciate that each transaction has its own private file block buffers. Let transaction A and transaction B be two transactions that both update QUANTITY ALLOCATED in the same

INVENTORY record. The sequence of events could be as follows.

1. Transaction A copies a block from the database in secondary memory to a file buffer block in immediate access memory and updates a QUANTITY ALLOCATED field within this file block buffer. Suppose for example that the updated value of QUANTITY ALLOCATED is 15.

2. Transaction A is held up for some reason *before* copying the updated block back to secondary memory. Transaction B takes over the CPU, reads the non-updated version of the block from secondary memory, changes the same QUANTITY ALLO-CATED field (e.g. to 20), and copies the updated block back into secondary memory.

3. Eventually Transaction A resumes control of the CPU and copies the block containing QUANTITY ALLOCATED = 15 from the file block buffer back into secondary memory, thus overwriting and destroying Transaction B's update. This is an example of the notorious *lost-update problem*.

8.3.2. Locks

To prevent any transaction reading or updating data that is being updated by another transaction we can use locks. A *lock* is a marker that indicates whether a unit of data is available for access. We can arrange that a transaction locks a unit of data whilst updating it, so as to prevent any other transaction from accessing this unit until it has been unlocked. Any transaction that attempts to access locked data is suspended from controlling the CPU and cannot regain control until the lock is undone.

A sophisticated DBMS automatically manages the locking and unlocking. When a transaction accesses a lockable unit of data a typical sequence of steps is as follows.

1. LOCK unit {unless it is already locked in which case suspend this transaction until this unit is unlocked}.
2. DO SOMETHING {with the unit}.
3. UNLOCK unit {so that the unit becomes available for locking by some other transaction}.

The greater is the unit of locked data, the larger is the number of concurrent transactions that may be suspended waiting for access.

For example if a whole file is a unit of data that is locked, all transactions attempting to access this file will be suspended. If only a few individual records in the file are locked, only transactions that attempt to access these few records will be suspended, so that we can expect fewer transactions to be suspended. The size of the lockable unit is the locking *granularity*.

The finer is the granularity, i.e. the smaller are the lockable units, the greater is the cost of implementation because lock-status data must be stored for each lockable unit. Between the extremes of locking whole files, thereby reducing possible concurrency, or instead locking individual records, thereby maximizing cost of implementation, a reasonable compromise is to lock individual blocks.

A useful refinement is to provide more than one type of lock. An *exclusive* lock gives a transaction exclusive access to a unit of data, which is thereby rendered completely inaccessible to all other transactions. A transaction should exclusively lock units of data that it updates to prevent any other transactions from concurrently reading or updating the same data, for reasons that we have already illustrated.

A transaction that merely reads from a unit of data, without changing its contents, need not prevent other transactions from reading (but not updating) this unit concurrently. A *read-only* lock is a lock that does not prevent concurrent read-only access, but does prevent any other transaction from being granted an exclusive lock on the unit until such time as the read-only lock is released. A read-only lock prevents concurrent update.

8.3.3. Livelock and deadlock

Typically a transaction is suspended if it attempts to lock exclusively a unit of data that is already locked. Many transactions may be suspended waiting for the same lock to be unlocked. These transactions *queue* for the lock, and we may be free to choose the sequence of transactions in this queue. If the sequence is such that a particular transaction is always overtaken by others and is never granted the lock then this transaction is said to be *livelocked*. A livelocked transaction is permanently suspended. It is easy to avoid livelock by ensuring that no transaction is invariably overtaken by others.

We must also contend with *deadlock*, which is illustrated by the following classical example that consists of four steps:

1. Transaction A locks Unit X;
2. Transaction B locks Unit Y;
3. Transaction A attempts to lock Unit Y and is suspended;
4. Transaction B attempts to lock Unit X and is suspended.

Transaction A is suspended at step 3, awaiting release of Unit Y by Transaction B. Transaction B will never release Unit Y because Transaction B is itself suspended at step 4 awaiting release of Unit X by the suspended Transaction A. Transactions A and B are *deadlocked* because they hold each other up forever.

TABLE 8.1
Example of a sequence in which transactions attempt to lock units

Step	Transaction	Unit	Suspended
1	A	W	No
2	B	X	No
3	B	W	Yes
4	C	Y	No
5	C	X	Yes
6	D	Z	No
7	D	Y	Yes
8	A	Z	Yes

The 'suspended' column shows whether an attempt results in suspension of the transaction.

More generally, deadlock involves Transaction A, a further Transaction B that is suspended waiting for a unit locked by Transaction A, a further Transaction C that is suspended waiting for a unit locked by Transaction B, and so on. At the end of this chain, Transaction A is suspended waiting for a unit that has been locked by a transaction that is suspended in the chain. Table 8.1 shows an example. Deadlock results from the sequence of the rows of a table such as Table 8.1 and can be prevented by constraining the ordering of rows. One possible constraint is that the rows must be sorted on transaction; this means that the first transaction locks *all* the units that it requires, then the next transaction locks *all* the units that it requires, and so on. In the example shown in Table 8.1 this constraint would prevent Transaction A from attempting to lock Unit Z that is locked by a transaction which is suspended as an indirect result of Transaction A locking Unit W. This constraint is generally not practical for database work because, for example, at the start of a join operation the units that will be accessed may be unknown.

An alternative constraint says that a transaction can access units only in a prescribed order. For the example in Table 8.1 this order could be alphabetical: W,X,Y,Z. An alphabetical ordering constraint requires that Transaction B must lock W before X. Transaction C must lock X before Y, and so on. It can be proved that this constraint prevents deadlock. We can enforce this constraint by rolling back any transaction that violates it. In practice this enforcement will often roll back transactions that would not have caused deadlock.

Instead of attempting to prevent deadlock in database systems, it is usually more cost effective to allow deadlock to happen and to cure it by rolling back a transaction. To detect deadlock a DBMS records which units are available and which units are allocated to, or requested by, each transaction. Any transaction that is only requesting available units is not deadlocked and can therefore be deleted from consideration, the units allocated to it becoming available for allocation to other units. This may result in deletion of other transactions from consideration, which in turn may result in further deletion, and so on. If, finally, no transactions remain under consideration then there is no deadlock.

8.3.4. Serializability

In Section 8.2.2 we said that a transaction is a section of program that is required to be executed as if no other transaction is being executed concurrently. In other words, we require that concurrency is invisible to transactions. The effect of a collection of transactions must be the same as if they had been executed in turn, in some order. If the sequence of operations of the computer system is such that this condition is satisfied then the sequence is said to be *serializable* even if transactions are actually executed concurrently. A sequence is serializable if and only if its final effect is the same *as if* transactions had been executed one after the other non-currently.

One way to ensure serializability is to insist that no transaction ever locks a unit after unlocking any other unit. A proof of this statement is beyond the scope of this text. Another way to ensure serializability is by timestamping.

8.3.5. *Timestamping*

Timestamping is a method that can be used instead of locking to prevent transactions from spoiling each other's work. We now outline an example of a timestamping system that uses roll back as in Section 8.2.3.

Successive transactions are numbered 1,2,3,... by the DBMS, so that each transaction has a unique transaction number. The DBMS maintains a list of transaction numbers of transactions that have started but not terminated.

The units of data are blocks. Each block has a header in which the DBMS places administrative information. This information includes the transaction number of the transaction that most recently started to update the block. This transaction number is known as a *timestamp*.

A transaction is rolled back if it attempts to change the contents of a block that bears the timestamp of a non-terminated transaction. Thus the lost-update problem is avoided.

For each block the DBMS maintains a list of timestamped before-images. A transaction is allowed to read any block that has not been modified since that transaction started. If a block has been modified since the transaction started, the DBMS ensures that the transaction reads a before-image of the block. This before-image is the block contents at the time that this transaction started. This arrangement ensures that no transaction is affected by any concurrent transaction. A block can be updated whilst a before-image of it is being read concurrently. This concurrency would not be allowed by a locking system, and generally timestamping may allow more concurrency than would be allowed by a locking system that has the same granularity.

8.4. Access control

8.4.1. *Database security*

Some or all of the data in a database may be confidential. For example, a database may contain accounting information that should be kept secret from a company's competitors. *Access control* is intended to determine who has access to what parts of a database for what purposes.

An alternative term for *access* control is *security* control. In this context security means preservation of secrecy and protection against unauthorized updates. In database literature the term *security* does *not* mean safeguarding against hardware and software faults, fire, and other misadventures.

We now briefly introduce various methods that are intended to provide security by controlling access.

8.4.2. Authorization tables

Access to a computer system can be controlled by insisting that a user identifies himself when logging in, by typing a login name and a password. Many systems go further than this and control access to specific units of data. For each unit of data a DBMS can maintain an *authorization table* that shows which username is allowed to access which unit of data and for what purposes. In this context, units of data may be files. Table 8.2 is a simple example of an authorization table, in which N signifies 'No access', R signifies 'Read only', and U signifies 'Unrestricted'. For example Table 8.2 authorizes user AY73M1 to update FNAME2 and FNAME3 and to read but not update FNAME4. The basic idea here is that the system 'knows' who is allowed to do what to which unit of data.

TABLE 8.2
An example of an authorization table

USER NAME	FILE NAME			
	FNAME1	FNAME2	FNAME3	FNAME4
AX4352	U	N	U	R
AY73M1	N	U	U	R
BE64M8	N	N	U	R
CF12S1	N	N	U	U
EK61HZ	R	R	R	R

8.4.3. Passwords

An alternative idea is that for each type of access (e.g. read only or unrestricted) to each unit of data the user is required to produce a separate password. In this context a password produced by a user is a *privacy key*, and a password demanded by the system is a *privacy lock*. Access is only granted to users who produce a privacy key that matches a privacy lock. For each unit of data the system now only has to store a privacy lock for each type of access, instead of a list of user names and access rights such as U, N, or R as in Table 8.2.

There are systems in which this idea has been developed by providing a separate privacy lock for each field of each record type for each kind of access (e.g. unrestricted or read only). Going a step further still, for each field of each record type there may be a separate privacy lock for each DML procedure such as FIND, INSERT, REMOVE, CREATE, DELETE. In a DML program, instead of simply writing something like FINDKEY (THISINDEX, KEYVAR, PTR) the DML programmer must now write something like

PRIVACYKEY FOR FINDKEY OF THISINDEX IS
'ABACADABRA';
FINDKEY (THISINDEX, KEYVAR, PTR)

where 'ABACADABRA' is the privacy key for this specific access. A PRIVACY KEY FOR... statement is placed in the program before each DML statement that requires database access.

8.4.4. Physical access

To prevent unauthorized persons from accessing data we can physically prevent them from entering a room and reaching a terminal. We may only allow people who have been physically identified to use terminals.

8.4.5. Encryption

Encyphering data means making data unintelligible to anyone who does not possess appropriate keys. Text is called *plaintext* before it has been encyphered, and *cyphertext* after it has been encyphered. We now briefly introduce two classical elementary methods of encryption, assuming for simplicity that plaintext contains only letters and spaces. Both of these methods work with *blocks* of text, a block being a set of consecutive characters. The number of characters per block is BLOCKLENGTH.

8.4.5.1. A transposition cypher

A transposition cypher uses a cypher *key* that is a permutation of
the set of ordinals 1,2,3,...,BLOCKLENGTH. For example, if
BLOCKLENGTH = 6 then a possible cypher key is 351462.
Another possible key is the permutation 453261. We shall store the
cypher key in an array

CYPHERKEY: **array** [1..BLOCKLENGTH] **of** 1..BLOCKLENGTH

The following encryption algorithm works with an array

BLOCK: **array** [1..BLOCKLENGTH] **of** CHAR;

Assuming for simplicity that the number of characters in the
plaintext file is a multiple of the block length, the following program
fragment inputs plaintext and outputs cyphertext:

```
RESET (PLAINTEXTFILE);
while not EOF (PLAINTEXTFILE) do
begin
   for i: = 1 to BLOCKLENGTH do READ (BLOCK [i]);
   for i: = 1 to BLOCKLENGTH do
   WRITE (BLOCK [CYPHERKEY [i]])
end
```

This algorithm produces cypher text by permuting the sequence
of plaintext characters within each block. For example, if
BLOCKLENGTH = 6, the cypher key is 341462, and the plaintext is
'ANGELS IN GUMBOOTS', then the cypher text is 'GLAESNNG
UIOTMOST'. A decyphering algorithm is

```
RESET (CYPHERTEXTFILE);
while not EOF (CYPHERTEXTFILE) do
begin
   for i: = 1 to BLOCKLENGTH do
   READ (BLOCK [CYPHERKEY [i]]);
   for i: = 1 to BLOCKLENGTH do WRITE (BLOCK [i])
end
```

The number of possible permutations increases rapidly as a function
of blocksize, giving better security.

8.4.5.2.　A substitution cypher

Before introducing a simple substitution cypher it is expedient to introduce two simple Pascal functions. The first of these converts letters 'A','B',....,'Z' to integers 1,2,...,26 and converts a space to zero:

```
function NUMBERIC (CH: CHAR): INTEGER;
begin
    if CH = ' ' then NUMERIC: = 0
    else NUMBERIC: = ORD (CH) − ORD ('A') + 1
end
```

We also need the reverse function

```
function LETTER (J: INTEGER): CHAR;
begin
    if J = 0 then letter: = ' ' else
    LETTER: = CHR (J + ORD('A') − 1)
end
```

We shall store a cypher key in an array

```
CYPHERKEY: array [1..BLOCKLENGTH] of 0..26;
```

We now allow more than one CYPHERKEY array element to have the same value; this is not permitted with transposition cyphers.

A substitution cypher substitutes plaintext letters with other letters determined by the cypher key as follows:

```
RESET (PLAINTEXTFILE);
I: = 0;
while not EOF (PLAINTEXTFILE) do
begin
    READ (CH); I: = I + 1;
    J: = CYPHERKEY [I] + NUMERIC [CH];
    if J > 26 then J: = J − 26;
    WRITE (LETTER (J));
    if I = BLOCKLENGTH then I: = 0
end
```

For example if BLOCKLENGTH = 3, if the cypher key is 142, and if the plaintext is 'ANGELS IN GUMBOOTS', then the cyphertext is 'BRIFPUAMPAKWNFQPXU'. The same cypher key is used in decyphering:

```
RESET (CYPHERTEXTFILE);
I: = 0;
while not EOF (CYPHERTEXTFILE) do
begin
   READ (CH); I: = I + 1;
   J: = NUMERIC (CH) – CYPHERKEY [I];
   if J < 0 then J: = J + 26;
   WRITE (LETTER (J));
   if I = BLOCKLENGTH then I: = 0
end
```

The principles of transposition and substitution cyphers can be combined to produce cyphers that are more secure.

8.5. Views and subschemas

Hitherto we have assumed that a DML programmer has complete knowledge of the database declaration of any databases that he uses. Actually the programmer could work with incomplete knowledge, for example knowledge of only some of the fields of some of the files. In this case the programmer would only be aware of a subset of the database declaration. Another possibility is that the programmer programs as if a file is included in the database but in fact only a non-loss decomposition is included, the file being reconstructed from the decomposition behind the scenes when required.

Yet another possibility is that the DBMS allows different programmers to use different names for the same database variables, particularly fields of records. Furthermore two programmers could work with the same variable as if its type were different. For example, one programmer could regard a field as comprising a string of four characters that are digits. Another programmer could see this same field as simply an integer field, not a string of characters.

The general idea here is that a DBMS can allow different users to have different *views* of a database. In the context of CODASYL DBTG the term *subschema* is used instead of *view*. A subschema is essentially a subset of a database declaration (i.e. schema) with names changed and types of variables changed where required, as long as interconversion between types can easily be done behind the scenes. A CODASYL subschema does not allow a DML programmer to work with a file that is represented only by a non-loss decomposition, but this facility does exist in various relational systems except that such a file is always read-only and cannot be updated.

Some advantages of views or subschemas are as follows.

(a) They provide the DML programmer with a simplified view of the database, thus facilitating his work.

(b) They improve access control: a DML programmer is prevented from accessing any part of the database that is excluded from his view. Ideally a view should be minimal, in that a programmer should not have unnecessary knowledge of the database.

(c) A user's subschema can remain unchanged when the schema itself is edited and amended, for example to include new files and access paths or to include new fields in existing records. Furthermore, a subschema can remain unchanged when fields, files, or access paths that are excluded from this subschema are deleted from the parent schema. If the user had to work with the full schema, instead of a subschema, then such changes would be unhelpfully visible. The insulation of a user from changes in a database is a kind of *data independence*, to which we shall return in Section 8.6.

For these reasons, Typico's various departments have different subschemas. For example, the Sales Department needs to know details of customers, but not of suppliers. The Sales Department uses a subschema for which Fig. 8.1 is a Bachman diagram.

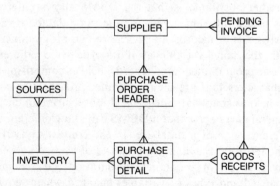

Fig. 8.1. Bachman diagram for Typico's Sales Department's subschema.

Compared with Typico's schema, this subschema has been simplified by omission of purchase orders and other irrelevant files such as the EMPLOYEES file. Because payments from Typico to suppliers are invisible in the Sales Department's subschema, there is no risk of confusion with payments to Typico from customers. The simplicity of this subschema makes the database easier for the Sales Department's staff to use, i.e. easier than working with the complete schema.

If Typico decide to incorporate into their database a new file showing the dimensions, location, and use of every room on all their sites, this development will be invisible to the Sales Department, and will therefore cause them no trouble. Furthermore this development will not affect the work of the Purchasing Department, whose subschema is shown in Fig. 8.2. The Purchasing Department's subschema has been simplified by omission of files relating to customers and their sales orders.

Generally the declaration of a view or subschema is similar to a DBD, but this declaration also specifies the relationship between the view and the parent database. This declaration may be the responsibility of a database administrator, to whom we shall return in Section 8.7.

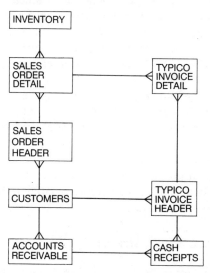

Fig. 8.2. Bachman diagram for Typico's Purchasing Department's subschema.

8.6. Data independence

Data independence means avoiding changes to DML or query language programs when the database is reorganized, for example when hash functions are changed, B-tree block size is changed, or indexes are provided or removed. Significant data independence can be attained even when views or subschemas are not used. For example in Pascal DML the B-tree block sizes could change without the programmer knowing. Data independence arises when the programmer is unaware of the internal working of DML procedures such as FINDKEY, INSERT, etc.

A query language such as relational algebra is at a higher level than Pascal DML in that it is further away from physical implementation. We can write in relational algebra without knowing which selection and join operations are speeded up by the provision of indexes. Indeed the provision of access mechanisms may be changed without the user knowing. The higher is the level of the query language, the greater are the possibilities for data independence.

To achieve data independence there must be some kind of mapping between a user's view of (all or part of) a database and the physical database. This mapping is required so that it, not the user's view, can be changed when the physical database is amended. If there are many different user's views or subschemas, then a separate mapping is required for each. One way to cope with physical changes in the database is to change all these mappings accordingly.

An ANSI/SPARC Study Group proposed an alternative way of coping *without* changing more than one mapping, but instead using indirection, as in Section 6.6.2. The idea is that there is a single mapping between the physical database and one unchanging abstract representation. There are separate mappings between the various user's views and this one abstract representation. When we change the physical database, we only need update the single mapping between the physical database and the one abstract representation, leaving unchanged the many mappings between the one abstract representation and the many user's views.

8.7. Database administrator

In Chapters 6 and 7 we wrote DBDs without worrying about administrative issues that have been introduced in the present chapter. In the present chapter we have seen that a sophisticated commercial DBMS has provisions for concurrency and access control and recovery from failure, and may provide different users with different views or subschemas.

A database system is a shared resource that must efficiently serve the diverse needs of many users. Commonly there is a professional person (or team) responsible for deciding what access paths to provide, what provisions to use for recovering from failure, and what access control methods to adopt. A professional who has such responsibilities is a *database administrator*. His job is to look after the database on behalf of all the users, arbitrating between conflicting requirements.

The database administrator, rather than a user programmer, is responsible for writing a DBD or schema. Indeed he may be the only person who knows the full details of the schema; users of the system may only have knowledge of subschemas or views. The database administrator monitors performance (e.g. response times) and tunes the access mechanisms of the DBMS to adapt to changing patterns of usage.

At Typico the database administrator is a senior member of the staff of the Data Processing Department. In various other companies, computerized data processing and database technology are seen as a constituent part of the total clerical function that includes non-computerized files and manual procedures. The entire computerized and non-computerized data management function is the responsibility of a *data administrator*. In this case the database administrator is a professional specialist who is normally subordinate to the data administrator.

8.8. Data dictionary

In a practical database and data-processing system the total number of names of fields, records, files, programs, reports, etc. may be so great that no one could remember them all, and instead we may wish to maintain a *data dictionary* that says how each name is used. Indeed the dictionary itself may be stored using a DBMS that provides query language facilities, concurrency and access control, and facilities for recovery from failure.

A data dictionary contains *meta data*, i.e. data about data. The meta data may be about non-computerized data as well as compu-

terized data. Furthermore, a data dictionary may include information about programs, and possibly also about programmers and
other personnel who access the data. Various different data dictionary systems are commercially available and they differ in their
facilities, aspirations, and terminology.

A rudimentary data dictionary may be introduced as a file that
has variable-length fields and various secondary indexes. Typical
fields are as follows.

SIMPLE DATA DICTIONARY field names

NAME {contrived to be unique, and used as the dictionary's primary
  key}
ELEMENT {e.g. FIELD, RECORD, FANSET, FILE, DATABASE,
  INDEX, SCHEMA, SUBSCHEMA}
DESCRIPTION {explanatory text that may be required to include key
  words such as CUSTOMER that may be useful for purposes of
  indexing}
BELONGSTO {e.g. if ELEMENT if a FIELD then BELONGSTO is a
  list of names of records to which this field belongs}
ALTERNATIVE NAMES {there may be good reasons for having more
  than one name to mean the same thing. Alternative names are listed in
  this field}
LENGTH {number of bytes required to store this element}
ACCESS PATHS TO OTHER ELEMENTS {this field lists all access
  paths, e.g. indexes, that lead from this element directly to any other
  element}
FREQUENCY OF ACCESS {to this element}
DATE AND TIME OF LAST READ-ONLY ACCESS
DATE AND TIME OF LAST UPDATE
BY WHOM WAS LAST ACCESS MADE {user name}
AVERAGE ACCESS TIME {for monitoring DBMS performance it is
  useful to have a measure of the time taken to access each element}
OWNER {who owns this element. If this element is a file then the
  OWNER is the file's owner. Another example is that if this element is a
  database then the OWNER is the database administrator}
ACCESS RIGHTS {this field says who is allowed to do what to this
  element}
PRIVACY LOCK {possibly an alternative to the previous field}

In this list the name of the second field is unsatisfactory because
there is not a generally accepted generic term to cover what may be a
file, or a field, or a record, or a subschema, or a complete database,

etc. In this context, ELEMENT is essentially anything that has a name in a data-processing system.

A data dictionary may also serve as a data directory, incorporating some of the functions of an operating system's file directory. In this case, for each ELEMENT that is in fact a file, the dictionary includes some kind of name of the file organization (e.g. hash) and physical addresses required for accessing the file.

A data dictionary helps the database administrator and others to live with what might otherwise be an overwhelming proliferation of names. Indeed the use of a data dictionary may help towards standardization of names. Another advantage of having a data dictionary is that its contents may contribute directly to the documentation that describes the data-processing system. Yet another advantage is in saving a DML programmer's time, for example by copying a complicated record declaration from the dictionary into the declaration part of a program. There are systems in which this kind of copying is made compulsory to enforce control over the use of names and to ensure that the dictionary itself is kept up to date.

9 Appendix: Pascal files, records, and pointers

9.1. Introduction

Chapters 4, 5, 6, and 7 presuppose knowledge of Pascal files, records, and pointers which are briefly introduced in the present chapter. This chapter forms an appendix to the main text because it deals with facilities of Pascal itself, and not with database or data-processing concepts. A firm understanding of these Pascal facilities is an essential prerequisite for understanding the second half of the main text.

We assume that the reader is already familiar with Pascal input and output from a computer terminal, and that this familiarity includes READ, WRITE, READLN, WRITELN, and EOLN. We also assume that the reader has used operating system facilities for creating, editing, and deleting files of text, such as files that contain Pascal programs. For example, we assume that the reader could create a text file named ROUTE1 containing the five lines

AYTON
DEEFIELD
EMBY
GREATHAM
BIGCHESTER

and could create a separate file named ROUTE2 containing the six lines

AYTON
BEEHAMPTON
GIDDLEWICK
HOLLYFIELD
GREATHAM
BIGCHESTER

In this example the two files contain the names of successive towns along different routes from AYTON to BIGCHESTER.

9.2. Files of text

If CH has been declared to be a variable of type CHAR, then the Pascal statement

READ (CH)

reads the next character from the terminal and assigns it to CH. The statement

READ (ROUTE1, CH)

reads the next character from a text file named ROUTE1 and assigns it to CH. Similarly the statement

WRITE (FNAME, CH)

writes the character CH to a text file FNAME, leaving CH unchanged. Thus we see that Pascal allows the programmer to make a program read from, or write to, a text file by using a simple extension of the READ and WRITE statements that are used for communicating with the terminal. The extension is that the file name is the first parameter of the READ or WRITE statement.

If CH1 and CH2 are variables of type CHAR, the statement

READ (CH1, CH2)

reads the next two characters from the terminal and assigns them to CH1 and CH2 respectively. Similarly the statement

READ (ROUTE2, CH1, CH2)

reads the next two characters from ROUTE2 and assigns them to CH1 and CH2 respectively. This illustrates the fact that READ and WRITE statements using files can have any number of parameters, just like READ and WRITE statements that communicate with the terminal.

The two statements

READ (CH1); READ (CH2)

have the same effect as the single statement READ (CH1, CH2). Suppose, for example, that the input data typed as one line at the terminal is

AYTON

and that READ (CH1) causes the first character A on this line to be read into CH1. After this character A has been read, a behind-the-scenes marker indicates that the next character to be read is the second character Y. If the statement READ (CH2) is executed immediately after READ (CH1), this Y will be assigned to CH2 because this Y is the character indicated by the marker. The marker now moves on to the T, which will be the next character to be read. The general idea is that successive READs cause movement along the sequence of data characters. The same idea applies to successive WRITEs. Indeed the same idea applies to successive READs and WRITEs for a text file, just as for a terminal.

A Pascal system needs some means of knowing that in a statement such as READ (ROUTE1, CH1) the first parameter is the name of a file, not a variable. For this and other reasons, the programmer must declare text files. For example, a program that uses variables CH1 and CH2, and also uses the text file ROUTE1, would have amongst its **var** declarations

var
    CH1, CH2: CHAR;
    ROUTE1: TEXT;

For use in declarations such as this, TEXT is the standard type of a text file.

Before the first time that a program writes to a file, the computer system must be notified that data will be sent *to* the file. The programmer issues this notification by writing a REWRITE statement with the name of the file as parameter. For example, the statement

REWRITE (THYFILE)

tells the system that the program is expected to send data to a file named THYFILE. Similarly the programmer must use the statement RESET, with the name of a file as parameter, to tell the system that the program is expected to read from that file. For example, the statement

RESET (MYFILE)

tells the system that the program is expected to read from a file named MYFILE; this RESET statement must be executed ahead of all statements that actually read from MYFILE. After execution of a RESET statement, the first character to be read will be the first character in the text file. If, after reading part of a file, a program is required to start reading that file again from the beginning, the programmer must again use the statement RESET (filename).

A standard Pascal program cannot read from a file at a point where it left off writing; when a program first reads from a given file, it always starts from the beginning of that file. Similarly a program cannot write to a file at a point where it left off reading; writing always starts from the beginning. In this sense, reading and writing are mutually exclusive.

To illustrate ideas that have been introduced so far, the following program counts the lines of text in our file named ROUTE1. We assume that text has previously been entered into this file by using operating system facilities.

```
program COUNTEX1 (ROUTE1, OUTPUT);
var
  COUNT: INTEGER;
  ROUTE1: TEXT;
begin
  COUNT: = 0;
  RESET (ROUTE1);
  while not EOF (ROUTE1) do
  begin
    READLN (ROUTE1); COUNT: = COUNT + 1
  end;
  WRITELN ('number of lines = ', COUNT)
end.
```

In this, EOF stands for end of file; EOF is a boolean function that returns TRUE if and only if the end of the file has been reached or the file is empty. If the file is not empty, EOF can only be true when the last character that was read was an end-of-line marker. The statement READLN (ROUTE1) causes a whole line of text to be read from ROUTE1, up to and including the end-of-line marker, so the character to be read next will be the first character on the next line, if indeed there are any more lines in the file. If there are no lines left then the next character to be read will be a special end-of-file marker, and EOF will return TRUE. Because ROUTE1 is the only parameter of READLN, the text that is read is not assigned to any variable but is in effect just skipped over.

As a further example, the following program computes the average number of characters per line in the text file named ROUTE2.

```
program COUNTEX2 (ROUTE2, OUTPUT);
var
    LINECOUNT, CHARCOUNT: INTEGER;
    ROUTE2: TEXT;
begin
    LINECOUNT: = 0; CHARCOUNT: = 0;
    RESET (ROUTE2);
    while not EOF (ROUTE2) do
    begin
        while not EOLN (ROUTE2) do
        CHARCOUNT: = CHARCOUNT + 1;
        READLN (ROUTE2); {skip to start of next line}
        LINECOUNT: = LINECOUNT + 1
    end;
    if LINECOUNT = 0 then WRITELN ('Empty file') else
    WRITELN ('average number of characters per line = ',
    CHARCOUNT/LINECOUNT:6:2)
end.
```

Note that EOLN has as its parameter the name of the text file in which an end-of-line marker is to be sought.

Sometimes it is convenient for a program to write to a file and subsequently read from this file, starting from the beginning. If before commencement and after termination of execution of the program this file does not exist then this file is said to be an *internal* file. An internal file exists only during the execution of a program. A file that exists in secondary memory before and/or after execution of a program is said to be an *external* file. The programmer must include in the **program** statement at the head of a program the names of all external files that the program uses. For example, ROUTE2 has been included in the parameter list of example program COUN-TEX2 because ROUTE2 is an external file that exists in secondary memory before and after execution of this program. The names of internal files should not be included in the parameter list of the **program** statement.

As an example to illustrate writing to a file, the following program copies the contents of text file MYFILE into text file THYFILE, although operating system facilities would normally provide a simpler way of doing this.

```
program COPY (MYFILE, THYFILE);
var
  CH: CHAR;
  MYFILE, THYFILE: TEXT;
begin
  RESET (MYFILE); REWRITE (THYFILE);
  while not EOF (MYFILE) do
  begin
    while not EOLN (MYFILE) do
    begin
      READ (MYFILE, CH); WRITE (THYFILE, CH)
    end;
    READLN (MYFILE); {to skip to first character on next line}
    WRITELN (THYFILE) {to output end-of-line marker}
  end
end.
```

The WRITELN statement is required because otherwise no end-of-line markers would be copied into THYFILE. In this example program, INPUT and OUTPUT are not included in the parameter list of the **program** statement because this program does not take input from or send output to the terminal.

9.3. Type declarations

The only way that a program can insert new data into a standard Pascal file is to read the file and write a new version of the file containing the inserted data. The new version cannot have the same name as the old, because a program cannot work with two files that have the same name. After the new version has been created, the old version can be deleted if it is not required for other purposes.

Similarly, to delete some of the data from a standard Pascal file, a program must copy into a new file those parts of the old file that are *not* to be deleted.

To illustrate deletion, and at the same time provide an example that will be useful for introducing type declarations, the following program reads the name of a town from the terminal and deletes this name from the file ROUTE2, the resulting new file being ROUTE3. If the program does not find this name in ROUTE 2 it outputs a message to say so, and in this case ROUTE3 is simply a copy of ROUTE2.

```
program CHOPTOWN (INPUT, OUTPUT, ROUTE2, ROUTE3);
var
   I, J: INTEGER;
   ROUTE2, ROUTE3: TEXT;
   DELETED, NAMEFOUND: BOOLEAN;
   WHICHTOWN, THISTOWN: array [1..10] of CHAR;
begin
   WRITELN ('please type town name with not more than ten letters');
   I: = 0;
   while not EOLN (INPUT) and (I < 10) do
   begin
      I: = I + 1;
      READ (WHICHTOWN [I])
   end; {WHICHTOWN now contains the name to be deleted}
   {The following loop puts in spaces if necessary to make
   WHICHTOWN contain exactly ten characters. Such spaces are known
   as *padding*}
   for J: = I + 1 to 10 do WHICHTOWN [J]: = ' ';
   RESET (ROUTE2); REWRITE (ROUTE3);
   DELETED: = FALSE; {to signify no deletion so far}
   while not EOF (ROUTE2) do
   begin
      I: = 0; NAMEFOUND: = TRUE;
      while not EOLN (ROUTE2) and (I < 10) do
      begin
         I: = I + 1;
         READ (ROUTE2, THISTOWN [I]);
         if THISTOWN [I] < > WHICHTOWN [I] then
         NAMEFOUND: = FALSE
      end;
      READLN (ROUTE2);
      if NAMEFOUND and (I > 0) then DELETED: = TRUE else
```

```
      begin
         for J: = 1 to I do WRITE (ROUTE3, THISTOWN [J]);
         WRITELN (ROUTE3) {to output end-of-line marker after the
         name}
      end
   end;
   if DELETED then WRITELN ('name deleted')
   else WRITELN ('name not deleted')
end.
```

To be practical, this program should check that names read from the terminal and from ROUTE2 contain not less than one and not more than ten characters. We omit such checks only to avoid cluttering up the program with detail.

Instead of declaring

```
var
   WHICHTOWN, THISTOWN: array [1..10] of CHAR;
```

the programmer can give a name to the type **array** [1..10] **of** CHAR by writing a *type declaration* such as

```
type
   NAMEARRAY = array [1..10] of CHAR;
```

Subsequently the programmer can declare

```
var
   WHICHTOWN, THISTOWN: NAMEARRAY;
```

and then WHICHTOWN and THISTOWN can be used in our example program without further modification. An effect of this **var** declaration is to create arrays named WHICHTOWN and THISTOWN which are arrays [1..10] **of** CHAR. In this particular example there is no advantage in using a type declaration, but in various other contexts, such as those for structured types of procedure parameters, type declarations are essential.

INTEGER, REAL, CHAR, and BOOLEAN are standard types in Pascal. *Standard* means that they can be used without being declared. Types that have to be declared are *user-defined* types. To provide further examples of user-defined types, note that in our program CHOPTOWN the variable I should be confined to the range 0..10, and J should be confined to the range 1..10. To help ensure that I and J are indeed confined to these ranges, the programmer can declare integer subrange types by writing, for example,

type
    BOUNDS = 1..10;
    CURSOR = 0..10;

Subsequently the programmer can declare

var
    I: CURSOR; J: BOUNDS;

I and J can now be used in our example program without further modification. An advantage of this is that, for example, any attempt to assign to I a value outside the range 0..10 will be detected immediately, and this will help the programmer to find out what has gone wrong.

After declaring the subrange type BOUNDS, the programmer can optionally use this in the declaration of the type NAMEARRAY:

type
    BOUNDS = 1..10;
    CURSOR = 0..10;
    NAMEARRAY = **array** [BOUNDS] **of** CHAR;
var
    I: CURSOR; J: BOUNDS;
    WHICHTOWN, THISTOWN: NAMEARRAY;
    DELETED, NAMEFOUND: BOOLEAN;

The body of our program can remain unchanged. In **type** declarations, the type name is followed by =, whereas in **var** declarations type names are preceded by :. Note also that Pascal insists that **type** declarations always precede **var** declarations. If there are any **const** declarations then **type** declarations must be placed between **const** declarations and **var** declarations.

Declared constants can be used in **type** and **var** declarations. For example

const
    MAXCHARS = 10;

type
    BOUNDS = 1..MAXCHARS;
    CURSOR = 0..MAXCHARS;

In an array of type NAMEARRAY, the elements are physically stored in a manner that permits relatively rapid access, but does not necessarily minimize the total storage required for the array. If the programmer wishes the storage required for an array to be minimized by the system, and is willing to pay for this by tolerating slower access to elements of the array, he should declare the array to be *packed*. The programmer uses packed arrays in just the same way as ordinary arrays, subject to the following exceptions.

A packed array of characters is a *string*. For example we can declare

type
    STRING10 = **packed array** [1..10] **of** CHAR;
var
    WHICHTOWN, THISTOWN: STRING10;

We can apply operators $>$, $<$, $<>$, $=$, $> =$, and $< =$ to compare strings. For example we can write

if WHICHTOWN < THISTOWN **then** STATEMENT1 **else**
STATEMENT2

and this will execute STATEMENT1 if and only if the contents of the string WHICHTOWN precede the contents of string THIS-TOWN in lexicographic sequence. This sequence is generally lexicographic rather than alphabetic because a string is not restricted to contain only letters; it can contain any characters, including punctuation and spaces.

Another special property of a string is that it can be written in its entirety by a single WRITE or WRITELN statement, such as WRITE (WHICHTOWN), without a character-by-character loop. To illustrate some of these features, here is a version of our previous program CHOPTOWN.

program CHOPTOWN2 (INPUT, OUTPUT, ROUTE2, ROUTE3);
const
    MAXCHARS = 10;

```
type
  BOUNDS = 1..MAXCHARS;
  CURSOR = 0..MAXCHARS;
  STRING10 = packed array [BOUNDS] of CHAR;
var
  I: CURSOR; J: BOUNDS;
  DELETED: BOOLEAN;
  ROUTE2, ROUTE3: TEXT;
  WHICHTOWN, THISTOWN: STRING10;
begin
  WRITELN ('please type town name with not more than ten letters');
  WHICHTOWN: = '          '; {this fills WHICHTOWN with 10 spaces}
  I: = 0;
  while not (EOLN (INPUT)) and (I < 10) do
  begin
    I: = I + 1;
    READ (WHICHTOWN [I])
  end; {WHICHTOWN now contains the name to be deleted}
  RESET (ROUTE2); REWRITE (ROUTE3);
  DELETED: = FALSE; {to signify no deletion so far}
  while not EOF (ROUTE2) do
  begin
    THISTOWN: = '          ';
    I: = 0;
    while not EOLN (ROUTE2) and (I < 10) do
    begin
      I: = I + 1;
      READ (ROUTE2, THISTOWN [I])
    end;
    READLN (ROUTE2);
    if THISTOWN = WHICHTOWN then DELETED: = TRUE
    else WRITELN (ROUTE3, THISTOWN:I) {:I causes only the first I
    characters to be output}
  end;
  if DELETED then WRITELN ('name deleted')
  else WRITELN ('name not deleted')
end.
```

This program writes the whole of string THISTOWN by means of a single WRITELN statement. Standard Pascal does not allow an entire string to be read by means of a single READ statement; instead the programmer must provide an explicit character-by-character loop, as has been done in the foregoing example CHOP-TOWN2. This explicit character-by-character programming is wise because it ensures that the programmer knows how padding spaces and other contingencies have been dealt with.

There are, however, many practical Pascal systems that permit the reading of an entire string by a single READ statement, and the present text uses this commonly availble short cut to make programs more easily readable. To illustrate this, the following is a final version of our program CHOPTOWN which will work correctly only if the string that is typed at the terminal and also the strings that are read from ROUTE2 comprise exactly ten characters, including padding spaces where necessary. The output file ROUTE3, like the input file ROUTE2, will have exactly ten characters per line, not counting end-of-line markers.

```
program CHOPTOWN3 (INPUT, OUTPUT, ROUTE2, ROUTE3);
type
   STRING10 = packed array [1..10] of CHAR;
var
   DELETED: BOOLEAN;
   ROUTE2, ROUTE3: TEXT;
   WHICHTOWN, THISTOWN: STRING10;
begin
   WRITELN ('please type town name with exactly ten characters');
   READ (WHICHTOWN); {WHICHTOWN now contains the name to
   be deleted}
   RESET (ROUTE2); REWRITE (ROUTE3);
   DELETED: = FALSE; {to signify no deletion so far}
   while not EOF (ROUTE2) do
   begin
      READ (ROUTE2, THISTOWN);
      if THISTOWN = WHICHTOWN then DELETED: = TRUE
      else WRITELN (ROUTE3, THISTOWN);
      READLN (ROUTE2)
   end;
   if DELETED then WRITELN ('name deleted')
   else WRITELN ('name not deleted')
end.
```

9.4. Pascal record types and variables

9.4.1. Record declarations

The declarations

type
  STRING6 = **packed array** [1..6] **of** CHAR;
  SOURCEREC = **record**
                ITEMREFNO: STRING6;
                SUPPLIERNO: 0..99999;
                PRICEPERUNIT: REAL
              end;
var
  CURRENT, CHEAPEST: SOURCEREC;

declare SOURCEREC to be a record type that has three fields, ITEMREFNO, SUPPLIERNO, and PRICEPERUNIT. ITEM-REFNO is of type STRING6, SUPPLIERNO is of the integer subrange type 0..99999, and PRICEPERUNIT is of type REAL. In general a record type is specified by a list of (field name, field type) pairs, enclosed between the reserved words **record** and **end**. As in the SOURCEREC example, successive pairs are separated by semicolons, but there is no semicolon immediately preceding **end**. Within each pair the field name and field type are separated by a colon.

In our example, CURRENT is declared to be a variable of type SOURCEREC. This means that CURRENT has three fields. The name of the first field is CURRENT.ITEMREFNO, and the type of this field is STRING6 because this is the type of the ITEMREFNO field in the SOURCEREC type declaration. The name CURREN-T.ITEMREFNO consists of the name of the first field of the SOURCEREC record type, qualified by CURRENT, which is the name of the record variable in this example. In general the name of a field of a record variable is the name of the corresponding field of the record type, qualified by the name of the record variable. *Qualified by* means that the field name is immediately preceded by a full stop which is immediately preceded by the qualifying name.

This is further illustrated by the second field of our record variable CURRENT. The name of this field is CURRENT.SUPPLIERNO and its type is 0..99999 because this is the type of the second field of the record type SOURCEREC. Similarly the name of the third field of CURRENT is CURRENT.PRICEPERUNIT, and its type is REAL. The field CURRENT.PRICEPERUNIT can be used in exactly the same way as any other variable of type REAL, the field CURRENT.SUPPLIERNO can be used just like any other variable of type 0..99999, and CURRENT.ITEMREFNO can be used just like any other variable of type STRING6.

Thus a record variable is essentially a collection of variables (fields) that are generally of different types. It is worthwhile to contrast this with an array variable, which is collection of variables (array elements) that must all be of the same type. The fields of a record variable are distinguished from each other by name, whereas the elements of an array are distinguished from each other by subscript.

At the beginning of this section we declared a second variable, CHEAPEST, of type SOURCEREC. Its three fields are CHEAPEST.ITEMREFNO, CHEAPEST.SUPPLIERNO and CHEAPEST.-PRICEPERUNIT. The use of the qualifying name CHEAPEST distinguishes the ITEMREFNO field of CHEAPEST from the ITEMREFNO field of CURRENT. This illustrates the purpose of qualification.

The entire multifield value of a record variable can be assigned to another record variable of the same type by means of a single assignment statement. For example

CHEAPEST: = CURRENT

achieves the same as the sequence of three statements

CHEAPEST.ITEMREFNO: = CURRENT.ITEMREFNO;
CHEAPEST.SUPPLIERNO: = CURRENT.SUPPLIERNO;
CHEAPEST.PRICEPERUNIT: = CURRENT.PRICEPERUNIT;

However, it is not legitimate to compare the entire contents of record variables as in

if CHEAPEST = CURRENT **then** DOSOMETHING

Instead, to accomplish any such comparison, the record variables must be compared field by field explicitly.

Cheapest source example. We now give an example of a program

that processes records of type SOURCEREC obtained from a text
file named SOURCES that tells us which supplier supplies which
item at what price. We assume that this file contains one record per
line. The first six characters on each line are an item reference
number. Then there is at least one space followed by a supplier
number followed by at least one space followed by a price. The space
between supplier number and price is necessary for the same reason
that there must be space or end of line between successive numbers
in input read from a terminal; otherwise there would be no satisfac-
tory demarcation between one number and the next. Examples of a
few successive records in the file SOURCES are

```
6PK9F1      733        86.14
F8431P      733       152.18
J496B5      218         9.95
```

The following program reads an item reference number from a
terminal and looks it up in the SOURCES file to find the supplier
number of the supplier from whom the item is available most
cheaply. The output also includes the cheapest price of the item and
the number of different suppliers of this item.

```
program SEEKCHEAP (SOURCES, INPUT, OUTPUT);
type
   STRING6 = packed array [1..6] of CHAR;
   SOURCEREC = record
                   ITEMREFNO: STRING6;
                   SUPPLIERNO: 0..99999;
                   PRICEPERUNIT: REAL
               end;
var
   SOUGHTREFNO: STRING6;
   CURRENT, CHEAPEST: SOURCEREC;
   HOWMANY: INTEGER;
   SOURCES: TEXT;
begin
   WRITELN ('please type item ref no: exactly six characters');
   READLN (SOUGHTREFNO);
   HOWMANY: = 0; {no suppliers of this item have been found yet}
   RESET (SOURCES);
   while not EOF (SOURCES) do
   begin
      READLN (SOURCES, CURRENT.ITEMREFNO,
```

```
   CURRENT.SUPPLIERNO, CURRENT.PRICEPERUNIT);
   if SOUGHTREFNO = CURRENT.ITEMREFNO then
   begin
      HOWMANY: = HOWMANY + 1; {a supplier of the sought item
      has been found}
      if HOWMANY = 1 then CHEAPEST: = CURRENT {if this is the
      first it must be the cheapest so far}
      else
      if CHEAPEST.PRICEPERUNIT > CURRENT.PRICEPERUNIT
      then CHEAPEST: = CURRENT
   end
end;
WRITELN ('number of supplier of ', SOUGHTREFNO, 'is',
HOWMANY);
if HOWMANY > 0 then
begin
   WRITELN ('cheapest supplier is ', CHEAPEST.SUPPLIERNO);
   WRITELN ('cheapest price is ',
   CHEAPEST.PRICEPERUNIT:10:2)
end
end.
```

9.4.2. With

Repetitive qualification of field names may make a program long-winded. For example, if NEXTINV is a record variable of the record type of Typico's inventory file then we would prefer not to write such a repetitive statement as

```
if
NEXTINV.QUANTITYINWAREHOUSE −
NEXTINV.QUANTITYALLOCATED + NEXTINV.QUANTITY-
ONORDER < NEXTINV.REORDERLEVEL
then
WRITELN ('reorder ', NEXTINV.ITEMREFNO, 'quantity ',
NEXTINV.QUANTITYTOORDER)
```

To achieve abbreviation, Pascal allows us to write a statement preceded by

with recordvariablename **do**

In the (possibly compound) statement that follows the **do**, every field name of this record variable is understood to be qualified by the

name of this record variable. When this is used our example can be
written more succinctly:

with NEXTINV **do**
if
QUANTITYINWAREHOUSE – QUANTITYALLOCATED +
QUANTITYONORDER < REORDERLEVEL
then
WRITELN ('reorder ', ITEMREFNO, 'quantity ',
QUANTITYTOORDER)

   Some of the fields of a record type may themselves be records. For
example

type
  COMPLEX = **record**
                    REALPART, IMAGPART: REAL
              end;
  ELECTROMAG = **record**
                    WINDINGS: INTEGER;
                    GAPWIDTH: REAL2;
                    ELECTRIC, MAGNETIC: COMPLEX
                 end;
var
  LEFTCOIL, RIGHTCOIL: ELECTROMAG

In this example ELECTRIC and MAGNETIC are fields that are
records. Pascal allows us to write

with LEFTCOIL **do with** ELECTRIC **do**
begin
  REALPART: = REALPART*2; IMAGPART: = IMAGPART*2
end

As an abbreviation that achieves the same thing, Pascal allows us to
write

with LEFTCOIL, ELECTRIC **do**
begin
  REALPART: = REALPART*2; IMAGPART: = IMAGPART*2
end

Furthermore, Pascal also allows us to write

with LEFTCOIL.ELECTRIC **do**
begin
  REALPART: = REALPART*2; IMAGPART: = IMAGPART*2
end

and this would be the best option in the present context, because it would not provide unnecessary generality.

9.4.3. Variant records

Hitherto we have only considered record types for which the list of fields is fixed. In fact Pascal allows us to declare a record type that includes a menu of alternative sublists of fields. Selection from this menu is accomplished by including in the record a special field called the *tag* field, which is used like the selector in a **case** statement. A record that includes a tag field and menu is said to be a *variant* record.

To illustrate this we consider a much simplified version of Typico's EMPLOYEES record type. Typico's employees are permanent, temporary, or probationary. Temporary employment means employment for a fixed duration, e.g. 1 year, with no commitment to Typico to continue employment at the end of that time. Probationary employment means employment on trial, to see how it works out: if it works out well it is upgraded into permanent employment; otherwise Typico may terminate the appointment. The work of probationary employees is reviewed at regular intervals. The following is a version of a simplified EMPLOYEES record type that is *not* variant:

```
EMPLORECTYPE = record
                 EMPLOYEENUMBER: 100000..999999;
                 SURNAME: STRING12;
                 FORENAMES: STRING24;
                 DATEOFENTRYTOTHISAPPOINTMENT:
                     DATETYPE;
                 TEMPORARY: BOOLEAN;
                 DATEOFEXPIRYOFTEMPORARY
                   APPOINTMENT:
                   DATETYPE;
                 PROBATIONARY: BOOLEAN;
                 DATEOFENDOFPROBATION,
                   DATEOFLASTREVIEWOFPERFORMANCE,
```

DATEOFNEXTREVIEWOFPERFORMANCE:
DATETYPE;
EMPLOYEENUMBEROFSUPERVISOR:
100000..999999
    end

This is wasteful because, for example, for permanent employees the
DATEOFEXPIRYOFTEMPORARYAPPOINTMENT field is
unnecessary. For permanent and temporary employees the
DATEOFLASTREVIEWOFPERFORMANCE and DATEOF-
NEXTREVIEWOFPERFORMANCE fields are superfluous. We
can eliminate superfluous data by using a variant record type, as
follows. Before declaring the record type in this example we declare
a type EMPSTATUS that we shall use as the type of the tag field.
This declaration of EMPSTATUS tells the system that any variable
or field of type EMPSTATUS will have three possible values:
PERMANENT, PROBATIONARY, TEMPORARY.

```
type
  EMPSTATUS = (PERMANENT, PROBATIONARY,
    TEMPORARY);
  EMPLORECTYPE =
  record
    EMPLOYEENUMBER: 100000..999999;
    SURNAME: STRING12;
    FORENAMES: STRING24;
    DATEOFENTRYTOTHISAPPOINTMENT: DATETYPE;
    case STATUS: EMPSTATUS of
      TEMPORARY: (DATEOFEXPIRYOFAPPOINTMENT:
        DATETYPE)
      PROBATIONARY:
        (DATEOFLASTREVIEWOFPERFORMANCE,
        DATEOFNEXTREVIEWOFPERFORMANCE,
        DATEOFENDOFPROBATION: DATETYPE;
        EMPLOYEENUMBEROFSUPERVISOR: 100000..999999);
      PERMANENT: ( )
  end
```

The field between **case** and **of** is the tag field. In this example the tag
field is STATUS, which is of type EMPSTATUS. If an EMPLOR-
ECTYPE record has tag value STATUS = TEMPORARY, the
programmer can use this record *as if* its fields had been declared
to be:

```
EMPLORECTYPE = record
                  EMPLOYEENUMBER: 100000..999999;
                  SURNAME: STRING12;
                  FORENAMES: STRING24;
                  DATEOFENTRYTOTHISAPPOINTMENT:
                     DATETYPE;
                  STATUS: EMPSTATUS; {which has the value
                     TEMPORARY}
                  DATEOFEXPIRYOFAPPOINTMENT:
                     DATETYPE
               end
```

Here only the single field DATEOFEXPIRYOFAPPOINTMENT
appears after STATUS, because this is the only field in brackets
after TEMPORARY in the variant record. The fields associated
with PROBATIONARY are not included when STATUS = TEM-
PORARY.

If an EMPLORECTYPE record has STATUS = PROBATION-
ARY then the programmer can use this record as if its fields had
been declared to be

```
EMPLORECTYPE = record
                  EMPLOYEENUMBER: 100000..999999;
                  SURNAME: STRING12;
                  FORENAMES: STRING24;
                  DATEOFENTRYTOTHISAPPOINTMENT:
                     DATETYPE;
                  STATUS: EMPSTATUS; {which has the value
                     PROBATIONARY}
                  DATEOFLASTREVIEWOFPERFORMANCE,
                     DATEOFNEXTREVIEWOFPERFORMANCE,
                     DATEOFENDOFPROBATION:
                     DATETYPE;
                  EMPLOYEENUMBEROFSUPERVISOR:
                     100000..999999;
               end
```

Here the fields that follow STATUS are those that appear in the list
in brackets after PROBATIONARY in the variant record. The field
associated with TEMPORARY is not included when STATUS-
= PROBATIONARY. When STATUS = PERMANENT the record type looks like

EMPLORECTYPE = **record**
                    EMPLOYEENUMBER: 100000..999999;
                    SURNAME: STRING12;
                    FORENAMES: STRING24;
                    DATEOFENTRYTOTHISAPPOINTMENT:
                      DATETYPE;
                    STATUS: EMPSTATUS {which has the value
                      PERMANENT}
        end

Here there is no field after STATUS because in the variant record the brackets associated with PERMANENT enclose nothing.

The part of a variant record that follows **case** is called the *variant* part, and it must be terminated by exactly one **end**. Pascal requires that the variant part is always the last part; no non-variant fields may come after it. A record type can have only one variant part, but this may itself have a variant part, and so on, nesting to any depth.

Throughout this text, record types should be assumed *not* to be variant, except where there is explicit contrary specification.

9.5. Binary files

A text file is a sequence of characters, normally stored in secondary memory. We now introduce the general idea of a *binary* file, which is a sequence of values of a type *other than* CHAR. A program must declare all binary files that it uses, just as it must declare all text files that it uses. For example we might declare a file of integers

type
    FTYPE = **file of** INTEGER;
var
    AYFILE: FTYPE;

or equivalently

var
    AYFILE: **file of** INTEGER;

In this case AYFILE will contain a sequence of integers, not necessarily in character code form but in a general binary representation. This is why a file of a type other than CHAR is said to be *binary*. Each value written to or read from AYFILE will be an entire integer; a single integer cannot be written to or read from a file of integers digit by digit. All the digits of a single integer appear to be written or read in one gulp. The programmer does not need to know how successive integers are demarcated in a binary file of integers.

Pascal allows binary files of records. For example

```
type
  RECTYPE = record
              X: INTEGER;
              Y: REAL;
              Z: CHAR
            end;
  SOURCEREC = record
                ITEMREFNO: STRING6;
                SUPPLIERNO: 0..99999;
                PRICEPERUNIT: REAL
              end;
var
  EXFILE: file of RECTYPE;
  BINSOURCES: file of SOURCEREC;
  CURRENT: SOURCEREC;
  EXREC: RECTYPE
```

READ and WRITE statements for binary files are the same as for text files, except that reading and writing cannot be done character by character. Indeed the single statement WRITE (EXFILE, EXREC) writes the entire multifield value of EXREC to EXFILE. Because EXFILE is binary (i.e. not text) EXREC cannot be written to or read from EXFILE field by field; all fields are automatically written or read at once.

Similarly the single statement READ (BINSOURCES, CURRENT) reads into CURRENT all the fields of the next record in the binary file BINSOURCES. In the example program SEEKCHEAP in Section 9.4.1, we read a record from the text file SOURCES field by field:

READ (SOURCES, CURRENT.ITEMREFNO,
CURRENT.SUPPLIERNO, CURRENT.PRICEPERUNIT)

The file SOURCES may contain the same data as the file BIN-SOURCES; in SOURCES these data will be represented by a sequence of characters, whereas in BINSOURCES they will have a general binary representation. An advantage of using a binary file such as BINSOURCES instead of a text file such as SOURCES is that reading and writing is not done field by field and is therefore simpler for a binary file. This advantage becomes more important the greater the number of fields in the record type. A further advantage is speed, because there is no conversion between the character form and the binary form of numbers.

When operating system facilities are used, the only kind of file that we can create by typing at a terminal is a text file because typing produces a sequence of characters. Similarly, the only kind of file that we can print on a printer or display on a visual display unit screen is a text file, because a printer or a VDU outputs a sequence of characters. It is, however, easy to write a program to read records in text form and output the records into a binary file, or to read data from a binary file and output the same data in text form.

Because a binary file does not contain text it does not contain end-of-line markers. Therefore READLN, WRITELN, and EOLN are illegal for binary files.

RESET, REWRITE, and EOF are the same for binary files as for text files. For example, before reading from BINSOURCES for the first time, or to start reading BINSOURCES again from the beginning, a program must execute RESET (BINSOURCES). The distinction between internal and external files is the same for binary and text files. The parameter list of the **program** statement must include the names of all external binary files used by the program.

9.6 File buffers

A *buffer* is an area of memory used for temporary storage of data that are on their way from somewhere to somewhere else. The **var** declaration of a file causes a file buffer to be made available for use with that file. For each file that is declared, a separate buffer is made available. For example, the declaration

FNAME: **file of** TYPENAME

causes automatic provision of a buffer for file FNAME. This buffer is actually a variable of type TYPENAME, and the name of this variable is FNAME↑. Generally the file buffer is a variable of the type that the file is **of**, and the name of the file buffer is derived by appending an up-arrow to the name of the file.

While a file is being used for read only, the file buffer contains the value that will be read by the *next* READ statement. Thus successive values are copied from the file into the file's buffer. The programmer may sometimes wish the next value to be copied into the file's buffer without execution of a READ statement. Pascal allows the programmer to achieve this by using the standard procedure GET, which has the name of the file as parameter. Thus GET (FNAME) gets the next value of type TYPENAME from the file FNAME and copies it into FNAME↑, overwriting the previous value of FNAME↑ and advancing along FNAME so that a second call of GET would get the next value from FNAME. If V is a variable of type TYPENAME then the two statements

V: = FNAME↑; GET (FNAME)

achieve the same as the single statement READ (FNAME, V). For a text file the file buffer is of type CHAR: integers and reals are automatically read via this buffer character by character, without the programmer seeing the details. Note that if, for example, V, W, and X are variables of type TYPENAME then the three statements

V: = FNAME↑; W: = FNAME↑; READ (FNAME, X)

cause the value that will be read into X to be assigned also to V and W. The assignments to V and W do not cause successive values to be read from FNAME; only the statements READ and GET cause movement to the next input value.

Analogous to the standard procedure GET, Pascal also provides a standard procedure PUT which has a file name as its parameter. The effect of PUT (FNAME) is to output the current value of FNAME↑ to the file FNAME, leaving FNAME↑ unchanged. Thus the pair of statements

FNAME↑: = V; PUT (FNAME)

achieve the same as the single statement WRITE (FNAME, V), unless FNAME is a text file and V is not of type CHAR.

Sum of money example. To illustrate the use of the file buffer of a text file, the following program reads through a text file AMOUNTS that contains real numbers, one per line. Each of these is an amount of money, not preceded on the line by any spaces. If the first character on the line is $ then the amount is in dollars, whereas if there is no $ sign the first character on the line is the first digit of the amount which is in sterling. The program outputs the total of all these amounts, given in sterling, assuming 1.50 dollars per pound.

```
program SUMS (AMOUNTS, OUTPUT);
const
  DOLLARSPERPOUND = 1.5;
var
  AMOUNTS: TEXT;
  DOLLARS, POUNDS, SUM: REAL;
begin
  SUM: = 0;
  RESET (AMOUNTS);
  while not EOF (AMOUNTS) do
  begin
    if AMOUNTS↑ = '$' then {amount is in dollars}
    begin
            GET (AMOUNTS); {so that the next character to be read
            will be the first digit of the amount}
            READLN (AMOUNTS, DOLLARS);
            POUNDS: = DOLLARS / DOLLARSPERPOUND
    end else READLN (AMOUNTS, POUNDS);
    SUM: = SUM + POUNDS
  end;
  WRITELN ('Total = ', SUM:8:2)
end.
```

The file buffer enables the program to look for $ without spoiling the number if $ is not there. If, instead, the program were to read the first digit on the line by using a statement such as READ (AMOUNTS, CH), and subsequently read the actual amount by a statement such as READ (AMOUNTS, POUNDS) then the most significant digit of POUNDS would be lost if it was the first character on the line. In this case the first READ statement would have caused movement along the input file so that the second character on the line would be the first to be read by the second READ statement.

File-merging example. File merging provides a classic example of the use of file buffers, illustrating the use of GET and PUT. The following program merges two binary input files into a single output file. In this example both the input files are files of STUDENT-COURSES records which have been sorted so that STUDENTI-DENTINO increases. That is to say, in an input file the STUDEN-TIDENTINO of any record exceeds the STUDENTIDENTINOs of all preceding records. The merge preserves the sorted order.

```
program EXMERGE (OLDMASTER, TRANSAC, NEWMASTER);
type
   STRING12 = packed array [1..12] of CHAR;
   STUDENTCOURSES = record
                          STUDENTIDENTINO: 1..9999;
                          COURSES: array [1..3] of STRING12
                       end;
var
   OLDMASTER, TRANSAC, NEWMASTER: file of
   STUDENTCOURSES;
   STOPLOOP: BOOLEAN;
begin
   RESET (OLDMASTER); RESET (TRANSAC);
   REWRITE (NEWMASTER);
   STOPLOOP: = EOF (OLDMASTER) or EOF (TRANSAC);
   while not STOPLOOP do
   begin
     if
     OLDMASTER↑.STUDENTIDENTINO < TRANSAC↑.
     STUDENTIDENTINO
     then
     begin
       NEWMASTER↑: = OLDMASTER↑; GET (OLDMASTER);
       STOPLOOP: = EOF (OLDMASTER)
     end
     else
     begin
       NEWMASTER↑: = TRANSAC↑; GET (TRANSAC);
       STOPLOOP: = EOF (TRANSAC)
     end;
     PUT (NEWMASTER)
   end;
   while not EOF (OLDMASTER) do
```

```
begin
   NEWMASTER↑: = OLDMASTER↑; PUT (NEWMASTER);
   GET (OLDMASTER)
end;
while not EOF (TRANSAC) do
begin
   NEWMASTER↑: = TRANSAC↑; PUT (NEWMASTER);
   GET (TRANSAC)
end
end.
```

In this program the first **while** loop does the actual merge. After termination of this loop, the one of the two files OLDMASTER and TRANSAC that is not exhausted is copied to NEWMASTER. This copying is done by one of the last two **while** loops. An advantage of using file buffers is that the program can compare STUDENTI-DENTINOs of the next records of OLDMASTER and TRANSAC without actually reading from (and thus moving along) either of these files. To see how much this simplifies the programming, it is worthwhile rewriting the program without using file buffers.

9.7. Exercises

The following exercises are concerned with a simplified INVOICE file that contains the following eight records:

INVOICENO	CUSTOMERNO	DATE	AMOUNT
1020	12	910621	302.61
1023	15	910621	57.81
1027	11	910622	652.34
1034	12	910622	81.72
1036	15	910622	24.00
1045	11	910623	775.00
1049	11	910624	61.55
1051	15	910624	81.17

The record type is

record
   INVOICENO: 1000..9999;
   CUSTOMERNO: 10..99;

DATE: 900101..991231;
AMOUNT: REAL
end

1. (a) Create a text file name TINVOICE containing the eight records shown above. Create this file using operating system facilities, without writing a program.
   (b) Write a program to read TINVOICE and output a binary file named INVOICE containing the same records.
   (c) Write a program to read the binary file INVOICE and output it to the VDU screen. Keep this program for use later.
   (d) By using operating system facilities, delete the file TINVOICE, but do not delete INVOICE.

2. (a) Write a program to output to the VDU screen the result of

   proj INVOICENO, DATE, AMOUNT (**sel** CUSTOMERNO = CX (INVOICE))

   where CX is a customer number typed on the VDU keyboard. Your program should start by reading CX and should then read through the file INVOICE outputting data from each record where the CUSTOMER matches CX. If there are no such records your program should say so.
   (b) Amend your program to make it read a customer number from the keyboard and output *only* the total (possibly zero) of the AMOUNTs of this customer's invoices. (Note that there is no relational algebra expression for this.)

3. (a) Use operating system facilities to make a copy of the INVOICE file, giving the copy a new name.
   (b) Write a program to read an invoice number from the keyboard and delete from the INVOICE file the record that has this INVOICENO. If there is no such record then your program should output a message to say so. The deletion is to be achieved by reading the original INVOICE file and outputting a new version of it with the specified record absent. Display the new version of the INVOICE file on the VDU using the program of Exercise 1(c). Keep your program for use in Exercise 4(b).
   (c) From the copy made in (a), use operating system facilities to restore the original contents of the INVOICE file.

4. (a) Write a program to read a new invoice record from the terminal and insert it into the INVOICE file in the correct place in sequence of increasing INVOICENO. The insertion is to be achieved by reading the original INVOICE file and outputting a new version of it that includes the new record. If the INVOICENO of the input record is the same as that of a record which is already in the file, do not insert the input record into the file but instead output a message to say what has happened. After inserting a record, display the new version of the INVOICE file on the VDU screen.

(b) Using your program of Exercise 3(b), delete from INVOICE the record that was inserted in (a). Display the resulting original version of the INVOICE file on the VDU screen.

5. Write a program to read from the terminal an INVOICENO followed by a letter that may be A or D. If this letter is D then the program should next read from the terminal a date and insert it into the DATE field of the record that the INVOICENO identifies in the INVOICE file, overwriting the previous value of this DATE field. If the input letter is A then the program should read from the terminal an amount and insert it into the AMOUNT field of the specified record of the INVOICE file, overwriting the previous value of this AMOUNT field. If the specified record is not found in the INVOICE file or if the input letter is not A and not D, then the program should output an explanatory message and terminate.

6. (a) As in Exercise 3(a), make a copy of the INVOICE file.

(b) Create a text file named DTRANSAC containing the INVOICENOs 1023, 1034, 1036, and 1049.

(c) Write a program to delete from the INVOICE file all the records whose INVOICENO is stored in DTRANSAC.

(d) Using the copy, restore the original version of the INVOICE file. Edit DTRANSAC so that it now contains 1023, 1024, 1036, 1038, and 1049.

(e) Repeat (c) but now outputting a message to the VDU each time a sought record is not found.

7. This is a repeat of Exercise 5, except that more than one INVOICE record is to be updated by a single run (i.e. execution) of your program. A text file named VTRANS is to contain the update information; its variant record type is

record
   INVOICENO: 1000..9999;
   case TAG: CHAR **of**
    'A': (AMOUNT: REAL);
    'D': (DATE: 900101..991231)
end.

The records in VTRANS are in sequence of increasing INVOICENO. You are required to make up the contents of VTRANS.

9.8. Pointers

9.8.1. Pointer types

A pointer is a kind of address that tells the computer where to find a variable. A pointer can itself be the value of a variable. In Fig. 9.1 P↑ is a variable of any type T. P is a variable whose value is a pointer to P↑. This pointer is represented diagrammatically by an arrow whose tail is in the variable P and whose head points at the variable P↑. The name P↑ can be regarded as meaning 'pointed at by P'. The variable P↑ can be used in exactly the same way as any other variable of its type.

Fig. 9.1. A pointer P pointing to a variable P↑.

A pointer variable can only point to variables of one type. A pointer variable that points to variables of type T must be declared to be of type ↑T. The type name ↑T can be regarded as meaning 'pointer to variable of type T'. For our example in which P points to P↑, if P↑ is of type INTEGER then P must be declared to be of type ↑INTEGER.
   The declaration

var
   I: INTEGER;

causes the system to create a variable named I for which the initial value is undefined. Similarly the declaration

var
  P: ↑INTEGER;

causes the system to create a variable named P, capable of having a
value that is a pointer to a variable of type INTEGER but having an
undefined initial value. This declaration of P does *not* cause the
system to create an integer variable P↑. Instead, the programmer can
explicitly tell the system to create this variable by calling the
standard procedure NEW. The effect of NEW(P) is to create a new
integer variable named P↑ and assign to P a pointer to P↑. NEW(P)
leaves the initial value of the new variable P↑ undefined. Subsequently P↑ can be used in exactly the same way as any other integer
variable.

Suppose, for example, that we have a program which starts

```
program PEXAMPLE (INPUT, OUTPUT);
type
   PCATCHTYPE = ↑CATCHTYPE; {it is legitimate for this declaration
   to precede the declaration of CATCHTYPE}
   CATCHTYPE = record
                  WEIGHT: REAL;
                  FISHCOUNT: INTEGER
               end;
var
   P, Q: ↑INTEGER;
   TRIP1, TRIP2: PCATCHTYPE;
begin
   NEW (P); NEW (TRIP1);
   READLN (P↑, TRIP1↑.WEIGHT, TRIP1↑.FISHCOUNT);
```

TRIP1↑.WEIGHT and TRIP1↑.FISHCOUNT are the names of the
fields of the record to which TRIP1 points. Suppose, for example,
that the result of this READLN statement is as shown in Fig. 9.2.
The assignment P: = TRIP1 is illegal because P and TRIP1 are of
different types. The assignment Q: = P is legal and makes Q point to
the integer variable that P is pointing at, as shown in Fig. 9.3. Q↑ is
now an alternative name for P↑. The assignment TRIP2↑: = TRIP1↑
is currently illegal because TRIP2 does not yet point to anything; the
record variable TRIP2↑ does not exist until it has been created by
calling NEW (TRIP2). The effect of the two statements

NEW (TRIP2); TRIP2↑: = TRIP1↑

is to create the record variable TRIP2↑ and copy the fields of TRIP1↑ into it, as shown in Fig. 9.4.

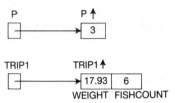

Fig. 9.2. Example of possible values of variables.

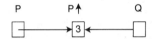

Fig. 9.3. Two pointers pointing to the same variable.

Fig. 9.4. Example values of TRIP2 and TRIP2↑.

Pascal allows us to assign to any pointer variable the special value **nil**. We can use this value to signify that a pointer is not actually pointing to anything. For example we might wish to assign TRIP2 : = **nil** before we call NEW (TRIP2) in order to signify that TRIP2 is not pointing to anything before the time of this call.

When we have finished using a variable that was created by calling the procedure NEW, we can eliminate the variable, thus making its memory area available for other use, by calling the procedure DISPOSE. For example, DISPOSE (TRIP1) undoes the effect of NEW (TRIP1). To avoid the possibility of chaos, the programmer should ensure that TRIP1↑ is not pointed to by any other pointer, in addition to TRIP1, when DISPOSE (TRIP1) is executed.

9.8.2. Linked lists

A linked list is a structure in which one record points to another, which points to another, which points to another, and so on, as shown in Fig. 9.5. The **nil** value of the final pointer field signifies that this is the end of the list: it does not point to anything. This *linked-list* structure has the advantage that a record can easily be deleted

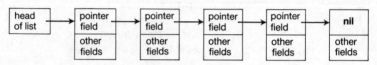

Fig. 9.5. An example showing the form of a linked list.

from the sequence by changing its predecessor's pointer as shown in Fig. 9.6. Furthermore a new record can be inserted by changing its predecessor's pointer as shown in Fig. 9.7. It is important that the programmer does not need to know the number of records in a linked list when the declaration part of the program is written. If a collection of records, all of the same type, are held in an array, the programmer needs to know the maximum number of elements when writing the array declaration (unless conformant arrays are used).

Car park example. We shall now put together, step by step, a program that maintains an up-to-date list of all the cars currently in a car park. The program allows us to look up any given car registration number in the list to find out whether or not this car is currently in the car park. The program also produces, when required, a list of registration numbers of all cars currently in the car park. This output list is alphabetically sorted on registration number to facilitate looking up any given registration number. The purpose of this example is to illustrate basic operations on a linked list

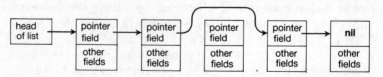

Fig. 9.6. A record removed from a linked list by making its predecessor point to its successor.

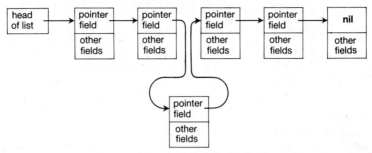

Fig. 9.7. A record inserted into a linked list by linking it into the pointer chain.

(although a linked list is actually not the most appropriate data structure for this problem).

The program asks the user to type a single letter to indicate what he wishes to do, e.g. insert into the list the registration number of a car that has just entered the car park, or delete from the list the registration number of a car that has just left the car park. It is easy to see how these single letters are used by the program:

```pascal
program CARWATCH (INPUT, OUTPUT);
type
    STRING7 = packed array [1..7] of CHAR;
    LISTPTR = ↑REGRECTYPE;
    REGRECTYPE = record
                        REGNUMBER: STRING7;
                        NEXTREG: LISTPTR
                    end;
var
    LISTHEAD: LISTPTR;
    SELECTOR: CHAR;
procedure INSERT; begin {declaration omitted} end;
procedure DELETE; begin {declaration omitted} end;
procedure LOOKUP; begin {declaration omitted} end;
procedure OUTPUTLIST; begin {declaration omitted} end;
begin {body of program}
    LISTHEAD: = nil; {to signify that list is initially empty}
    repeat
        WRITELN ('if you wish to insert please type I');
        WRITELN ('if you wish to delete please type D');
        WRITELN ('if you wish to look up please type R');
        WRITELN ('if you wish to output the list type L');
```

```
    WRITELN ('if you wish to terminate the program type X);
    READLN (SELECTOR);
    case SELECTOR of
      'I': INSERT;
      'D': DELETE;
      'R': LOOKUP;
      'L': OUTPUTLIST;
      'X':
    end
  until SELECTOR = 'X'
end.
```

We now provide the missing procedures, starting with OUTPUT-LIST, because this is the simplest:

```
procedure OUTPUTLIST;
var
  CURRPTR: LISTPTR;
begin
  CURRPTR: = LISTHEAD;
  if CURRPTR = nil then WRITELN ('list empty') else
  repeat
    WRITELN (CURRPTR↑.REGNUMBER);
    CURRPTR: = CURRPTR↑.NEXTREG
  until CURRPTR = nil
end;
```

To illustrate the working of this procedure, suppose for example that the list contains the four registration numbers 'A136PTK', 'A783AFC', 'B276PPC', and 'B304PTC'. Just before the first execution of the loop, CURRPTR points to what LISTHEAD is pointing to, as shown in Fig. 9.8. WRITELN (CURRPTR↑.REGN-UMBER) outputs the first registration number 'A136PTK'. The assignment   CURRPTR: = CURRPTR↑.NEXTREG   makes CURRPTR point to the record that the 'A136PTK' record is

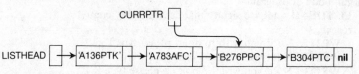

Fig. 9.8.   Pointer values before the first execution of the loop.

pointing to; therefore just before the second execution of the loop the pointers are as shown in Fig. 9.9. The statement WRITELN (CURRPTR↑.REGNUMBER) now outputs 'A783AFC'. Just before the third execution of the loop the pointers are as shown in Fig. 9.10. When, eventually, CURRPTR = **nil**, all the registration numbers have been output.

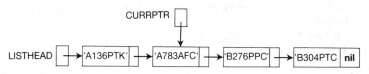

Fig. 9.9. Pointer values before the second execution of the loop.

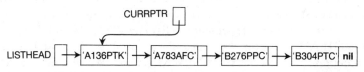

Fig. 9.10. Pointer values before the third execution of the loop.

The procedure INSERT is more complicated, and we shall only write part of it to start with:

```
procedure INSERT;
var
   NEWREGPTR: LISTPTR;
   REGISTRATION: STRING7;
begin
   READLN (REGISTRATION); {assuming that exactly seven
   characters are typed}
   NEW (NEWREGPTR); {NEWREGPTR now points to a newly
   created record}
   NEWREGPTR↑.REGNUMBER: = REGISTRATION; {to put the
   input registration number into the REGNUMBER field of the newly
   created record}
   if LISTHEAD = nil then
   begin {in this case the list is empty}
      LISTHEAD: = NEWREGPTR; {to make LISTHEAD point to the
      newly created record}
```

LISTHEAD↑.NEXTREG: = **nil** {to signify that the newly created record does not yet have a successor}
end
else {the list is not empty and we next check whether the newly created record should be inserted as the first record in the list}
if REGISTRATION < = LISTHEAD↑.REGNUMBER **then**
begin {the input registration number alphabetically precedes the first registration number in the list}
NEWREGPTR↑.NEXTREG: = LISTHEAD; {explained in the text below}
LISTHEAD: = NEWREGPTR
end else {continued later}

Suppose for example that the input registration number is 'A136PTK' and that the first registration number that is already in the list is 'A783AFC'. In this case, just before execution of the last compound statement shown above, the situation is as shown in Fig. 9.11. After execution of the statement NEWREGPTR↑.NEXTREG: = LISTHEAD the situation is as shown in Fig. 9.12, and after execution of LISTHEAD: = NEWREGPTR the situation is as shown in Fig. 9.13. Note that the assignment LISTHEAD: = NEWREGPTR makes LISTHEAD point to what NEWREGPTR

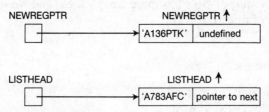

Fig. 9. 11.   Pointer values before execution of the last compound statement.

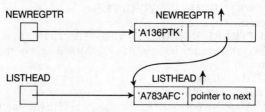

Fig. 9.12.   Pointers after LISTHEAD has been copied.

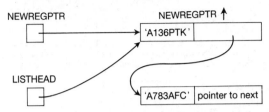

Fig. 9.13. Pointers after the assignment to LISTHEAD.

was pointing to, but does *not* assign LISTHEAD↑: = NEWREGPTR↑. Thus the contents of the record NEWREGPTR↑ do not overwrite the contents of the record LISTHEAD↑. Instead, both these records are preserved in the list.

We now continue writing the procedure INSERT to take care of the case where the new record should be inserted somewhere after the first record in the list, possibly to become the final record. For this purpose we shall define two further pointers, CURRPTR and PREVPTR, of type LISTPTR. We use a **repeat until** loop that makes CURRPTR point to successive records in the list. The following is a simplified version of the loop which rashly assumes that the input registration number will not be the last in the list:

```
CURRPTR: = LISTHEAD;
repeat
   PREVPTR: = CURRPTR;
   CURRPTR: = CURRPTR↑.NEXTREG
until CURRPTR↑.REGNO > REGISTRATION;
PREVPTR↑.NEXTREG: = NEWREGPTR;
NEWREGPTR↑.NEXTREG: = CURRPTR;
```

Suppose, for example, that the first three registration numbers in the list are 'A136PTK', 'A783AFC', and 'B304PTC'. Suppose that the input registration number now is 'B276PPC'. After the first execution of the loop the pointers are as shown in Fig. 9.14. After the second execution of the loop the pointers are as shown in Fig. 9.15. The loop now terminates because CURRPTR↑.REGNO > = REGISTRATION which shows that the input registration number should be inserted before the third in the list. After execution of the two statements

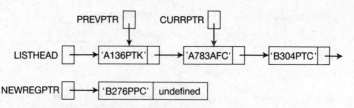

Fig. 9.14. Pointers after the first execution of the loop.

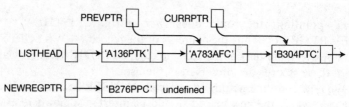

Fig. 9.15. Pointers after the second execution of the loop.

PREVPTR↑.NEXTREG: = NEWREGPTR;
NEWREGPTR↑.NEXTREG: = CURRPTR

the pointers are as shown in Fig. 9.16 and 'B276PPC' has been
inserted into the correct place in the list.

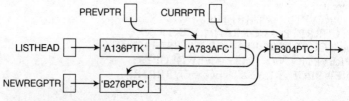

Fig. 9.16. Pointer values when the procedure terminates.

The following is a complete version of the procedure INSERT,
which takes care of the possibility that the new record should be
inserted at the end of the list. The Boolean variable DONE serves to
indicate when the loop should terminate.

procedure INSERT;
var
    NEWREGPTR, CURRPTR, PREVPTR: LISTPTR;

```
   REGISTRATION: STRING7;
   DONE: BOOLEAN;
begin
   READLN (REGISTRATION);
   NEW (NEWREGPTR);
   NEWREGPTR↑.REGNUMBER: = REGISTRATION;
   if LISTHEAD = nil then
   begin
     LISTHEAD: = NEWREGPTR;
     LISTHEAD↑.NEXTREG: = nil
   end else
   if REGISTRATION < = LISTHEAD↑.REGNUMBER then
   begin
     NEWREGPTR↑.NEXTREG: = LISTHEAD;
     LISTHEAD: = NEWREGPTR
   end else
   begin
     CURRPTR: = LISTHEAD;
     repeat
       PREVPTR: = CURRPTR;
       CURRPTR: = CURRPTR↑.NEXTREG;
       if CURRPTR = nil then DONE: = TRUE
       else DONE: = CURRPTR↑.REGNO > = REGISTRATION
     until DONE;
     PREVPTR↑.NEXTREG: = NEWREGPTR;
     NEWREGPTR↑.NEXTREG: = CURRPTR
   end
end {of procedure INSERT};
```

DONE is used to avoid testing whether CURRPTR↑.REGNO >
= REGISTRATION in the case where CURRPTR = nil, because
this would fail.

A version of procedure DELETE is

```
procedure DELETE;
var
   CURRPTR, PREVPTR: LISTPTR;
   REGISTRATION: STRING7;
begin
   if LISTHEAD = nil then WRITELN ('the list is empty') else
   begin
     READLN (REGISTRATION); {the registration number to be
     deleted}
     CURRPTR: = LISTHEAD;
     if CURRPTR↑.REGNUMBER = REGISTRATION then
```

```
        LISTHEAD: = CURRPTR↑.NEXTREG {this makes LISTHEAD
        point to the second record in the list, thus missing out and thereby
        deleting the first record}
      else
      repeat
        PREVPTR: = CURRPTR;
        CURRPTR: = CURRPTR↑.NEXTREG
      until (CURRPTR↑.REGNO = REGISTRATION) or
      (CURRPTR↑.NEXTREG = nil);
      if CURRPTR↑.REGNO = REGISTRATION then
      begin
        PREVPTR↑.NEXTREG: = CURRPTR↑.NEXTREG;
        DISPOSE (CURRPTR) {to release memory space that was
        occupied by the unwanted record}
      end else WRITELN (REGISTRATION, 'is not in the list')
    end
end;
```

Suppose for example that the list contains 'A136PTK', 'A783AFC', 'B276PPC', and 'B304PTC', and that the registration number to be deleted is 'B276PPC'. In this case when the loop terminates the pointers are as shown in Fig. 9.17. Just before the call of DISPOSE the pointers are as shown in Fig. 9.18.

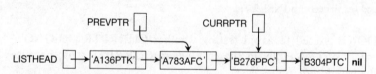

Fig. 9.17. Pointer values when the loop terminates.

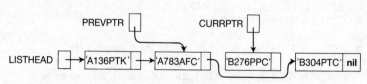

Fig. 9.18. Pointer values just before the call of DISPOSE.

Our last procedure is LOOKUP, which should be self-explanatory:

```
procedure LOOKUP;
var
  CURRPTR: LISTPTR;
  REGISTRATION: STRING7;
  FOUND: BOOLEAN;
begin
  if LISTHEAD = nil then WRITELN ('the list is empty')
  else
  begin
    READLN (REGISTRATION); {registration number to be looked
    up}
    FOUND: = FALSE; {registration number not yet found in the list}
    CURRPTR: = LISTHEAD;
    while (CURRPTR < > nil) and not FOUND do
    begin
      FOUND: = (CURRPTR↑.REGNUMBER = REGISTRATION);
      CURRPTR: = CURRPTR↑.NEXTREG
    end;
    if FOUND then WRITELN ('FOUND') else
    WRITELN ('NOT FOUND')
  end
end;
```

Indexed invoice table example. As further illustration of the use of pointers and linked lists, we now consider an example in which a program reads a simplified INVOICE file into immediate access memory, and then reads a customer number from the terminal and outputs the INVOICENUMBER and AMOUNT of all of a specified customer's invoices. For efficiency we use an index which, for each customer number, takes us to all of this customer's invoice records. For simplicity the program does not check that the input data are within declared range.

The simplified invoice record type is

```
INVRECTYPE = record
                INVOICENUMBER: 10..20;
                CUSTOMERNUMBER: 10..15;
                AMOUNT: REAL
             end
```

The program starts by reading records from a binary file of INVRECTYPE into an array INVOICETABLE: **array** [10..20] **of** INVRECTYPE, putting each record where the array subscript is the same as the INVOICENUMBER. An array of records is sometimes called a *table*. The contents of our table might for example be as shown in Table 9.1. The top row shows field names; these names are not actually stored in the table. The first column of the table shows the array subscript (which for simplicity we shall unnecessarily include within the table). Associated with the table we have an index that shows, for each CUSTOMERNUMBER, the array subscripts of all of this customer's invoices in the table. For our example the contents of the index are as shown in Table 9.2. Again the field

TABLE 9.1
Example of contents of invoice table

INVOICENUMBER	CUSTOMERNUMBER	AMOUNT
10	14	65.73
11	12	78.10
12	14	19.50
13	15	35.33
14	12	61.80
15	10	69.90
16	14	12.30
17	15	30.00
18	12	13.29
19	14	50.92
20	14	88.00

TABLE 9.2
An index on CUSTOMERNUMBER for Table 9.1

CUSTOMERNUMBER	ARRAY SUBSCRIPTS
10	15
11	**nil**
12	18,14,11
13	**nil**
14	20,19,16,12
15	17,13

names are not actually contained in the index. Corresponding to
each CUSTOMERNUMBER there is a variable number of array
subscripts. Because these numbers are variable it is convenient to
store these subscripts in linked lists; pointers to these lists are stored
in an array that has CUSTOMERNUMBER as its subscripts, as
indicated in Fig. 9.19.

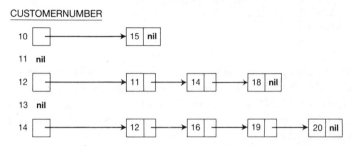

Fig. 9.19. A linked-list implementation of the index shown in Table 9.2.

Here is a program; we shall provide the missing procedures later.

```
program CUSTIND (INVOICE, INPUT, OUTPUT);
type
    CUSTOMERRANGE = 10..15;
    INVRECTYPE = record
                    INVOICENUMBER: 10..20;
                    CUSTOMERNUMBER: CUSTOMERRANGE;
                    AMOUNT: REAL
                 end;
    MEMPTRTYPE = ↑MEMBERTYPE;
    MEMBERTYPE = record
                    INVOICENUMBER: 10..20;
                    NEXT: MEMPTRTYPE
                 end;
var
    INVOICE: file of INVRECTYPE;
    INVOICETABLE: array [10..20] of INVRECTYPE;
    CUSTINDEX: array [CUSTOMERRANGE] of MEMPTRTYPE;
    CUSTOMER: CUSTOMERRANGE; CH: CHAR;
procedure LOADTABLEFROMFILE; begin {declaration omitted} end;
procedure FINDINVOICESOF (CUSTOMER: CUSTOMERRANGE);
begin {declaration omitted}
end;
```

```
begin {body of program}
  LOADTABLEFROMFILE;
  repeat
    WRITELN ('please type a customer number in the range 10..15');
    READLN (CUSTOMER);
    FINDINVOICESOF (CUSTOMER);
    WRITELN ('type C for another customer',
    'anything else to terminate the program');
    READLN (CH)
  until CH < > 'C'
end.
```

The procedure LOADTABLEFROMFILE inserts an entry into the index when it inserts a record into the table. Initially all the elements of the index CUSTINDEX are set to **nil** to signify that the index is empty. For simplicity we shall not now discuss initialization of the INVOICETABLE.

```
procedure LOADTABLEFROMFILE;
var
  CUSTOMER: CUSTOMERRANGE; INVNO: 10..20;
  ENTRY: MEMPTRTYPE;
  INVRECORD: INVRECTYPE;
begin
  for CUSTOMER: = 10 to 15 do CUSTINDEX [CUSTOMER]: = nil;
  RESET (INVOICE);
  while not EOF (INVOICE) do
  begin
    READ (INVOICE, INVRECORD);
    INVOICETABLE [INVRECORD.INVOICENUMBER]: =
    INVRECORD;
    NEW (ENTRY); {to be inserted into the index, at the head of the
    list because this is easiest}
    ENTRY↑.INVOICENUMBER: =
    INVRECORD.INVOICENUMBER; {this identifies the record in the
    INVOICETABLE}
    ENTRY↑.NEXT: =
    CUSTINDEX [INVRECORD.CUSTOMERNUMBER];
    CUSTINDEX [INVRECORD.CUSTOMERNUMBER]: = ENTRY
  end
end;
```

If the last three statements of the **while** loop require explanation, it will be worthwhile to work through a specific example to see the detailed effect of each statement.

The procedure FINDINVOICESOF (CUSTOMER) uses the input CUSTOMER number as the subscript of the array CUST-INDEX and thence obtains access to the list of relevant subscripts of the INVOICETABLE.

```
procedure FINDINVOICESOF (CUSTOMER);
var
  CURRENT:MEMPTRTYPE;
begin
  CURRENT: = CUSTINDEX [CUSTOMER];
  while CURRENT < > nil do
  begin
    with INVOICETABLE [CURRENT↑.INVOICENUMBER] do
    WRITELN (INVOICENUMBER, AMOUNT);
    CURRENT: = CURRENT↑.NEXT
  end
end;
```

The output of this procedure can be expressed in relational algebra:

proj INVOICENUMBER, AMOUNT (**sel**
CUSTOMERNUMBER = CUSTOMER (INVOICE))

The index is intended to speed up the selection operation by avoiding linear search through the INVOICETABLE to find all records containing the specific customer number.

9.9. Exercises

1. (a) Use operating system facilities to create a text file named MONTHS containing twelve records such as

    1   January
    2   February
    3   March

which give the number and name of each month of the year. Keep this file for use in subsequent exercises.

(b) Write the missing procedures MINSERT and OUTPUTNAME-FORMONTHNO for the following program that starts by reading the records from the file MONTHS into a linked list of records of type MONTHRECTYPE. The program then reads a month number from the terminal and outputs the name of that month, and does this again and again until the number read from the terminal is 0, which causes the program to terminate.

```
program MONTHEX (INPUT, OUTPUT, MONTHS);
type
    MONTHRANGE = 1..12;
    STRING9 = packed array [1..9] of CHAR;
    MONTHPTR = ↑MONTHRECTYPE;
    MONTHRECTYPE = record
                        MONTHNUMBER: MONTHRANGE;
                        MONTHNAME: STRING9;
                        NEXTMONTH: MONTHPTR
                    end;
var
    LISTHEAD, CURRMONTH: MONTHPTR;
    NUMBER: MONTHRANGE;
    NUMIN: INTEGER;
    MONTHS: TEXT;
procedure MINSERT; {to be written as an exercise}
procedure OUTPUTNAMEFORMONTHNO (N: INTEGER); {to be
written as an exercise}
begin {program body}
    LISTHEAD: = nil; {the list is initially empty}
    RESET (MONTHS);
    for NUMBER: = 1 to 12 do
    begin
        NEW (CURRMONTH);
        with CURRMONTH↑ do
        READLN (MONTHS, MONTHNUMBER, MONTHNAME);
        MINSERT {inserts record pointed to by CURRMONTH at head
        of list because this is the easiest place for insertion}
    end;
    repeat
        WRITELN ('type month number or 0 to stop program');
        READLN (NUMIN);
        if NUMIN in [1..12] then
        OUTPUTNAMEOFMONTHNO (NUMIN)
    until NUMIN = 0
end.
```

2. The following program allows you to input a sequence of words and output these to your terminal. You can insert into, and delete words from, this sequence. Each word may have up to ten letters. To simplify program-

ming, the sequence of words is stored in a linked list that includes the dummy word 'ZZZZZZZZZZ'. The last record in this list points to the first.

```pascal
program TOYEDITOR (INPUT, OUTPUT);
type
  WORDTYPE = packed array [1..10] of CHAR;
  WORDPTR = ↑WORDRECTYPE;
  WORDRECTYPE = record
                     WORD:WORDTYPE;
                     NEXTWORD: WORDPTR
                  end;
var
  PREVIOUSWORD, CURRENTWORD: WORDPTR;
  SELECTOR: CHAR;
procedure INSERT (CURRENTWORD: WORDPTR); {to be written as
an exercise}
procedure DELETE (PREVIOUSWORD: WORDPTR; var
CURRENTWORD: WORDPTR); {to be written as an exercise}
begin {program body}
  NEW (CURRENTWORD);
  CURRENTWORD↑.WORD: = 'ZZZZZZZZZZ';
  CURRENTWORD↑.NEXTWORD: = CURRENTWORD;
  PREVIOUSWORD: = CURRENTWORD;
  repeat
    WRITELN ('to find next word type N, to insert a new word type I');
    WRITELN ('to delete a word type D, to stop program type X');
    READLN (SELECTOR);
    if SELECTOR in ['N','I','D','X'] then
    case SELECTOR of
    'N': begin
          PREVIOUSWORD: = CURRENTWORD;
          CURRENTWORD: = CURRENTWORD↑.NEXTWORD;
          WRITELN (CURRENTWORD↑.WORD)
       end;

    'I': begin
          WRITELN ('type the new word, then press the return key');
          INSERT (CURRENTWORD)
       end;
    'D': DELETE (PREVIOUSWORD, CURRENTWORD);
    'X': WRITELN ('program terminating')
    end;
  until SELECTOR = 'X'
end.
```

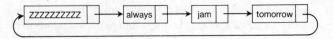

Fig. 9.20.   An example of the contents of the ring structure.

For example if you start by inserting the three successive words 'always jam tomorrow' the list structure should be as shown in Fig. 9.20. A list like this, which ends by pointing back to its beginning is called a *ring*. The exercises are as follows.

(a) Write the procedure INSERT (CURRENTWORD) which reads a new word from the terminal and inserts it into the ring immediately following the word pointed to by CURRENTWORD, leaving CURRENTWORD unchanged.

(b) Write the procedure DELETE (PREVIOUSWORD, CURRENTWORD) which deletes the word pointed to by CURRENTWORD and leaves CURRENTWORD pointing to the next word.

(c) Use the completed program to input some words that make up a sentence, and then delete some words and insert further words so that you can see the program working properly.

(d) Amend the program so that as well as the options N, I, D, X you now provide a further option T which causes all the words to be output on a single line, starting with the word that follows 'ZZZZZZZZZZ', not outputting 'ZZZZZZZZZZ', and placing exactly one space between successive words.

3. Amend the indexed invoice table example of Section 9.8.2 so that invoice records are stored in a linked list instead of a table. You will now be able to increase the range of allowed values for invoice numbers, for example to 1000..9000, which would have made the array of invoice records undesirably large.

Index